PRAISE FOR RUSHING

"Amid the noise of acceleration, *Rushing Headlong* reminds us that progress without purpose is peril. Its stories are urgent, universal, and deeply human—offering clarity for anyone determined not just to keep pace, but to shape the future with intention."

~ Stéphane Bancel, CEO Moderna

"A tour de force... a master class on how information technology, policy, and the best and worst of intentions can combine to under-mine patients and the physicians who care for them. *Rushing Headlong* should be required reading for doctors, patients and anyone who cares about the future of technology in healthcare."

~ Pauline W. Chen, MD
Author of *Final Exam: A Surgeon's Reflections on Mortality*

"Yin Ho brings thirty-years of experience in healthcare IT and common sense to the conversation about the impact of AI on healthcare. While providing a realistic survey of the history of healthcare IT, AI, and its limitations, she offers a hopeful vision for the engagement of physi-cians and patients in determining the most impactful applications for AI in healthcare."

~ Nancy J. Brown, MD, Dean of Yale Medical School

"Today, generative AI is full of promise to unlock new cures and better care. Will it deliver– or just like Electronic Records and the Internet itself– be constrained by old practices? *Rushing Headlong* details how despite revolutionary advances, decades of policy, profit incentives, and fragmented systems have left patients, clinicians, industry, and researchers struggling to access and use the very data meant to transform care. Physician-entrepreneur Yin Ho documents personal and corporate lessons learned with a call to action– and an optimistic way ahead for the future. An important read for everyone in health-care with the will to confront structural obstacles, rethink incentives, and harness technology with courage and intention in the interest of better patient care."

~ Peter Frishauf, Founder Medscape and Godfather of <u>Osmosis.org</u>

"Dr. S. Yin Ho's *Rushing Headlong* presents a comprehensive 25-year history of healthcare information technology (HIT) in the United States, written from the unique perspective of someone who participated in many of its defining moments. The book traces the evolution from the early optimistic days of healthcare IT through today's generative AI revolution, revealing how good intentions and market forces created a system that prioritizes billing and transactions over patient care and medical research. This book is a must read for practitioners, academics, researchers, and policy makers and will become a milestone in the field. Great and pioneering effort. Much needed."

~ Ayman El-Mohandes, MBBCh, MD, MPH
Dean, CUNY Graduate School of Public Health & Health Policy

"Yin Ho doesn't rush. She thinks hard, smart, and outside the prover-bial box. Then she acts—boldly, creatively, intuitively, strategically. That's why she arrives ahead of the curve, precisely positioned for disruptive success in the swiftly changing healthcare ecosystem. There is nothing artificial about her intelligence."

~ Peter Pitts, President, Center for Medicine in the Public Interest, Visiting Professor, University of Paris School of Medicine, Former Associate Commissioner, U.S. Food and Drug Administration

"As a Chief Patient Officer for pharma and biotech, I have seen firsthand how the patient journey is hindered by a fragmented and broken U.S. healthcare system. The solution is more than innovation, it demands systemic change. *Rushing Headlong* shows why decades of fragmented health IT have hindered progress, yet also why responsible AI could offer us a rare chance to unite care and research. As someone who has dedicated a lifetime to patient advocacy, I find Dr. Ho's work not only compelling, but essential reading for anyone touched by the health system– which is all of us."

~ Jodie Gillon, CEO BioCT

"This book is essential reading for anyone who cares about the future of healthcare. It brilliantly traces the evolution of health IT over the past three decades and makes a compelling case for how generative AI can finally unlock the promise of data to improve care, accelerate research, and transform the system."

~ Bunny Ellerin, CEO Digital Health New York

"Despite decades of investment, healthcare IT remains frustratingly broken—patients can't access their records, clinicians battle clunky systems, and promising innovations stall before making real impact. In *Rushing Headlong*, Dr. Ho delivers an unflinching examination of how economic incentives and regulatory capture created today's fragmented system, while asking the critical question: 'Can generative AI finally bridge these gaps so we can finally have more transparency in our own health?'"

~ Deborah Perry Piscione, Silicon Valley-based serial entrepreneur and co-author *Employment is Dead: How Disruptive Technologies are Revolutionizing the Way We Work* (Harvard Business Review)

"Dr. Yin Ho has written the book our industry has been waiting for: an unflinching history of health IT and a clear-eyed roadmap for the future. Her insights on data curation, policy, and generative AI are not only timely, but essential for anyone who believes healthcare can, and must, work better for patients. *Rushing Headlong* is both a cautionary tale and a call to action. I am deeply grateful for Yin's mentorship and proud to count her as a friend. This book will challenge and inspire leaders across healthcare and technology alike."

~ Shashi Shankar, Co-Founder and CEO, Novellia Inc.

"Data and the lack of a research-oriented infrastructure remain the bottlenecks for healthcare innovation, and this book perfectly articulates why, while shedding new light to what's possible. Healthcare data is primarily captured for billing, creating significant challenges when trying to make secondary use to accelerate data-driven clinical research and access to new treatments. A thought-provoking masterpiece that will inspire many and catalyze progress forward."

~ Xinkun Nie, PhD, Founder and CEO, Lighten Inc.

"Dr. Yin Ho brings a wealth of information and expertise to shed light on the history and evolution of healthcare IT that makes it what it is today. She brings to life the challenges and opportunities in this space through concrete examples and stories. *Rushing Headlong* is a great resource for healthcare and technology innovators who want to have real impact on our health system."

~ Dr. Carri Chan, PhD, John A. Howard Professor of Business & Faculty Director, Healthcare and Pharmaceutical Management Program at Columbia Business School

"Rushing Headlong: Health IT's Legacy and the Road to Responsible AI is a review of the origins and evolution of health information technology in the U.S. From the earliest attempts to computerize manilla charts in doctor's offices, to e-prescribing and the multiple failed attempts to achieve industry-wide data interoperability, Dr. Ho gives a personal front row seat as a Harvard/Yale trained ER doctor and health IT entrepreneur to the complexities of our fragmented healthcare system and the various attempts to streamline it with technology. About halfway through the book, you realize there are two distinct IT systems that do not play well together: one for care delivery and the other for clinical research. Dr. Ho reviews these two systems in depth and then delivers us to the present time where the promises of Generative AI are being tested and applied and leaves us with a glimmer of hope for the possibility of a whole new crop of health IT companies.

This book is a must read for anyone starting a new health tech startup, incumbent players lobbying for payment reform or even the earliest graduating medical students who are getting ready to care for patients."

~ Missy Krasner, former Senior Advisor, to the inaugural Office of National Coordinator for Health IT, U.S. Department of Health & Human Services, venture capitalist and executive at Amazon, Google and Box.

RUSHING HEADLONG

Health IT's Legacy
and the Road to Responsible AI

S. YIN HO, MD, MBA

Edited by Jennifer S. Wilkov at Your Book is Your Hook LLC

Cover design and layout by Susie Ward at SGW Design

Printed in the United States of America
First Printing, 2025

ISBN dust jacket: 979-8-9935373-0-6
ISBN casebound: 979-8-9935373-1-3
ISBN paperback: 979-8-9935373-2-0
ISBN ebook: 979-8-9935373-3-7

For Henry, Viola, and Talia

CONTENTS

Chapter 10: Physicians (continued)

PART II: DATA AND RESEARCH

Chapter 11: Data Is the New Oil 129

Chapter 12: Evidence-Based Medicine............................... 137

Chapter 13: How Do I Compare Thee? 147

Chapter 14: "Real World" Evidence 157

Chapter 15: Clinical Trials and Patients 165

FOREWORD BY J.D. KLEINKE

It is 2025 and I am checking in for my first visit at a primary care clinic in our new city. When the harried receptionist turns to make a photocopy of my laminated health insurance card, I notice the row of fax machines on the countertop behind her. One is idle, one is buzzing with an incoming fax, and the third with an outgoing fax.

The receptionist comes back with my card and hands me a pen and the clipboard with the new patient forms, including one where I check off all my medical problems for the past sixty-three years, and another where I sign off on a 20-page HIPAA Procedures & Compliance Policy. I had already filled these forms out online, of course. But she can't seem to find them on "the computer", a hulking cream-white monitor that fills her desk.

Obviously, I am not here at this new clinic because of its cutting-edge use of health information technology. I am here because this is the primary care practice in our new city with the shortest waitlist for new patients. (It took only six months for this first appointment.)

My doctor is running forty-five minutes late, so I have plenty of time to think back to an odd business meeting I had last year with executives from one of several companies that provide routing services for those very faxes – forms that go back and forth between providers and health plans, generating annual revenues in the hundreds of millions of dollars and profits in the tens of millions.

Why the time warp? Why was the rest of the world not just "computerized" but connected in real-time while so much of our health care "system" was still stuck somewhere in the mid-1990s? It has taken me three decades of working in both health policy and health care information technology to figure out the answer. This is something no health IT sales representative, entrepreneur, or "implementation" consultant – armed with a pitch deck full of dazzling groove charts – wants to hear: health IT problems are not information technology problems; they are health care system problems. Full stop. The U.S. healthcare "system" isn't a system at all, but a $5 trillion-dollar-per-year battle royale of raw, economic conflict.

No evil genius, mindless government bureaucracy, or self-serving mega-corporation designed the health care "system" this way, though it may seem that way to many. Every attempt to "reform" any part of it is another patch sewn onto a patchwork quilt that is just that—all patches. As a result, every new government health care program, new private health insurance product, and attempt to belatedly organize providers into "health care delivery systems" is additive; chaos ensues, and the fax machines keep humming.

This is the vast, embattled, economic landscape – peopled by case managers, medical records technicians, billing specialists, utilization reviewers, "chart chasers," claims adjudicators, *et al., ad infinitum* (not to mention half a million exhausted primary care physicians who spend their evening hours listening to health insurer authorization line hold-music) – that my colleague and friend, Yin Ho, has spent her career attempting to help modernize with information technology.

The book in your hands, *Rushing Headlong,* is the summation of her efforts. It is an unvarnished account of the complexities and hard lessons she learned in the process as well as how every turn in her fascinating career has come to inform her hard-headed, clear-eyed analysis of the way AI is likely to play out across this messiest of all landscapes.

I know Yin was "in the room" for many of the biggest promises and even bigger failures of health IT because I was there with her in several of them. I met her in 2001, when she was a young health IT executive dancing with giants: IBM, Microsoft and Pfizer, as she recounts in the pages that follow. Most recently, she was "in the room" when the AI health care evangelists first came calling.

What makes Yin nearly unique among the many dedicated physicians-turned-health IT entrepreneurs I have met over the decades: she has had the rare opportunity to work inside not just one of the many different kinds of parties to healthcare transactions listed above, but in nearly all of them. People in health care tend to specialize, to spend much or all of their career in one or another of health care's warring economic sectors. In the process, they become fully captive of its particular self-interest.

By contrast, Yin's career has been unusually far-flung across the sprawling health care IT landscape. As importantly, she was often the only voice for the role of the physician and, by extension, the patient. She recognized that most technology innovations were being forced on physicians – in many cases, even by physician-turned-informaticians themselves. Yin's overriding perspective, which I have always shared: The health care "system," if it could have been designed, should have been done so to meet the needs of physicians and patients, not business prerogatives of the Keepers of the Fax Machines.

She has worked not only on "the pipes" – as we call the software and systems that move medical and claims data around in cyberspace – but also on "the content": the dense, complex, and critical data that runs through them. While the pipes and the content may be obviously related, they have always been managed in two very different worlds, with their own distinct (and often conflicting) economic imperatives, business models, and corporate cultures.

And Yin, for better or for worse, has a knack for finding the frontier of both of those worlds. She has worked with one of the earliest electronic health records (EHRs) for community physicians with a research focus. She helped develop one of the first exchanges to facilitate patients finding clinical trials. She was the first executive in a corporate position to make a strategic investment in SureScripts, now the national system for routing prescriptions. She was among the first to build a company focused on the data-driven analysis of how we evaluate drugs in the U.S. and across the world. And she was the first to lead an EHR company to acquire AI capacity.

What you will find in the pages to follow are her notes from the battlefield – a *de facto* history of health IT's biggest fights, weirdest wins, and wildest misses. From the earliest attempts to computerize clinical practice, to the false promises of the internet, to the billions of dollars wasted trying to mash together routine patient care and clinical trials, the bittersweet professional tales that drive *Rushing Headlong* are told in the authentic voice of someone who always thought, first and last, about what was best for patients, their physicians, and the future of medicine. No spoilers here, but in the pages that follow, Yin offers an odd glimpse of hope of what is possible.

Ultimately, this is a rare, unique, and fascinating story about the real world of health IT and the coming collision with AI. Although the complexity of health care's many competing interests may make you despair for our U.S. health system and the prognosis for healthcare IT, I can promise you one thing: a surprise ending. Yin takes us to a place where I least expected her to go – and for the sake of all of us, I hope she is right.

J.D Kleinke
Providence, Rhode Island
June 28, 2025

INTRODUCTION

In the fall of 1998, on the precipice of the dot com era, I started my first year at Harvard Business School as one of ten physicians, the largest number of physicians in an HBS class at that time.

I had just walked away from my medical training after completing two years of residency in emergency medicine, enough to get a medical license, and I was rushing headlong toward an uncertain future in an industry that had barely begun: health information technology* (HIT).

At the time, I had just spent the past six years learning how to become a doctor. I scarcely understood any business terminology, had scant knowledge of economics, and had only had a brush with entrepreneurship when I ran a small catering business in college many years earlier. But here I was determined to enter and shape the nascent world of HIT.

Two events had led me to this moment. I recalled how my excitement and imagination had been fired up three years earlier in the spring of 1995 when Medscape, the famous website with a radical concept: free access to medical information previously only available through professional journals to anyone, had burst onto the scene. At that moment, I was a year away from graduating from Yale Medical School and soon to start my residency in emergency medicine. However, I also remembered my disappointment, frustration

---

* Health Information Technology (HIT), also called healthcare IT (HCIT), refers to the field that uses information technology and data management to support clinical care, operations, and public health through electronic systems that store and manage healthcare data across medical organizations.

and anger several years earlier in 1993 when as a first-year medical student, I watched Hillary Clinton pull together a task force on healthcare reform without including a single physician in her leadership team.

When I look back, it was those two events that shaped my desire to leave medicine and join this new undefined world, a world of solutions afforded only by the recent widespread availability of the internet. Physicians had been cut out of the conversation as new policies and business models were emerging. I knew I needed to find a way in—not only as a physician but as someone with ideas about how to make healthcare better and possibly find a way to re-insert clinical experience and expertise into the mix. To have a say in the business of medicine.

I believed strongly and rather naïvely that by simply making healthcare information more widely available and creating capabilities to collect and organize patient data, we would be able to develop new tech solutions to solve age-old problems in medicine and healthcare: in particular, the speed at which medical discovery would make it into routine care. I had been trained as a physician when evidence-based medicine was making the rounds and the most commonly quoted statistic was: it took seventeen years for a discovery to make it into clinical care.

But I had one small challenge: I didn't know how to begin.

On the advice of a friend, I applied to business school as an entryway into the "business" world. Surely this would get me into one of those new health companies experimenting with the internet.

During business school, while trying to learn a new language and way of thinking, I couldn't wait to get to work. I even joined forces with a few of my classmates to create an early business plan for an e-care website to manage your information and healthcare purchases. We won an Arts Alliance scholarship in a venture capital sponsored competition, but we never finished building out the idea. It wasn't until after I graduated in 2000 when I would join my first real startup: emergingmed.com, a web application to connect patients to cancer clinical trials. This experience was the beginning of my career in healthcare IT, discovering and trying to close gaps with technology, content, and later data.

I would also learn something crucial: that in U.S. healthcare, you need to first understand policy before you can understand the business.

The stories told in the following pages are more than just my journey. My work has given me a front-row seat for each major technological leap and every well-meaning (and often misguided) government intervention. At times, I have been an observer, witnessing how the healthcare system and its key players have reacted to new capabilities and policy changes. At other times, I have been an active participant, leading teams to develop information technology solutions aimed at bridging the persistent and new gaps between research, data, decision-making, patient care, and even the equity of care options.

I wrote this book to share a firsthand history of healthcare IT, because to be intentional about where we are going, we first have to understand how we got here. This isn't just about avoiding past mistakes; it is about recognizing and understanding deep-seated structural issues and powerful interests that have made our healthcare ecosystem such a challenge.

The latest technological leap is generative AI, and it is already creating a new crop of healthcare IT companies. But generative AI isn't entering a vacuum. As this technology develops at lightning speed, it will inevitably be shaped and constrained by the same power dynamics that have defined healthcare for decades.

The danger in AI is that without intentional direction, these powerful tools can hurt patient care and further entrench the current inefficient and costly system—one in which large players prioritize revenue management over advancing research or patient care. This risk is significant, as these large, powerful incumbents are best positioned to absorb the immense costs of development, meeting regulatory requirements, and scaling AI, effectively cementing their advantage.

To make things even more complex and as you will read throughout the book, our healthcare system faces many structural challenges in how patients, physicians, payments, research, data, decisions, and transactions interact and function. A little-recognized reality is that we actually operate with two separate health IT ecosystems: one for care delivery and another for clinical research. Although both rely on the same patients and sometimes the same data, there is still no meaningful bridge connecting them.

Book Structure

Rushing Headlong is structured into three parts.

Part I begins with the early, optimistic days of healthcare IT and the desire to create a digital infrastructure with electronic records as the backbone. The overall goal was to have a digital set of "pipes" to support and underpin the U.S. healthcare ecosystem. But most of what will happen during this first decade will end up emphasizing transactions in healthcare. In addition, the application of government incentives and penalties will accelerate adoption of electronic records and distort the marketplace, leaving us with a healthcare IT infrastructure that disappoints and dis-empowers both physicians and patients.

Part II begins with the second decade of health IT and shortly after widespread adoption of electronic records. There is renewed interest in the rising importance of the data (the water flowing through the pipes) and the ability to harness this data for greater understanding of disease and to support the development of new therapies. But the transactional nature of the digital infrastructure and the primacy of patient privacy has made the ability to access meaningful clinical data difficult and only possible through a series of complex work-arounds. Meanwhile new medical discoveries and scientific progress will continue to widen this gap.

Part III begins part-way through the third decade of health IT with the advent of generative AI. A generational opportunity to change the system presents itself. The speed and scale of generative AI technology could allow us to double down on a digital infrastructure that doesn't work well and is transactional in nature OR it may provide a chance to change the direction of the digital infrastructure to support a care-research orientation. The combination of new entrants, re-empowered physicians, and digital native patients creates a tantalizing scenario. Can we move beyond today's fragmented, transaction-heavy, zero-sum U.S. healthcare system? Are we able to responsibly develop AI tools to shift our healthcare digital infrastructure to be more research focused, allowing us to reap the benefits of improved individual and population health?

While the business of U.S. healthcare relies heavily on first under-standing healthcare policy, the impact of technology relies on knowing the power dynamics, the state of the existing infrastructure, and having a clear-eyed view of the goal. Otherwise, generative AI efforts could easily become subsumed and harden the same long-standing structural problems that have defined U.S. healthcare and plagued healthcare IT.

In fact, the modern health IT ecosystem exists because of key events and milestones over the past few decades that fundamentally changed the distribution of power among patients, physicians, health systems, and payers.

You will learn how the wonky term, *interoperability*, which is the connecting of disparate IT systems so they can talk to one another for information exchange and transactions, is not just a technical term. It is a concept dependent on the voluntary cooperation of all stakeholders. It will become the obsession of six presidential terms and is facing a renewed push once more today.[1]

Our healthcare system is messy and complex, but there are many moments of optimism, innovation, and excellence driven by successive waves of new entrepreneurs applying new technology to solve both small and large identified problems. For those of us who have lived within the healthcare IT ecosystem, some of these problems remain frustratingly perennial.

Generative AI, though, gives us pause. Although still in its early days, it represents a breakthrough of a different magnitude. It is a transformative technology, both in functionality and who can develop and use it. Will this latest technology leap finally break the stalemate of interlocked interests and close long-standing gaps in care to truly empower both patients and physicians? It could — if we don't screw it up.

Hopes

For many years, I believed deeply in the potential of health IT to accelerate our shared understanding of disease and treatment, and to support better decision-making—much like Medscape, which opened access to medical knowledge beyond the traditional boundaries of academia and industry.[2] My vision was a connected ecosystem that resembled a feedback loop using clinical data to deepen our understanding of disease, accelerate research, and empower patients with their own health data already present in their electronic records. In fact, many of us imagined a system purposefully designed to support medical discovery.

Instead, the healthcare systems we built are exceptionally good at managing the revenue cycle. Anyone who has had to sift through health insurance claims data and deal with billing codes (e.g., CPT, ICD-10) to determine a patient's journey knows this all too well. It didn't have to be that way.

At the same time, our need to safeguard patient privacy meant creating complex workaround processes to access and utilize data for research. These same regulations designed to protect patients have not always adapted at the speed of technology change and this lag has resulted in making it actually administratively and systematically harder for patients to access their data, manage their care, participate in a clinical trial, or obtain and evaluate a second opinion.

The frustrating reality is that while health information technology could ease the flow of data to support our ability to improve, instead it is too often a transactional morass that has turned physicians into accountable scribes and forced patients to have to jump through many hoops to benefit from the digitization of their records.

Ultimately, the history of healthcare IT can be seen as a story of competing priorities, where the initial vision for an infrastructure that prioritized research, patient empowerment, and reducing preventable errors has been progressively reshaped by the powerful economic imperatives of a transaction-based ecosystem. The relentless focus on billing within the electronic systems has changed the behavior of physicians and the options available to patients. Worse, this infrastructure has largely been subsidized by government and private incentives.

The healthcare IT systems, in a nutshell, operate like an "accounting system"— aligning activity and outcomes to payment. The only players in the industry who could meet the increasingly complex government compliance requirements are the largest ones. Their main value proposition is to promise timely and accurate payments to their customers.

Creating A New Future

Reflecting on this history, it is interesting to consider how the landscape might have been different with the tools generative AI is now making available. The capabilities of today's generative models are already creating a more direct link between the clinic and the lab, offering a tangible way to connect the daily work of a physician with the needs of a researcher or to translate a patient's experience into data that can inform the development of new treatments.

The promise of generative AI lies in its potential to simplify the process for physicians simultaneously caring for patients and beginning the process of answering current and future research questions.

BUT...

A reliance on generative AI also means taking into account a whole new set of risks, given this new technology's tendency toward bias and hallucinations.

Over twenty years ago, I gave a panel talk at the American College of Physicians emphasizing the need to protect the patient-physician relationship by evaluating healthcare IT tools using a filter of decision-support versus decision-control. My stance was that any responsible evolution of healthcare IT should be determined "by what we wish to protect, what we wish to enhance, and what risks we may be opening ourselves to."[3]

Today, I would say the same sentiment applies for generative AI. We are collectively responsible for how models are trained and applied. We bear the consequences of any decision made from the output. And the *zeitgeist* to use AI to further automate transactions by reducing administrative burden may actually turn into a form of decision control.

However, if we are intentional in developing generative AI to *augment* clinical and professional judgment and empower patient preference, we may end up with a wholly different result.

By actively involving patients and physicians in shaping clinical care systems and *jointly* organizing patient data to drive future research, we can build the structural framework and the impetus to *support* better decisions and speed up learning from real-world experiences.

This can only succeed if we approach it responsibly and ethically, designing AI tools with clear intention. Restoring agency to both patients and physicians is at the heart of this effort. What we learn could not only strengthen the patient-physician partnership but also help shorten the time between today's care and tomorrow's research—a goal that many share.[4]

New technologies always come with bold promises. Experience shows while many are eventually realized, the path is rarely direct. Still, the potential of generative AI feels different. The sheer speed and scope creates real possibilities.

The greatest opportunity may be to finally bridge the clinical care we provide today and the clinical research we conduct now and in the future. By creating a continuous learning feedback loop using AI models and thoughtful tools, we can accelerate the translation of discoveries into practice. That seventeen-year time interval for a discovery to make it into clinical care may finally be shortened while expanding our knowledge along multiple directions. We may be looking at a renewed opportunity to pursue the goals that many of us in the field have had from the very beginning.

Now is the time when we should close the gap.

Yin Ho
New York City
September, 2025

PART I: THE DIGITAL INFRASTRUCTURE

*"Drowning in data
and starving for wisdom."*

~Peter Frishauf,
founder of Medscape

CHAPTER 1:

CURATION

On my first day of sixth grade, my teacher asked my class, "What if I told you there was one place you could go to find out all the known information in the world?"

I am sure that my teacher did not say that the encyclopedia is a collection of carefully curated information, but he nonetheless explained the importance of this resource whose origins began millennia ago.

He unfortunately took his excitement a bit too far, saying, "If you take these encyclopedia sets, and you read each one from beginning to end, there would be nothing more I could ever possibly teach you."

People in my age demographic (GenX) are among the last of the "encyclopedia generation". Before the loosely curated Wikipedia was accessible on our smartphones, before dial-up internet interrupted our ability to make phone calls, there were shelves of books that contained information on everything from aardvarks to zebras.

My family had the World Book Encyclopedia set and I was curious about my teacher's comment. I approached the bookcase and selected the book with the letter "A". I believe many of my classmates did something similar.

I opened this first of many volumes and learned about the eating habits of aardvarks, followed by Abraham Lincoln, adrenal glands, the Aegean Sea, agriculture, and amphibians. I remember shutting the book, feeling bored and tired, and thinking "This is stupid."

I didn't know how to connect one piece of information to the next, since it was all sorted alphabetically. There was no common connection. There was no game I could conjure in my mind to make this alphabetical exercise any less boring and more meaningful to me.

I went back to my teacher and told him, "I tried your method but it didn't work. Even if I read every volume of the encyclopedia, I am not sure I would gain knowledge." He thought about it for a moment, agreed with me, and moved on.

At the age of eleven, I didn't know that the word for what I needed to organize this information was "curation".

A museum curator manages and preserves historical artifacts — acquiring, authenticating, organizing, and displaying antiquities for the public good.

But curators exist in many forms. Archeological curators oversee collections from ancient civilizations. Ethnographic curators manage cultural artifacts and indigenous art. Academic curators research, publish, teach, and create educational programs within universities.

Across these roles, the expectation remains consistent: curators exercise judgment. They distill complex material and present it in a way that others can access, understand and appreciate.

So it stands to reason that medical information should also be curated too, so we can better understand it and ultimately extract value from it.

Physicians have long practiced their own form of curation; through journal groups, grand rounds, or weekly meetings with colleagues. In these settings, they may discuss relevant cases, journal articles, the most recent research findings, best practices, and interesting case reports—filtering and synthesizing information to inform better care.

Why Peer Review Matters

The term "peer review" is often used as shorthand to indicate that a paper has been vetted. It is a practice that aligns with scientific self-correcting mechanisms and has been the foundation for the curating of scientific works, particularly around the validation of quality, currency and relevancy.

Curation in science has the twin fold requirement to both be compelling as well as accurate. But who determines what is compelling?

Peer review began in the European Enlightenment. The first documented review took place in 1731 at the Royal Society of

Edinburgh. In this inaugural review, the Society's members reviewed the manuscripts of its own journal, *Medical Essays and Observations,* anonymously.[5] Later in 1752, the Royal Society of London established a "Committee on Papers" which employed a secret ballot (also among its members) to determine what could be published in their journal *Philosophical Transactions* Around the same time, the French Académie Royale des Sciences also used committees to evaluate submissions. But it wasn't until the 19th century that the modern peer review, the solicitation of independently written reports, emerged. It would take another century for the use of external reviewers to become widespread.[6]

At its core, peer review is built on the concept of independent assessment to create a correcting mechanism for accuracy. On the flip side, the main challenge is ensuring that new ideas have a chance to see the light of day, a function often highly dependent on the breadth of the reviewer pool. When peer review was concentrated in the hands of a few distinguished experts, there was a perverse incentive for competitive work to be snuffed out.

With the rapid growth of science and subspecialties, there was a corresponding need for more reviewers. The volume of work was increasingly difficult for journal editors to manage by themselves. And the peer review process we know today became a hallmark of scientific journals beginning in the 1970s.

Though far from perfect, peer review has continued to evolve, broadening to include more anonymous and diverse voices. It has created a pathway for lesser-known researchers to experience greater equity while publishing work. The practice has also established a measure of quality control for scientific and medical literature and created a framework to showcase new discoveries.

In the mid-1990s, as the internet became more widely accessible, the demand for even greater specialized information began to grow quickly.

In healthcare, this demand could not be satiated by simply opening up access to medical journals or putting textbooks online. Accessibility also depended on the material being *understandable* to a non-clinically trained individual. Without a navigator to help determine which sources were appropriate or a guide to understand terminology and context, it was clear that a mere translation was insufficient. There needed to be curation.

Enter the new curators of healthcare information: internet content companies and media outfits were the first to start making medical information accessible to patients. In 1995, Peter Frishauf launched Medscape, the first commercially viable healthcare information company on the internet. It would eventually become the most well-recognized brand in healthcare information. When Medscape combined with WebMD ten years later, it was granting more CMEs* to physicians than any other institution in the world.

Medscape

On May 22, 1995, the name Medscape first appeared in a notice on an electronic bulletin board:

Medscape — the online resource for better patient care.

---

*CME (Continuing Medical Education) includes activities that keep medical professionals updated on advances and help them maintain licensure.

A new, free Web site for health professionals and interested consumers. Practice-oriented information is peer-reviewed and edited by thought-leaders in AIDS, infectious diseases, urology, and surgery. Highly structured articles and full-color graphics are supplemented with stored literature searches and annotated links to relevant internet resources. From SCP Communications, Inc., one of the world's leading publishers of medical journals and medical education programs.[7]

As a writer, journalist, and visionary, Peter had realized that the emerging power of the internet and its online forums would provide the meeting ground where healthcare professionals could find peer-reviewed information and CME materials.

Part of Peter's brilliance was recognizing that access to the latest health information would benefit far more than just simply physicians and other medical professionals. He opened access to empower motivated consumers and patients.[8]

Prior to this point, few patients ever asked where they could read about diseases, new treatments, or even their own health status. There was a conventional assumption that patients wouldn't understand this information anyway, so they might as well not ask. But once it was made available and consumable, demand began to take off.

Part of Peter's brilliance was recognizing that access to the latest health information would benefit far more than just simply physicians and other medical professionals. He opened access to empower motivated consumers and patients.

The writers and journalists at Medscape did more than curate the latest studies, they translated complex medical information into clear, accessible language. Their work helped the public understand their diseases, treatments, and choices. In early 2002, Medscape merged with WebMD, cementing its role in shaping how we seek health information online.[9]

If we look at the cultural, technological and clinical impact of Medscape/WebMD, we can trace the origin story of how people learned to "Google" their symptoms. These platforms didn't just provide answers; they taught us how to ask the questions. As digital curation evolved, it increasingly focused on the most common concerns and frequently searched conditions.

Demand for More Knowledge

As medical knowledge became more accessible, patients were also gaining greater agency—researching their own conditions, seeking second opinions, and finding community. Advocacy and patient groups started to form as the internet made it easier to find one another.

Patients were now asking for access to their own health information and records. Those who suffered from diseases with few treatment options also began to seek research opportunities and clinical trials.

In 2000, right after I graduated from Harvard Business School, I joined a small startup company called emergingmed.com as its ninth employee. The company's mission was to match cancer patients to clinical trials. The business approach was to create an exchange. On one side were patients and their corresponding advocacy groups; on the other side, clinical trial eligibility criteria. Between them was a simple matching technology.

At that time, clinicaltrials.gov was the only publicly available database on clinical trials. It contained academic, government and non-profit sponsored trials. There were no private, pharmaceutical or biotechnology trials. The information listed about any one trial tended to be basic information including size, study question, geographies or sites, and the inclusion and exclusion criteria.

The internet at that time was accessible via direct cable modems, ethernet, and in many places, dial-up through home phone lines. Our interfaces were clunky, and it was difficult to organize information easily into fields without also needing new software to manage the different variables. We were simply thrilled to be able to fill out a form online and wait for the information in those fields to be matched appropriately across multiple dimensions.

And what was available to curate in clinical trials was sparse; it was still an open playing field, and the quest to amass data was only beginning. Many companies' business models were focused on building various trial databases by directly approaching biopharmaceutical companies as fast as they could and then selling access to their new databases to both companies and, sometimes, consumers.

Clinicaltrials.gov, the only widely available database for consumers and patients, had the least amount of information.

Every trial information company was creating its own proprietary trial database which contained information NOT included in clinicaltrials.gov. These supplemental databases focused only on one or a few specific disease conditions. You can only imagine what this was like for patients or anyone searching for a trial: a new landscape of some companies having better and more complete clinical trial information than others, but only in specific disease areas. There was no easy way of knowing who had what. Clinicaltrials.gov, the only widely available database for consumers and patients, had the *least* amount of information, both in terms of missing the total universe of trials (no industry trials) and the lack of depth and timeliness of information (basic trial information updated without any regularity).

When I first joined emergingmed.com, my job was to visit every biopharma company sponsoring an oncology clinical trial, convince them to allow us to list their trials' eligibility criteria in our proprietary database, and give us permission to match patients to their trials.

In exchange for finding some potentially eligible patients looking for a trial, I was asking these companies to help us build our database of oncology trials. One barrier I had not expected at the time was I had to *convince* these companies that by posting eligibility (inclusion and exclusion) criteria, they were not giving away proprietary information.

The idea that eligibility criteria were proprietary, and therefore not publicly shareable, would persist for several more years.

It was not until five years later that circumstances changed, triggered by an unfortunate event that led to the establishment of a new federal requirement.

A Drug Withdrawal Leads to More Clinical Trials Information

In 1998, Merck submitted an application to the FDA to approve a new drug called Vioxx, a new kind of non-steroidal anti-inflammatory drug (NSAID) that was more targeted and less likely to cause gastrointestinal distress than ibuprofen or aspirin. Vioxx was part of a new class of drugs called the COX-2 inhibitors and it was ultimately approved by the FDA in 1999 and went on to be one of the largest blockbuster drugs in the marketplace, earning billions for Merck. While there were other COX-2 inhibitors which also came onto the market over the next few years, new epidemiology studies showed an increased risk in cardiovascular events including strokes and heart attacks associated with the use of Vioxx. A series of lawsuits followed.

In September 2004, Merck voluntarily withdrew Vioxx from the market.[10] Much of the cardiovascular risk had appeared post FDA approval and after a longer period of time than the initial timeframe studied in clinical trials (an average of about eighteen months). But there were also reports of patients suffering cardiovascular events shortly after beginning the therapy.

Throughout the five years that Vioxx was on the market, there were many disputes about the studies, around the data, the cutoff dates and, more importantly, who knew what when. The editor of *The New England Journal of Medicine* at the time also pointed out that combined safety data from multiple arms of a trial had not been fully available due to a cut-off date that was selected before the primary trial was completed.

NEJM editors who had published the original data started calling for data correction and in January 2005, the medical journal *Lancet*, using a mathematical model and a retrospective analysis of data from Kaiser Permanente, *estimated* that 88,000 Americans had heart attacks from taking Vioxx and 38,000 of them died.[11]

The voluntary withdrawal of Vioxx goes down in history as the largest prescription drug withdrawal. The events demonstrated a need to monitor drug effects for a longer period in the real world beyond clinical trial timelines. This would later shape additional criteria for future trials, and subsequent FDA policies would focus predominantly on cardiovascular side effects.

But a notable consequence was what led to a change to clinicaltrials. gov.

In the wake of Vioxx's withdrawal, the International Committee of Medical Journal Editors (ICMJE) in 2007 began to require clinical trial registration as a condition of publication.[12] Around the same time, the FDA Amendments Act (FDAAA) of 2007 would mandate the listing of all pharmaceutical trials on clinicaltrials.gov, including inclusion and exclusion criteria.

This change provided the very information that emergingmed.com and similar companies (HopeLink, Veritas Medicine, Acurian) had been pursuing only a few years before—to benefit patients looking for trials.

However, with the new federal mandate, new clinical trial companies and even financial organizations began capitalizing on the expanded listings at clinicaltrials.gov. These companies supplemented the information with additional information gained from their own secondary research.

Large groups of financial analysts as well as clinical trial watchdogs began tracking new clinical trial results and followed data presented and discussed in medical and industry conferences.

As the ranks of those tracking and gathering supplemental clinical trial information grew, a new data information industry was born. Their proprietary databases became a curated product, sold with analytical services and directly to biopharma companies and other clinical trial information companies, including ones that serviced the same biopharma companies.

These emerging information brokers grew increasingly sophisticated, leveraging new tools and software to integrate supplemental data, enhance visualization, and enable more effective risk assessment and opportunity identification.

Sadly, clinicaltrials.gov never gained any of the additional information gathered by these companies, nor did the National Library of Medicine (a branch of the National Institutes of Health) improve the overall technology functionality of this public database.

"Although health is an information-intensive industry... it is natural to resist information technology, because it changes roles and the social order."

~ 1999 Scientific Symposium of the
American College of Medical Informatics[13]

CHAPTER 2

THE EMERGENCE OF HEALTH INFORMATION TECHNOLOGY

Patients Left on the Sidelines

When someone is actively looking to enroll in a clinical trial, they often have the most at stake: their health and, often, their future. Despite that, patients tend to have the *least* access to the very information that determines whether they can enroll.

Clinicaltrials.gov may have a reasonably up-to-date list of current clinical trials, but the website often fails to indicate whether trials are still open for enrollment or if there are any modifications.

Patients, unlike companies that can purchase access to more complete and richly detailed proprietary databases, must navigate this clunky public site that lacks real-time updates and nuanced filtering. The ability to extract meaningful knowledge remains maddeningly elusive.

This information gap has life-altering consequences.

In January 2025, the *Washington Post* ran an article[14] about a woman in her early thirties who received a Stage IV eye cancer diagnosis with only sixteen months to live. While the prognosis was grim, she was prescribed an immunotherapy therapy, brand named Yervoy.* Her father, who was a physician, immediately insisted on finding a clinical trial and for her *to delay* the start of her prescribed therapy.

Over the next several years, she enrolled in a total of four clinical trials, an unusually high number to be granted eligibility. Three years later, having made it through all the challenges, failures, and costs, this woman is cancer free. She is one of the lucky ones, and her success is largely because her physician father was able to navigate the frustrating and opaque world of clinical trials.

What is most striking about this story is not that the woman needed a physician's help to find appropriate clinical trials, but that her physician-father realized starting the prescribed (and standard of care) cancer therapy at the time of diagnosis would have made his daughter *ineligible* for the first trial she ultimately enrolled in.

Twenty-five years earlier, when I was traveling from one biopharma company to another, trying to convince each organization to list their eligibility criteria into our fledgling database, I didn't realize then that we were "curating" one of the most important pieces of information that could help inform a patient about what was truly available to them.

---

* Yervoy (ipilimumab) is an immunotherapy checkpoint inhibitor for advanced melanoma, lung, kidney, and some colorectal cancers, made by Bristol Myers Squibb. It is not approved for eye cancer but may be used off-label by physicians.

Electronic Records - Capturing Data

While patients and medical professionals may have gained additional ways into more health information through greater access to journals and publications, the health information technology industry was simultaneously emerging from a patchwork of new and disconnected systems built to collect and utilize *patient* data.

Although health IT is typically defined as the intersection of healthcare, IT, and data management to support clinical care and operations within hospitals and clinics, its scope actually extends further. Health IT is a wider industry focused on developing, deploying, and maintaining *digital systems* for storing, managing, and exchanging healthcare data.

Notably, from the very beginning, systems designed for healthcare delivery and those built for clinical research were developed independently of each other, despite sharing a common need for healthcare data. This historical separation has led to the persistence of two parallel, largely disconnected

Systems designed for healthcare delivery and those built for clinical research were developed independently.

ecosystems: one for patient care and another for research, each with its own infrastructure, processes, and workflows, even as the underlying data needs have remained fundamentally linked.

Both electronic medical records (EMRs) for documenting clinical care and electronic data capture (EDCs) for collecting patient data in clinical trials have roots in the closed computer systems of the 1970s and 1980s, but each would take a different path to adoption and development.

For EMRs, two external forces would drive greater adoption: 1) the federal government's desire for greater connectivity (later becoming interoperability) to enhance patient safety and reduce medical errors; and 2) the desire to enact insurance payment reform. Future government financial incentives aimed to accelerate adoption will put EMRs further along a trajectory separate and distinct from EDC.

The adoption of EDC systems in clinical trials was driven mainly by the growing complexity of trial designs and the expanding roles and requirements. In addition, there was a growing desire to include more physician practices as clinical trial sites.

Initially, the adoption of EDC systems was limited to large contract research organizations (CROs) and biopharma companies seeking more effective tools to manage clinical trial data, but these systems soon became distributed among clinical trial sites. Many of these sites were clinics and hospitals. In fact, you would sometimes see within a clinic: one computer used for electronic medical records and another one used for electronic data capture. If a clinical trial site was doing multiple trials, every biopharma sponsor would often require a *separate* computer for their own electronic data capture. The end result was simply many computer terminals in a doctor's office, each with its own individual purpose.

For those of us who have straddled the two health IT worlds of clinical care and clinical research operations, there was always an underlying hope that the patient data collected during clinical care could one day be used for purposes beyond its original intent, specifically to support clinical research and the development of new treatments.

However, it would not be until the mid 2010s with the rise of real-world evidence when the patient data from electronic medical records would be considered a useful source of research data to support the development of new therapies.

Importance of Context

Context is everything. The meaning and relevance of information depends entirely on the context in which it is considered. That is why curation isn't just about selecting the most useful data or insights; it is about deliberately shaping the context that allows for clear evaluation and understanding.

In clinical care health IT, much of what has been considered progress has tended to be focused on measuring efficiency and productivity within the healthcare setting. It has often been about optimizing administrative operations, efficient care, transactions, and making sure activity is properly coded, billed, and reimbursed.

But when it comes to understanding data on new therapies, context plays a much bigger part. Understanding what the clinical data represents or what might be happening to a patient means trying to discern what context everything is occurring in. The metadata, or the data about the data, becomes important for understanding the meaning of the clinical data. Metadata is the information that describes what kind of data we are looking at or where it can be found. An example is a timestamp of when an observation happened. Curating clinical data requires context or metadata to help us understand a patient's journey, their disease progression, and their response to therapy.

It was February 2010, and I was sitting in the living room at Peter Frishauf's home on the Upper West Side of Manhattan, catching up with our friend, health technology economist J.D. Kleinke. Over the past several months, I had been deep in research about a relatively new concept called health technology assessment (HTAs). I was eager to share and discuss.

Across much of the world, health technology assessments (HTAs) serve as crucial, government-initiated reviews that examine clinical trial evidence and outcomes to determine whether a new therapeutic (such as a new drug) is considered cost-effective enough to offer at the population level. These reviews are conducted by HTA agencies (government or quasi-government agencies) that then provide recommendations to help a country government negotiate the price of therapies directly with the pharma company. This evaluation does not happen in the U.S. at a federal level and instead versions of this kind of analysis occur among various payers and institutions.

The evaluations conducted by these HTA agencies are published in the form of dense, narrative-heavy, large and sprawling reports, making the end recommendations unnecessarily complicated and inefficient to read.

What if you could create a comparison, especially with context? If there could be a tool that would allow you to search and compare decision factors and recommendations at a glance, that would at least make these reports more efficient to read and easier to understand. If we had this information in a comparative format without losing context, we could go to the next step and directly compare these drug evaluations across countries and across time.

All the expert analysis and the key decision-making criteria was locked within a long report, and pharma companies had been hiring consultants *to simply read* and determine what was important.

When J.D. Kleinke commented that "the context" in the report was often missing in any spreadsheet of criteria, suddenly the solution came into focus.

The next month, I would found and start a company called Context Matters Inc., where the mission was to provide the ability to quickly compare the context and criteria of all those HTA decisions to help improve trial and study design.

With a team of public health graduates who had specialized in health economics and epidemiology and a small group of software developers, we built a software platform and process to tackle those dense reports.

We developed methodology and mechanisms to accurately extract, organize, and continuously update the essential details from those global HTA reports. Our platform could deliver timely HTA intelligence in a user-friendly interface on the most important criteria and economic factors to various countries. We could even link these criteria back to the original clinical trials for our customers, the health economics teams at biopharmaceutical companies.

By making it easier to understand what factors mattered in a head-to-head comparison, our customers could plan both future clinical trials and their strategy around how to demonstrate the most optimal health economics and outcomes that truly mattered for health systems. In essence, they could focus on what data needed to be collected and curated.

In essence, we provided a data visualization *lingua franca* for both decision-makers (HTA agencies) and innovators (biopharma companies) as to which data and what context would best represent the effects of a drug within a population. This kind of approach to information would resonate with both.

Only with context and curation can data become the knowledge that drives progress.

Data alone is meaningless. Only with context and curation can data become the knowledge that drives progress.

I think there's data, and then there's information that comes from data, and then there's knowledge that comes from information. And then, after knowledge, there is wisdom. I am interested in how to get from data to wisdom."

~ Toni Morrison,
1993 interview with the *Harvard Advocate*

CHAPTER 3

DATA DATA EVERYWHERE

On a warm Manhattan evening in October of 2010, we held an event at the Chelsea Market Manhattan offices of Google. We were celebrating the first anniversary of NYC Health Business Leaders, an organization my friend, Bunny Ellerin, and I co-founded in the fall of 2009, to bring New York City together as a healthcare innovation capital.*

Together with Google, we were hosting a panel about the state of electronic records.[15] I was the moderator and the first panelist on my left was Aaron Brown, the product director for Google Health. My first question to him was why patients should trust Big Tech with their healthcare data.

---

* New York City Health Business Leaders (NYCHBL) was founded to showcase NYC as a hub for healthcare innovation by connecting leaders from across the health sector, fostering collaboration, and positioning the city as a leader in health business and innovation.

His answer was that the vision of Google Health was to create a service giving people access to their personal health information while encouraging them to take a more active role in managing their care and wellness. The belief was that Google's strength in consumer-centric product development would make it easier for patients to start using these new tools to take charge of their daily health experiences.

Google was the third in a line of Big Tech companies to try to launch a personal health record. Five years prior (2005), Steve Case, the founder of AOL, launched Revolution Health.[16] A couple of years later (2007), Microsoft would launch HealthVault.[17] The very next year (2008), Google launched Google Health.[18] All three would eventually close their doors. Google ended Google Health first in 2011, Revolution Health closed in 2012, and Microsoft HealthVault shuttered in 2019. All three failed due largely to low uptake.

Although the scale of large tech seemed promising, wariness about these giants having access to personal health information was a barrier not easy to overcome.[*]

In the following years, there have been many post-mortem discussions about why these efforts failed. Some felt that the timing may have been too early. Some believed it was the limited ability for systems to talk to one another (interoperability) and the difficulty for patients to access their data from electronic health systems used by their doctors, hospitals, and clinics. Others believed that the personal health records' inability to include additional health data collected by the patient was the culprit. Still others argued that these personal health records didn't incorporate mobile technologies fast enough to meet consumer behavior.

---

[*] Google Health 2011

Perhaps the real issue was society's discomfort with allowing Big Tech access to *any* personal health data.

Patient Data Privacy

An inherent tension exists between patient privacy and the desire to learn from patient data. Knowledge of patients' health conditions has been used as a way to discriminate for health insurance, employment, eligibility for public services, and many other aspects of life. In fact, this was far more prevalent in the 1980s and 1990s and directly affected people's opportunities and quality of life. As someone who graduated from medical school in 1996, I remember commending the *intention* behind the passage of the Health Insurance Portability and Accountability Act (HIPAA), the 1996 legislation known best for protecting patient privacy.

Although the scale of large tech seemed promising, wariness about these giants having access to personal health information was a barrier not easy to overcome.

Unfortunately, at that time, there was no way to realize the future impact of how the internet, the advent of mobile technologies and social media, and the speed of technology innovation would change society's expectations. We could not foresee the society's growing comfort with sharing personal information online, nor how it would ultimately affect our ability to interact with both institutions and one another.

The authors of HIPAA couldn't have anticipated all the consequences in their attempt to codify patient privacy nor would they have been able to advocate for necessary, rapid adaptations in a fast-changing ecosystem. At best, future policies were merely reactive and, at times, an unexpected millstone for research.

Future healthcare legislation would continue to try to plug some of the holes or address the unintended consequences of strict privacy requirements. There were many "exemptions."

Big Tech, mobile technologies, and social media are not fully covered by HIPAA.

Big Tech, mobile technologies, and social media are not fully covered by HIPAA. Consumers' unease with Big Tech accessing patient data was not unfounded.

The marketplace's ability to move quickly with new information technology meant that large amounts of personal health data could be collected through consumer or health devices. Some of this data could be sold to third parties, not too dissimilar to how data on one's credit card history or shopping habits could be sold. This meant that companies could use and monetize health care data legally, often without explicit patient consent.

Regulation only applies to patient data handled by healthcare providers and traditional healthcare entities. Most patient data in consumer apps or tech platforms are not covered, leaving patients little recourse if this data is breached, misused, or leaked.

It's no surprise that patients were wary of trusting Big Tech with their health records. High-profile breaches and privacy lapses only deepened their unease, especially around the fear of being identified or targeted for specific conditions. When Big Tech's personal health record ventures eventually collapsed, the conversation shifted toward how to build safeguards that would let *patients* manage and control their own data.

At the same time, patients as consumers were growing more digitally savvy—managing finances, travel, and personal data effortlessly online. It seemed natural for them to want to do something similar with their own health data.

So why did healthcare remain so frustratingly hard to navigate despite having digital systems and health records already in place? The usual, and deeply unsatisfying, answer was usually summed up in one word: HIPAA.

In 2018, another Big Tech giant, Apple, launched Apple Health Records to connect health data collected from the Apple Watch to a platform where patients could monitor their own conditions. Apple's product emerged at a time of better connectivity, standards, mobile technology, and APIs.[19] It also arrived at a time when consumers had a more casual attitude toward privacy when using sophisticated, mobile applications. Despite all this, adoption initially remained lower than expected.

A different issue became apparent. Health data needs context. Getting a full picture of your health status involves bringing together many disparate pieces of information, which are often located in multiple places. Aside from locating all the pieces, the format of the data can be a barrier. Even gains in interoperability are unable to overcome inconsistent formatting and a general lack of willingness to share among institutions and companies. While technology may have progressed further since 2018, giving us better and smarter tools, analysis isn't straightforward nor helpful without benchmarks or context.

Furthermore, managing, stewarding, and curating your own health data can be overwhelming unless you have a strong personal interest, a user-friendly system, or a compelling reason to knit it all together.

Data Curation

Data curation has been defined as the organization and integration of data collected from various sources, involving annotation, publication, and presentation to maintain the value of the data over time. Data needs to be validated, managed, and available for re-use or preservation. There also needs to be an intention to continually determine what is worth saving and for how long.[20]

In the digital age, data curation is complex and complicated. Examples include maintaining research findings, determining which evidence is appropriate for indexing and what should be catalogued, as well as how to maintain and manage algorithms, digital assets, and internet content.

In healthcare, large volumes of data are generated every moment and accumulated over time, but data tends to be used only for single purposes and the focus is more about centralized storage.

The types of data captured, generated, and stored range from clinical to administrative, lab and images, instrument-recorded (e.g., a glucose monitor) to patient-reported. Patients are cared for by several different professionals or members of a care team, each of whom will record their information separately. And even today, some data will be transmitted via fax and stored electronically or sometimes on paper.

The electronic medical or health record has become a central hub for storing information. Despite the growth in both the volume and types of data, these systems still function much like modern filing cabinets.

These systems still function much like modern filing cabinets.

Data is not curated as much as it is assembled to be read or reviewed.

"We seem to have lost the wisdom of the indigenous people, which dictated that in any major decision, the first consideration was 'How will this decision we're making today affect our people in the future? These days, decisions are made based on the bottom line."

~ Jane Goodall, 2018

CHAPTER 4

STEWARDSHIP

Inside healthcare organizations, data over the past thirty years includes hundreds of millions of patient records, billions of insurance claims, and countless other types of sources including lab and test results, radiology, pathology, and prescriptions. All this patient data, along with the advent of new genomic classifications, new therapies, and patient-collected information have made curation more difficult and stewardship more challenging.

Data stewardship is about safeguarding the integrity of the data while also ensuring compliance as to how the data are handled. Data provenance is being able to trace back to the original source and track all changes to the data.

Maintaining integrity and trust in the clinical data demands stewardship and clear provenance to protect patient rights and privacy.

A patient's protected health information (PHI) includes their medical diagnosis, treatment, and health status. Patients technically have ownership rights over their PHI and are guaranteed by law to have the ability to access the data, ask for corrections, request copies, and grant rights around sharing.

The *physical* health record, however, is owned by the health system, meaning the physician's office, a clinical practice, or a hospital or hospital network.

Consider what else is contained in this record, namely the clinical note generated during a patient visit. While the record may contain a patient's clinical information, the note is also the *work product* of their treating physician and the health system where the physician practices.

Although physical health records are owned by healthcare providers in all fifty states, ownership of *electronic* health records varies by state, sometimes belonging to the physician, the patient, or both.[*] But regardless of ownership, all healthcare entities are required to comply with HIPAA privacy regulations as a baseline for safeguarding privacy, including access.

Privacy laws can be rather confusing, especially as there are also state privacy laws that can sometimes be more stringent than HIPAA and will take precedence within their jurisdictions.

For example, California's recent amendment to the Confidentiality of Medical Information Act (effective July 1, 2024) mandates special protections for data related to abortion, contraception, and gender-affirming care, particularly concerning data shared across state lines and legal contexts. Similarly, Maryland's Electronic Health Record

---

[*] Appendix IV: Medical Record Ownership by State

Data Privacy bill (Senate Bill 786) restricts disclosure of reproductive health information, including abortion care, to shield patients and providers from legal risks when procedures are performed in states where lawful.

Beyond reproductive health, several states have long required heightened safeguards for sensitive information categories such as HIV/AIDS, mental health, and substance abuse, reflecting the ongoing complexity and regional variability in healthcare data privacy.

As healthcare continues to move toward nationwide interoperability, a balancing act remains — to facilitate secure data sharing while respecting patient privacy.

From a technology perspective, there are new advancements to segment health data while enabling sensitive information to be tagged and controlled without impeding clinical care. For example, HL7* privacy policies support the use of security labels and "break-the-glass" functionality, which permits clinicians to override data restrictions in emergencies to ensure patient safety.

The federal government also emphasizes patients' rights to specify which data can be shared and which will require stricter privacy. The goal is to protect individuals from harm or discrimination, especially in sensitive cases such as those involving domestic violence.

So now consider the contradiction when various state laws designate specific procedures as illegal and therefore can invoke other legal justifications to demand *access* to patient data.

---

* Appendix VI: Standards of Interoperability

Organizations use specialized and standardized vocabularies (e.g., ICD-10-CM, LOINC, and SNOMED) to codify and tag sensitive data accurately. This, in turn, promotes compliance with HIPAA, state laws, and evolving data-sharing regulations, all while maintaining seamless and secure information flow.

In light of the high stakes around data rights and the protection of sensitive data, the role of a data steward or stewardship program is constantly increasing in scope. A data steward[21] is someone or a team who manages and safeguards sensitive patient information and clinical data. They function within institutions, organizations, and even as support for electronic information systems, and are responsible for:

➤ data quality and integrity (validation processes for accuracy and procedures for handling data)

➤ data security and compliance (encryption, access controls, and even de-identification of data)

➤ data accessibility and usability (standardization, organization, integration)

➤ data governance (authorized access, establishing purpose of use)

Data stewards are also responsible for facilitating the communication and coordination of data for interdepartmental use and storage.

So what happens when we want to do analysis on the data, either internally or for third parties to aggregate and analyze? In either scenario, data stewards remove duplicates and ensure that there is no conflict with the data. They ensure it is up-to-date and consistent, fit for its intended use, and can connect with other data streams, all while ensuring the data is protected from unauthorized use.

Perils of Access

From the earliest days of Healthcare IT, we have cared greatly about who can access and share content, who can make decisions, and who may change these decisions downstream. We have conceived of information as flowing through pipes, built hardened security gates, and enacted laws, policies, and rules around managing protected health information (PHI).

From a policy maker's point of view, patient safety and safeguarding patient data are of paramount importance, but so too is the need to ensure proper utilization of resources.

When HIPAA was first enacted and outlined standards for electronic exchange, privacy, and security of health information, the original intention was actually to increase insurance coverage. Focusing on privacy allowed the beginning of de-linking insurance from employment.

At the time, insurance coverage for care was gated by what was termed as "pre-existing" conditions. HIPAA provisions about safeguarding patient health data was a way to keep insurance companies from discriminating.

"Pre-existing" conditions were a real barrier to insurance coverage. Having a chronic disease associated with expensive future care increased your odds of being rejected for any insurance coverage or subject to higher premiums. There was a lot of anxiety around people losing their health insurance if their health conditions were made known. Patients were rightfully very sensitive to their medical information being kept private and protected.

Diseases like HIV carried immense societal judgment. Popular culture further amplified these concerns. In 1994, Tom Hanks won an Oscar for his role in *Philadelphia*, a film that powerfully portrayed a gay lawyer dying of AIDS and the discrimination he faced in the workplace.

That same year, *Rent*, Jonathan Larson's groundbreaking musical, opened audiences' eyes to the brutal reality of AIDS, once again exposing the healthcare system's cold disregard (and sometimes denial of care) for those in need.

Mental health struggles were also heavily stigmatized. And I can still remember the advice circulating among my fellow physicians. If any of us had a family member suffering from a mental health condition, we were advised to pay cash to keep it "off the record".

HIPAA's privacy focus pre-dated the explosion of mobile and decentralized technology as well as voluntary sharing of personal information (social media). Hence, the reach of HIPAA was limited almost as soon as it was passed. Future legislation would continue to try to "plug the holes" that had not been previously anticipated.

Legislative priorities are often bundled together to ensure passage. The HIPAA "plugs" later combined into other larger legislation that, at times, worked at cross purposes. The challenge of using amendments to address circumstances that didn't exist at the time of the previous legislation is that there is seldom any review process to determine whether the gap-plugging is simply creating newer impediments.

For example, later legislation will require health systems working with electronic record vendors to comply with certain certification requirements. These requirements will increase the number of steps (more permissions needed) to access data. The end result will be additional administrative steps for patients to share even their own health information with family members, caregivers, and sometimes to elicit a second opinion.

One workaround is to leverage legal authorization, rather than direct HIPAA consent, to obtain data access. Under the HIPAA Privacy Rule, only the patient or their personal representative (as defined under state and federal law) can access PHI. This can be done with a patient assigning HIPAA authorization to a representative (e.g., family member) for a defined purpose. There is also the healthcare power of attorney (POA) designation which legally empowers a representative to make medical decisions and view records on the patient's behalf.

In fact, today, many people are appointing healthcare powers of attorney as a proactive measure, so medical decisions can be made on their behalf if they are unable to do so. Parents of college-aged children are using this approach to gain access to their children's medical records, in the case their children become incapacitated or mentally compromised. Similarly, POA is also being used to assist with managing care for elderly relatives who may suffer cognitive decline. Companies like Mama Bear Legal Forms have emerged to help consumers tap into these legal authorizations to manage HIPAA's restrictions.

But access to health data is more than just what is covered by HIPAA. As mentioned earlier, personal health data from mobile apps and social media are not protected by HIPAA. Sensitive information that patients *voluntarily* share also remains outside HIPAA's reach. So while HIPAA can enforce strict controls over patient records within the healthcare infrastructure, large and growing swaths of personal health information remain unprotected elsewhere.

"Confidentiality, Integrity, and Availability"

Three Principles of Security,
National Cybersecurity Center of Excellence,
December 2020[22]

CHAPTER 5

ELECTRONIC RECORDS 101

In 2005, Hurricane Katrina ripped through New Orleans. The devastation included paper medical records that were stored in offices, basements, hospitals, and clinics. Newt Gingrich, the former Speaker of the House known from the Clinton-era health reform days, was then leading a coalition to drive technological change in healthcare— and he came out swinging.

This was THE case study in favor of Electronic Medical Records (EMRs). "Paper kills" was his mantra. Gingrich and Dr. David Brailer, the head of the newly formed Office of the National Coordinator for Health Information Technology (ONCHIT), made the case that electronic versions of health records were vital to security and as a backup to support care.

Gingrich also stated that mere digitization of a record was simply not enough: "Health IT should be a dynamic system that makes use of access to information, not simply passive records."[23]

In addition to the medical record, which primarily contained physician's notes, other documents such as lab tests, prescriptions, and radiology also needed to be stored electronically. In reality, these were often located in different places. The early electronic medical records served as the base chart while scans, faxes and other additional information were mostly kept outside of the clinical record. This necessitated integration with practice management and electronic health systems.

With the accelerated adoption of electronic records and the digitization of more information, the need for an electronic infrastructure was reaching a critical state. However, there was no appetite for a centralized system. Rather, the goal was to create *interoperability* standards that would enable different systems to "talk to one another" and exchange information.

> **The determination to protect patient privacy prevented us from creating a national patient identifier.**

The goal in the U.S. was to foster a sense of competition for the purpose of driving innovative improvements while also ensuring that the various players in the healthcare ecosystem could still communicate and exchange information.

This goal was complicated to execute and compounded by both our decentralized health care system and dogged determination to protect patient privacy. Together, these forces prevented us from creating a *national patient identifier* that could bridge across the various health care systems.

Rather, future systems would be connected through cross-checking and "masking" patient identity through assigning privacy "tokens" – ensuring the data was appropriately tagged to the same individual.

The Electronic Medical Record (EMR)

Although there were many experimental installations with electronic record systems (in some form or another) at various academic institutions with the help of government throughout the 1960s, the first Electronic Medical Record (EMR) is frequently credited to Regenstrief Institute in Indianapolis under the leadership of Dr. Clem McDonald in 1972.[24] The primary goal was to unify scattered patient information into a comprehensive electronic database.

In 1975, the Veteran Affairs (VA) health system designed a system to integrate clinical, financial and administrative functions into a single database which became known as the Veterans Health Information Systems and Technology Architecture or VistA.[25] Using consultants from the National Bureau of Standards, the VA requested the use of a computer language known as MUMPS (Massachusetts General Hospital Utility Multi-Programming System) which had a hierarchical architecture and nodal design that allowed multiple functions to run at the same time. The goal was to form the basis of a hospital system information technology architecture that could weave multiple functionalities together. VistA would later be deployed across all VA hospitals and become an integrated system for all VA patients, servicing more than 9 million veterans, win awards for computer excellence, but remain only within the VA health system.

By the late 1970s and early 1980s, commercial electronic medical record systems became available to hospitals but did not offer the kind of fully integrated capabilities of the VA system. There were also no real standards or best practices around which or how functions should be integrated.

In 1991, the Institute of Medicine (IOM) published the Computer-Based Patient Record: An Essential Technology for Health Care.[26] This was the first document to examine the possibilities inherent in electronic medical records (EMRs) by defining twelve functions *focused* on the patient and physician, as opposed to simply the technology.

The twelve functions in the document included:

> ➤ Support a problem list

> ➤ Measure health status and functional levels

> ➤ Document clinical reasoning and rationale

> ➤ Provide dynamic links to other patient records

> ➤ Guarantee confidentiality, privacy and audit trails

> ➤ Offer continuous access for authorized users

> ➤ Support simultaneous multiple user views

> ➤ Facilitate clinical problem solving

> ➤ Support direct data entry by users

> ➤ Support practitioners in measuring costs and improving quality

> ➤ Support the existing and evolving needs of clinical specialties

It is interesting that not one of these functions mentions that the inherent value of the clinical data from a patient could support research and potential cures for common diseases.

When electronic *medical* records (EMR) were first created and deployed, particularly in clinics and in hospital systems, the records were stored the way you would store information in files. A patient's digitized records, reports, test results and clinical notes were simply placed in the same electronic folder. The format didn't really matter.

The challenge came later when you wanted to analyze the information contained in that folder, whether you wanted to view their progress or symptoms or values over time or look at a group of patients with similar conditions. Even in digital form, the information was either uploaded, needed to be manually entered into fields, or extracted separately to be included in a chart or table.

Within the digital folder are many clinical notes and every note is a narrative: the physician's observations or thinking and the patient's answers to questions. These notes show up within a free text field, and every clinician has their own style of writing. Notes can have a lot of variability which can make it difficult to standardize when extracting or converting into data. If the notes come from multiple sources (e.g., multiple offices or labs), this only compounds the data complexity.

When a clinical note is created, it is difficult to structure it *a priori*. The importance of an observation may not be determined until later. Unlike a list of medications which can be easily assembled into a table, documented observations require time, thought, and expertise before being combined with other observations to describe what is happening with the patient. In other words, conversion to data without context will guarantee something will get lost in translation. And so, EMRs remain with large text fields.

For example, a physician's note may contain the following: "The patient was able to stand firmly on both of her feet but could not stand on either foot without losing her balance and falling to the side. She also began swaying when asked to close her eyes. She was able to walk the distance of the hallway (approximately 30 feet in length) in about 2 minutes' time. But she also complained that she felt dizzy while walking." All the details are important to the physician, but only some of this information is useful in a structured field- for future analysis. How can you tell from the outset?

An Early EMR to Help Physicians

In mid 2001, I joined Pfizer and a new group called eHealth within the U.S. Planning and Business Development Department. The mission of the group was broad, deep, and innovative. We were to explore, invest in, support, and influence the emerging sweep of e-Health: internet-related and electronic health initiatives which could shape the pharma business and overall healthcare marketplace.

The first initiative was to launch an electronic medical record company for small independent physician practices.

On October 10, 2001, the headline in the Wall Street Journal announced our joint venture: "Pfizer, IBM, Microsoft Launch Healthcare Software Venture."[27,28]

At the time, internet access was spotty and servers were still locally housed. Few physicians were using electronic medical records as most practices were not interested in paying implementation and maintenance costs.

However, as independent physicians felt the growing administrative reach of managed care and the documentation paperwork burden, the thought of an electronic system was intriguing to many, but the cost was too high to justify.

Because these practices were independent, the physicians who owned or worked in them still had a great deal of autonomy. Here was Pfizer suggesting that an electronic medical record tailored to their needs would keep them independent, a common goal shared by both physicians and the pharmaceutical industry.

Pfizer's bold move was trying to provide *affordable* technology that would alleviate the administrative pain these physician practices were experiencing. The administrative pain was ascribed to too much paperwork and not enough time to think.

Pfizer's focus on time for physicians to think and being independent was also related to their experience with working with physicians as scientists. Perhaps more than any other entity in healthcare, the pharmaceutical industry's interaction with physicians was multifold including working with them as researchers.

As Pfizer wasn't in the business of providing hardware or software, a partnership with IBM and Microsoft, the reigning giants in their respective fields at the time, was the way to go, especially if the goal was to accelerate adoption at affordable prices. Starting out with a small pre-existing electronic medical record called PenChart along with these two blue-chip partners, Pfizer forged ahead to create a new electronic medical record company called Amicore.

Record Keeping and Unstructured Data

Amicore was not the first EMR vendor targeted at community or independent physicians.

Recall that early systems were closed computer systems designed with the input of early-adopter physicians and designed for users to be able to enter, retrieve, compile, and more importantly, keep information up to date. Prior to the internet, these were simply electronic record keeping systems and were predominantly deployed in hospitals.

In the 1990s, a number of new EMR vendors appeared in the market, with many focused on community physicians and standalone practices. These small EMR vendors were confined to specific geographic areas. As most care took place within their respective confined areas and often within a single building, servicing tended to be a local endeavor and connectivity wasn't necessarily an issue. As the internet became more prevalent, so did the desire for greater connectivity, both technologically and for expertise.

In 2001, when we launched Amicore, we were still dealing with onsite servers, though we did have local area networks (LANs). Despite improvement in broadband expansion in the mid-2000s, there were still internet dead zones all over the U.S. Cloud infrastructure did not emerge as an option until the early 2010s.

Gathering information was slow, but for those early adopter physicians, there was a lot of excitement and willingness to put in the effort to enter the information in an electronic format. But we couldn't get away from the large free text fields, not if we were trying to align with the physician's workflow.

Taking care of patients and documenting their care is a holistic process and doesn't naturally lend itself to the data entry flow. Physicians are not simply treating; they are also observing and sleuthing out what is happening.

In the process of a visit, they are considering potential diseases and disorders, noticing details, asking questions—and then constructing a narrative and documenting in a clinical note. It is difficult to both chronicle observations and problem-solve simultaneously. Consider the following: thinking about what is happening to the patient, documenting what you are learning, and performing data entry — all at the same time, in real time.

Meanwhile, the electronic record is designed primarily for data entry.

A physician's clinical note will be organized but not necessarily housed in structured data fields. When you are

The electronic record is designed primarily for data entry.

trying to capture clinical observations and make assessments in real time, you will type into the record in a single field as text. Later, someone will read the text and pull out the relevant information.

Physicians are scientists and they are also detectives. They begin by listing key identifiers and obvious observations, then move on to more subtle details, such as how a patient speaks or moves.

Using this information, the physician then builds a preliminary assessment to determine if the details match the pattern of a few diagnoses they are contemplating. They may ask more questions to determine the patient's context and circumstances. They may order more tests or observe a patient for a longer period of time. Their preliminary hypothesis, known as a differential diagnosis, will be written at the end, followed by potential options for treatment (including pros and cons). Finally, they will put forth a plan that they think may best suit the patient or elucidate further details that may inform treatment.

So how does this entire process get captured in a data-entry oriented electronic system?

It is broken up across time. Usually, a physician will take notes in front of the patient. Think of how many of us have had a computer terminal between us and our physician. They may make a quick decision and order some tests or give a prescription at the end, but often they return to those notes later in the day and think it through further and write out or amend their narrative. Either way, it becomes documentation at a later point in the day, and even then, it isn't necessarily entered into structured fields.

What happens when your physician, managing multiple patients, starts wondering if they may be seeing patterns across their patient population. There is no easy way to review the records in aggregate or in a systematic way. The data will not magically convert into a tabular or graphic form, retain meaning, and allow for any easy way to discern a pattern.

To demonstrate how difficult this is, try this exercise: Listen to a talk or have a discussion and try to take organized clinician-level notes. Your ability to capture the information accurately and comprehensively while also creating the categories of what you are hearing is almost impossible. You don't know what will be said, so you start writing in a narrative form. Maybe you categorize a few pieces of information in a list format, but generally, you won't be able to synthesize and categorize these ideas until later. The same difficulties plague physicians trying to use electronic records. While their thoughts and observations may be captured in a note, the classification doesn't happen simultaneously.

Workflows

Electronic recordkeeping initially meant maintaining the electronic version of paper files. Designed to record, file, and retrieve information, the process was workable, but awkward.

However, as new requirements emerged, electronic records slowly stopped trying to follow the workflow of the physician. For these software vendors, if they came up against workflow incongruence, they could either modify the software, which could be expensive, or change the workflow.

However, it wasn't until the health IT market expanded and large vendors began to dominate when modifying software to fit physician workflows became a lower priority. External pressures, such as the need to track billing, measure performance, and meet new regulations, pushed vendors to focus more on compliance than customizing to meet clinician's needs.

As a result, physicians were forced to modify their own workflows to accommodate the software, and the prioritization of one type of workflow (billing and payments) would ultimately change the behavior of both physicians and patients.

Taking a step back, what is workflow and how do you capture data within one? Walk through a visit and you will notice all the points when data is captured. What information is gathered from a patient when they first check in? Or check out? How does the physician capture what is happening in the encounter?

How many of you have sat in a physician's office with a computer in between you and a physician typing in their notes as they speak to you? Those who don't do it in front of you will end up writing or dictating the information right after your visit. During the visit, who else will need to interact with the electronic record before, during, and after a visit? In addition, medical subspecialties may have specific protocols concerning the order in which information is elicited and data is captured.

Electronic record systems were *meant* to support the practice of medicine by optimizing efficiency of data capture and, more importantly, avoid creating unnecessary and unnatural steps in the process of caring for patients.

That is not what happened. Instead, the most prioritized workflow was the one that captured data that could enable efficient coding for billing, payment, and compliance with regulation. Because the billing process depended so much on documentation, physicians had to focus on recording details. To keep up, many began typing notes during patient visits.

The most prioritized workflow was the one that captured data that could enable efficient coding for billing, payment, and compliance with regulation.

The tragedy here is that many of the early, experimental EMR systems, which were designed with physicians' needs in mind, disappeared once market forces and government incentives began pushing for widespread adoption at any cost. The loss of that experimental spirit came at a high cost; it prevented the field from using emerging technologies to improve clinical workflows and strengthen the connection between care and research.

Birth of the Electronic *Health* Record (EHR)

Recording clinical information about a patient in a record was never sufficient for a healthcare ecosystem. There was also a need to exchange information, assemble data from tests, labs, procedures, and hospital stays across multiple systems, gather clinical notes and orders from all physicians or teams caring for a patient, and, finally, ensure transactions were properly coded and transmitted for payment, authorization and reimbursement.

When the medical record started including these capabilities to exchange information, the electronic medical record (EMRs) then became referred to as "electronic *health* records" or EHRs.[29]

*"Show me the incentives,
and I'll show you the outcome."*

~ Charlie Munger,
Psychology of Human Misjudgment speech
at Harvard University, 1995

CHAPTER 6

MARKETPLACE DISTORTION

Government Initiatives

In 1996, the Health Insurance Portability and Accountability Act (HIPAA) was passed *primarily* to increase the number of people with health insurance and enhance healthcare efficiency. It also became the federal law best known for protecting the privacy of patient health care information.

In 2009, the American Recovery and Reinvestment Act was passed under then-President Barack Obama. Within this act was another act focused on healthcare IT known as Health Information Technology for Economic and Clinical Health Act (HITECH). This single act changed the marketplace of electronic records and would also attempt to correct the shortcomings of the original HIPAA by creating greater penalties for violation of patient privacy.

Included in HITECH was a new program known as Meaningful Use. The purpose was to push rapid adoption of electronic health records through a combination of incentives and penalties.

The aspect that pertained to closing a gap in HIPAA: requiring use of a *certified* set of EHRs operating with consensus standards for information exchange. The goal was to rapidly create a nation-wide network in which patient information could be safeguarded throughout.

Of course, implementing this first required physicians and hospitals to use electronic records.

To improve quality, safety, and efficiency seemed sensible from a digital infrastructure point of view, but the entire underpinning of it completely depended on EHR ubiquity. Once that was achieved, the assumption was that there would be demand for interoperability across other healthcare software functionalities and systems.

Ubiquity is achieved through speed of adoption. Up until 2009, EHR/EMR adoption had been extremely low and only 10-18 percent adoption across physician practices and hospitals, largely due to the cost of implementation and difficulty to use.

So to drive widespread and rapid EHR adoption, the Meaningful Use program was designed primarily to *compel* healthcare providers to incorporate EHR into their practice within a short timeframe.

The term "meaningful use" referred to the requirement that hospitals and practices had to use technology certified by the U.S. Health and Human Services (HHS) department, which held certain reporting capabilities and could connect to various services such as ePre-scribing. EHRs would become the linchpin and nodes of the entire digital infrastructure for U.S. healthcare.

All public and private physicians and healthcare providers were *required* to adopt and demonstrate "meaningful use" of electronic medical records by January 1, 2014, in order to maintain their existing Medicaid and Medicare reimbursement levels.

A key misstep in the Meaningful Use program was the decision to mandate *certified* EHR use, penalizing physicians who used *any* EHR, regardless of functionality or effectiveness.

Physician practices and hospitals were required to install an HHS-certified EHR that would *demonstrate* adherence to "meaningful use" criteria. This immediately favored certain EHR vendors, those who could ensure they met this criteria, while placing at a disadvantage those who might prioritize physician preferences or workflows. The thumb was on the scale in favor of the large EHR vendors.

A key misstep in the Meaningful Use program was the decision to mandate certified EHR use, penalizing physicians who used any EHR, regardless of functionality or effectiveness.

Certification creates winners and losers and, coupled with incentives, tends to spark a "gold rush" mentality. The EHR vendors that would benefit were the larger entities because, incidentally, the "meaningful use" criteria were almost *identical* to what the larger entities were already developing.

To give a sense of how big this effort was, HITECH had a federal incentive pool of $27 billion to encourage EHR adoption[30] and more than $38 billion was ultimately distributed to eligible providers to *purchase* certified EHR systems. If they did not, then the physicians faced penalties ranging from losing 1-5 percent of Medicare payments.

ACA Double Downs

A year later, in 2010, when the Affordable Care Act (ACA, also known as ObamaCare) passed, there was a "doubling down" on this mandate as well as on the financial incentives.

The ACA built upon the HITECH Act by further expanding the EHR adoption incentives (Medicare EHR incentive program) and clarifying the definition of "meaningful use-compliant" and "certified" EHRs. The criteria included:

➤ Improving quality, safety, efficiency, and reducing health disparities

➤ Engaging patients and family (allowing patients to access their EHRs)

➤ Improving care coordination and population and public health

➤ Maintaining privacy and security of patient health information

This list at first appears reasonable, but the devil is in the details. How does one prove they have met this criteria unless the information can be *tracked* and measured? What metrics do you use to determine whether there is improvement? With vague wording, what gets measured is simply activity, which is then used as a proxy for goal achievement.

If the criteria is tied to payment and reimbursement (Medicare, Medicaid penalties), this also distorts the market, as it drives involved parties to avoid financial penalties instead of focusing on better metrics for providing individual care and supporting clinical-based rationales in decision-making.

The ACA went further to emphasize interoperability standards, security guidelines, and rules around health data exchange and aggregation, particularly around "quality reporting." It also created an additional burden for physicians by integrating reporting measures under the Physician Quality Reporting Systems (PQRS), which fell under the "reporting requirements" of the Medicare EHR incentive program.

Distorted Marketplace: User Preferences Ignored

EHR vendors large and small were required to create networks or facilitate integration with other systems (prescribing, labs, data exchange with other EHRs). Many of the small vendors couldn't accomplish these tasks, and the industry rapidly became consolidated and defined by a few large players.

Since the entire focus was on proving "meaningful use" via specifically HHS-certified EHR systems, physicians' needs, preferences, workflows, and even their data needs took a back seat. Vendors didn't have to consider the user preferences, as the money came from the government and they only had to meet infrastructure criteria focused heavily on population metrics.

The government incentives created to offset the cost of technology adoption for physicians had truly created a bonanza for EHR vendors and organizations associated with interoperability, effectively diminishing the role of physicians in healthcare.

How did it work? The HITECH Act could authorize up to $27 billion in Medicare and federal Medicaid payments over ten years to eligible providers who adopted certified EHR systems and demonstrated meaningful use. The incentive payments to physicians ranged from $18,000 to $63,750 over five to six years. Hospitals could receive initial incentive payments between $2 million and $6.37 million annually, adjusted by Medicaid volume.

EHR vendors, spurred on by this new money, started moving quickly. A few, like GE Health's Centricity EHR product, even started charging the physicians almost the exact same incentive amount to implement their systems, but with a particular financing structure.[31] The more experimental vendors lost market share to the larger ones who were cutting deals and getting more savvy and sophisticated when it came to taking advantage of these incentives and subsidies.

The end result was bigger systems that were mediocre in both functionality and user experience, with high costs for implementation and service.

Aside from enriching a number of EHR vendors, the penalties were squarely aimed at the physicians. If physicians did not adopt a certified EHR before 2015, they were penalized 1 percent of Medicare payments, which would increase to 3 percent over the following three years, and then 5 percent in later years.

In addition, HIPAA violations by physicians could include civil fines up to $1.5 million for repeated violations and criminal penalties up to ten years in prison for "intentional wrongful disclosure of protected health information" as well as termination of Medicare and Medicaid billing privileges.

Needless to say, systems prioritized designs to both meet the meaningful use criteria (and get certified) as well as be built with a series of HIPAA violation triggers. Eventually, the system complexity and heavy implementation time made the cost of switching EHR systems too great for physicians and hospitals. This, in turn, created an almost permanent EHR customer installed base for the vendors who got there quickly.

The concept of improving user experience for physicians, medical professionals and patients disappeared.

HITECH accomplished the goal of rapid EHR adoption. By 2015, there was 95 percent adoption for hospitals (from 10 percent pre-HITECH) and 75 percent for physician practices (from 18 percent).

> This created an almost permanent EHR customer installed base for the vendors who got there quickly.

Furthermore, the attention to avoiding HIPAA violations made it more difficult to access data and inadvertently created a barrier to developing a better research infrastructure. The irony is that sections of this legislation pertaining to HIPAA were written to support clinical research.[32]

"While it will be desirable to achieve planned results, it will be even more important to avoid unplanned disasters."

~ John Kenneth Galbraith,
The Affluent Society

CHAPTER 7:

THE MARKET RESPONDS, RAPIDLY

Rise of the Big Players

In 2009, Judy Faulkner, the Founder and CEO of Epic Systems, was appointed to the health IT policy committee established under then-President Obama's American Recovery and Reinvestment Act. This was a committee generally dominated by medical informatics professionals, academics, policy wonks rather than large EHR vendor CEOs.[33]

Faulkner built Epic Systems in 1979, as an integrated and closed electronic records system. In 2003, she landed Kaiser Permanente as her largest client. From there, her program expanded across U.S. hospital systems and their clinics. Privately held, it has never acquired nor integrated another company and builds all its software in house. Its mantra is producing software that works.

Today, it is the largest hospital-based electronic health record company. With 2024 revenues at just under $5 billion, Epic Systems is a juggernaut. Epic's software is used in health systems that cover more than half of the hospital beds in the U.S. and counts several of the largest academic medical centers as its customers.

In spite of its reach and influence, however, the company has been controversial over the years due to its stance on interoperability, its reputation for playing hard with smaller companies, and its unwillingness to share healthcare data.[34]

Epic was one of the biggest beneficiaries of the government incentives from legislation in 2009 and 2010, namely HITECH, which supercharged electronic health record adoption. Its greatest gains came from this federal subsidization and at the cost of physicians being put in a regulatory and legal bind. Its outsized role in healthcare IT infrastructure, bolstered by government regulations, has allowed it to become one of the most deeply entrenched players in the industry.

Although the healthcare IT ecosystem is more than just EHRs, having a dominant EHR company with such a sizable market share of patient information does tend to distort what is possible. A large player deciding not to cooperate with others means more systemic healthcare problems will continue to go unsolved.

The end result is closed, private systems within an open ecosystem framework. Perhaps more concerning is that this closed system was bolstered by federal regulations, the same regulations meant to level the playing field.

During a CNBC segment in 2017 in a discussion about data access, then-Vice President Joe Biden questioned Judy Faulkner about the rationale for limiting patient access to their medical records. Faulkner responded, "Why do you want your medical records? There are a thousand pages, of which you understand 10."[35]

While some consider this response to be clear evidence of an incumbent with enormous market power being flippant, it is important to remember that at the time of the federal subsidies, few accountability measures were put into place.

However, it has been the patients and physicians who have suffered the most. Physicians had no true choice. To remain independent in practice meant choosing not to be hospital-based, not to be attached to a hospital covered by a large EHR system, or turning away Medicare and Medicaid patients in order to be exempt from having to use an *HHS-certified* electronic health record system.

This lack of choice is partially responsible for why the gap between clinical care and clinical research remains so wide. And the medical records are difficult to review.

But Epic Systems is not the only large EHR player who benefited from the government's initiatives to boost healthcare IT.

Neal Patterson, Cliff Illig, and Paul Gorup, three colleagues from the Arthur Andersen consulting firm in Kansas City, started PGI & Associates in 1979 with the intention of applying "software" to healthcare. Their breakthrough moment came when they were hired to fix a billing system for a pathology practice.

The company would go on to be rebranded as Cerner Corporation in 1984, the same year they would launch their first commercial laboratory information system called PathNet. From there, they would go on to build a broader Health Network Architecture (HNA) and lay the groundwork for integration of their own healthcare IT applications.

Through the next decade, they would develop a suite of applications for various clinical departments but then started to shift their focus to providing solutions for the evolving managed care environment. Their choice of name, Cerner, was to signify they believed in helping clients make better decisions with data by being more discerning or *cernere* (Latin).

Cerner would take a very different path from Epic and become a public company in 1986. With the additional funds available, they quickly expanded internationally and launched a unified software platform on a single architecture in 1997 called Cerner Millenium.

Just like Epic, Cerner would also experience an unexpected boon from HITECH and Meaningful Use subsidies. Cerner's win rate for new contracts was above 50 percent during the peak of this incentive-driven adoption, and sales grew by 60 percent during the three-year period following HITECH authorization; Cerner's revenue was greater than $2.2 billion by 2011.[36]

Cerner's growth trajectory was also different from Epic's—and included growth through acquisitions. Starting first with Siemens AG's health information technology business (acquired in 2014 for $1.3 billion), they rapidly expanded their hospital client base.

Throughout the 2010s, Cerner would continue to solidify their position as a global leader in healthcare IT for hospital and health systems. By 2018, Cerner and Epic together controlled 54 percent of all U.S. acute care hospitals.

While ostensibly only having the second largest market share in the U.S. hospital EHR market, Cerner also chased high profile contracts, particularly with the U.S. Department of Defense and other government agencies. By 2021, government contracts made up 18 percent of their revenue, at that time around $990 million. In 2022, Oracle Health would acquire Cerner as their largest to date healthcare IT acquisition.

Glen Tullman took over Allscripts in 1997. Up until this point, the company had focused primarily on electronic prescribing. Under his leadership, the company grew largely through acquisition, by rolling up smaller EHR vendors throughout the 2000s.[37] By 2008, Allscripts had begun merging with competitors of similarly sized EHR systems.

In 2010, Allscripts merged with Eclipsys, a large hospital EHR and practice management vendor whose main product was Sunrise Clinical Manager. This merger allowed Allscripts to help clients tap into the $30 billion of the HITECH funding for EHR adoption.[38] By 2012, the difficulty in software platform integration and the increasingly competitive landscape prompted Tullman to step down after a fifteen-year run.[39]

In the fall of 2022, Allscripts sold off its hospital EHR business and refocused exclusively on providing EHRs to independent clinics (unaffiliated with large hospitals and health systems) under its new brand name, Veradigm.

Today, it is one of a handful of companies, including Meditech, AthenaHealth, eClinicalWorks, and NextGen Health, who primarily focus on independent clinics and independent physicians.

While both Epic and Cerner have expanded beyond hospitals to include clinics, most of their installations are affiliated with larger health systems.

———

The EHR landscape has been a marketplace primarily consisting of these large players who have benefitted enormously from the HITECH and Meaningful Use government incentives. In fact, this structural advantage continues through today as the scale of these EHR vendors have also made it difficult for physicians or health systems to avoid using their systems. There is almost no room for a new startup to come in and disrupt this oligopoly of EHR vendors.

In addition, as independent clinics and practices have been acquired or rolled up over the years by private equity, the practices' EHR purchasing decisions have also tended to favor the large players.

There is, however, a subset of independent practices, who have charted their own course and work instead with a group of smaller and more specialized EHR vendors. Many of these EHR vendors are relatively newer companies and did not benefit from government incentives for adoption. Instead, they have gained a following due to their attention to specific specialty workflows with the support of physician champions.

Billing First, Patients Last

After the emphasis on connectivity and interoperability, insurance payments, and demonstrating "value" from ObamaCare, EHR vendors quickly recognized that the key ongoing revenue stream was to help create an efficient way to bill for care. The real and long game was about *creating efficiency in billing and practice management.* To borrow a term from the dot com era, payment or revenue management became the "killer application." Healthcare went into transactional hyperdrive.

For physicians, the widespread use of EHRs and the connection to better billing perversely ratcheted up their administrative burden. Soon, physicians were devoting more time and attention to entering data during patient visits, dealing with documentation after hours, and filing insurance appeals on behalf of their patients.

Physicians were losing time and attention to administrative headaches caused by new regulations and the need to *maintain* electronic records.

The mandate to work with EHRs increasingly centered around documentation for payment and resulted in physicians creating workarounds to support patients. It also altered their behavior with patients. Physicians found themselves being pushed to follow standardized clinical workflows because these were easier to track and even easier to get paid. The ability to exercise independent professional judgment was becoming more challenging.

The rapid push toward EHR utilization by physicians has resulted in a vicious cycle. Between their need to exercise independent judgment, spend time with patients, and meet the growing demands of a healthcare information tech system where physicians were responsible for both the input and output of information, it is no wonder physician burnout began to climb.

Worse still was the fact that the healthcare information technology system, supposedly intended to decrease medical errors and improve coordination, was also creating a "race to the middle" in terms of providing care and addressing inexorable payment demands.

Not only was this maddening to patients and physicians, but it also created the emergence of the healthcare information technology industrial complex, which would make the health system even more hostile to everyone who came in contact with it.

Unintended Consequences: A Faustian Bargain

In U.S. healthcare, you need to understand policy before you can understand the business. "Business structure in this industry is driven by the architecture of policy in America."[40] This is particularly true of healthcare IT.

> In U.S. healthcare, you need to understand policy before you can understand the business.

In an attempt to reform health insurance and fortify gaps in patient privacy within a digital world, the government was laser-focused on using legislation (ACA and HITECH) and subsequent policymaking to force the adoption of EHRs.

In the process of driving EHR-adoption, the government failed to take into consideration the physician's role, the patient-physician relationship, and how medical learning and research are interconnected.

The unintended consequence of "bribing" and "punishing" the hospitals and physicians to adopt digital systems faster than the marketplace was a distortion of market dynamics. When vendors did not have to compete to win over physicians, nor adapt their product to meet physician user needs, the natural evolution of product-market fit and supporting customers was upended and rendered unimportant.

By insisting that certified EHRs' primary goals were to a) capture and manage data mainly for billing and insurance purposes, b) eliminate waste, and c) ensure safety and patient privacy, the *overall* effect was to transform physicians from autonomous medical professionals into interchangeable service providers.

Physicians and clinicians were not only responsible for providing care, they were also responsible for meeting the criteria of new documentation—documentation that didn't necessarily support care nor research. The meaningful use criteria ultimately handcuffed physician practices to specific vendors and software that would allow them to get paid and be able to pay their staff.

The long-term unintended consequence of the government's pro-EHR movement was the ultimate deprioritization of the larger purpose of electronic medical and health information.

The unspoken goal of electronic medical information had been to *improve* outcomes and patient care, which necessitated a "feedback loop" of clinical data to help inform research, both in the context of caring for an individual and when it came to longer-term studies.

It was a bit of a Faustian bargain. In literature, a Faustian bargain refers to the legend of Faust, who makes a deal with the devil and acquires short-term earthly riches in exchange for the eternal sacrifice of his soul. In business, it refers to any deal in which we opt for a short-term gain at the expense of a long-term consequence.

The short-term gain here is the achievement of near ubiquity of electronic records among physicians and hospitals. The long-term consequences are that we sacrificed supporting physicians in their professional ability to care for patients and that we missed a perfect opportunity to structure collecting data in a way that would have bridged clinical care and clinical research.

In the end, the original promise of healthcare information technology from the heady early days of closing the information gap was forgotten and completely paved over.

"Regulation is the friend of the incumbent."

~ Bill Gurley, Benchmark Capital,
All-In-Summit, September 2023

CHAPTER 8:

REGULATORY CAPTURE

In 1982, George Stigler won the Nobel Prize for Economics for his work on regulatory capture. In 1971, he published a seminal paper entitled "The Theory of Economic Regulation"[41], in which he challenged the idea that regulation primarily serves the public interest. He argued instead that regulation often benefits the industries being regulated, as these industries can bias the regulatory processes to their advantage and hinder potential new competitors.

In 2009, HITECH was a case in point. Its incentives, along with the rules defined by the Federal Government's Office of the National Coordinator on HIT (ONCHIT), ultimately enriched the large players and allowed them to use the meaningful use criteria (regulation) to their advantage. The small EHR market was decimated.

In addition, there was a naïve assumption that if we achieved widespread EHR adoption, then interoperability would follow.

The reality was a much greater challenge than anticipated. Smaller organizations might want interoperability to offer more to their customers, while larger organizations would prefer to create walled gardens for their customers. There was no system-wide incentive for the various companies and organizations to cooperate.

U.S. Government Tries to Coordinate

On April 27, 2004, then-President George W. Bush, through executive order, established the Office of the National Coordinator for Health Information Technology (ONCHIT) within Health and Human Services. Dr. David Brailer was tapped as its first coordinator. Later, under the Obama Administration, Congress included this office in HITECH and ACA legislation.

ONCHIT was created to lead national health IT efforts. The rationale to create a federal entity responsible for coordinating national efforts around health information technology and electronic exchange of health information was driven from the prevailing wisdom that the marketplace could not, and would not, achieve interoperability on its own.

In the beginning, I remember thinking that the impetus behind ONCHIT (in 2004 and pre-HITECH) made some sense as a standards-setting organization and as a convener of stakeholders. In fact, anything intended to help encourage data exchange was something I considered rather positive. Nonetheless, I also remember being worried about how the patient-physician relationship might be affected. I held reservations about future mandates, and I found it odd that the benefits of data exchange barely touched research and instead focused mainly on quality metrics and certification.

The move to create ONCHIT was hopeful, but not without peril.

Pushing for a single set of standards for data exchange ultimately resulted in the need to "certify" HIT systems. While certified systems might meet technical requirements, these systems can still fail to address real-world safety, usability, and workflow needs. Mandating certification can often create a false sense of security, result in additional costs for small vendors, and may not actually meet the larger goals of quality and safety. In the end, overall costs tend to increase as a result.

Like most government entities, the initial promise can easily become mired in the marketplace reactions, stakeholder conflicts, and new legislation.

Mandating certification can often create a false sense of security.

At inception, ONCHIT focused mainly on using standard setting and convening various interests as a way to encourage EHR adoption. When 2009's HITECH Meaningful Use and 2010 ACA created large EHR giants, the office found that the ability to enforce cooperation and information flow became much more difficult.

In addition to being in the certification business, the office's primary priorities shifted to the development of Health Information Exchanges (HIEs) as it continued to push hard for interoperability standards with a focus on consistency and security. When giants are created almost overnight, market power can make it difficult to use regulation to enforce rules of fair play. In fact, much of the health IT ecosystem recognized and argued for explicit rules from the office and the government to prohibit large entities from blocking information flow and to support patients.

In 2016, the 21st Century Cures Act was passed. This was a wide-ranging act, but one key area and focus was around information integration and patient-centered health information technology. Within the legislation was a push for EHRs to be able to operate seamlessly with other third-party applications (e.g., smartphones) through standardized application programming interfaces or APIs.

In 2018, ONCHIT would finally publish the first draft of an agreement called the Trusted Exchange Framework and Common Agreement (TEFCA) as a step to achieve full interoperability among systems so that information could be seamlessly exchanged between various electronic health systems. The framework tried to encourage greater health information exchange by creating data sharing *networks* known as Qualified Health Information Networks (QHIN).

TEFCA ran into issues almost immediately when it was first blocked by Epic Systems on the basis of being unable to ensure patient privacy. The stance of protecting patient privacy was difficult to counter, despite many in the industry considering it an excuse for information blocking.

The issues also ran deeper than simply a lack of cooperation. In 2020, Epic went further than simply standing up for patient privacy; the company launched an all-out effort to block the outflow of data from its software into applications.[42] Urging its health system customers and the largest health system CEOs to take a stand against HHS's proposed rules, the federal government found itself unable to enforce its own interoperability requirement.

Only ten years prior, HITECH and ACA together had provided more than $28 billion in EHR adoption incentives, with most going to the largest EHR vendors. However, the incentives were only around adoption of EHRs, and the penalties were only directed at the physicians and hospitals. These legislative acts were not designed to ensure interoperability among different systems. Incentives drove immediate, but not long-term, behavior.

In December 2023, an Epic Systems' subsidiary, Epic Nexus, gained the *first* designated Qualified Health Information network (QHIN) status. Epic Systems subsequently changed its stance to become a willing participant and leader in driving interoperability within TEFCA's framework.[43] Their lead position was secure.

Regulatory capture does indeed favor the incumbent.

Collateral Damage: Data for Research

Despite a growing interest in the clinical data contained within EHR systems, few vendors have focused on developing tools for physicians to perform their own analytics, and none have invested in making the data from their clinical records usable or structured for research purposes. Instead, they have continued to add functionalities that simply support, track, and manage payments for healthcare transactions.

> Few vendors have focused on developing tools for physicians to perform their own analytics.

EHR vendors have integrated both practice management and revenue cycle management software into their existing products to continue to support the healthcare financial infrastructure. Was there a missed opportunity to create a pathway for clinical care data to support clinical research? Design centered entirely around payment at best gave lip service to physician needs, and the data captured was not refined for research. Ultimately, it was a double loss.

EHR "improvements" continue to demand more documentation from physicians in order to smooth out processes such as revenue cycle management. No real dashboards or workspaces were created to support physicians or patients from a research point of view. Rather, both physicians and patients became cogs in a transactional system. Payment claims, the paper trail of what was billed and paid for, became the main throughline when it came to determining what happened with patients as they interacted with the health system. Additional software solutions were developed to integrate with EHRs to try to close gaps between care given and payment received.

The irony is that as EHRs have evolved to support billing and claims – invoices for tests and treatments – these claims have become the imperfect proxies for actual clinical care provided. There is an entire industry dedicated to aggregating and de-identifying claims data and then selling it as research datasets.

Had EHRs evolved in a way that tethered them to research pathways, there may not have been the need to infer a patient journey from claims data or impute what actually happened from a collection of invoices and billing codes.

For the sake of a rapid EHR adoption, we sacrificed long-term success. We forgot that the clinical data captured in the EHR could have and should have supported physicians, patients, and research simultaneously. More importantly, we forgot about the role of the physician and physician-scientist.

Privacy and National Patient Identifier

The focus on privacy has also made it difficult to bridge care and research. In fact, legislation focused on privacy concerns also contributed largely to how we ended up with a system where work-arounds abound, just to even determine if we are looking at the same patient.

As discussed earlier, there is an inherent tension between protecting privacy of personal health information and decision-making between physicians and patients versus the need to access data to improve care and research for both patient and population.

Although HIPAA may have been created with the right intentions, I have discussed how the rapid speed of progress and innovation made this piece of legislation inadequate or not easy to adapt.

Privacy also extended to the difficulty of developing a national patient identifier, a unique number or identifier that could be assigned to a patient and used to pull together information about that patient (not too dissimilar to a social security number). While the benefits may seem obvious, the concerns around privacy became sacrosanct.

In fact, so great were the concerns, the idea of a national patient identifier was literally *banned* within a House appropriations spending bill in fiscal year 1999–known as Section 510. Section 510 specifically prohibits any federal funding to "promulgate or adopt any final standard for providing for the assignment of a unique health identifier for an individual until legislation is enacted specifically approving the standard." In fact, the original rider was inserted by then Representative Ron Paul of Texas into a budget bill in 1999. It has continued to remain standing, mainly due to the efforts of his son, Senator Rand Paul, M.D., of Kentucky. The main arguments preventing a national or universal patient identifier (UPI) or even the centralizing of patients' health information has revolved around the threat of theft by foreign bad actors or the interference of the trust within a patient-physician's decisions.[44]

Over the last few decades, many healthcare organizations including the American College of Surgeons and the American College of Physicians have continued to clamor for a universal patient identifier, even suggesting the option to make it voluntary. They cite the issue of medical errors, loss of information, duplicative records, and an undue impediment to both streamlining of care as well as the workarounds to conduct research.[45] Multiple attempts to pass legislation to remove or to blunt the effects of Section 510 have failed.

And so, the debate continues around the merits of UPI versus privacy concerns, and the number of organizations pushing for a UPI continue to grow.[46] So as physicians, patients, healthcare organizations, and research efforts continue to work around the lack of a UPI, this state of affairs perpetually fuels a cottage industry of blinding/unblinding data for multiple healthcare and research purposes and the sale and use of various "tokens" to ensure privacy concerns remain met.

The VA Swaps its Long-Time Custom-Built Electronic System to Buy From a Big Player

In 2018, the U.S. Veterans Administration (VA) signed a $10 billion contract with Cerner, now Oracle Health. The administration had decided to give up its forty-year-old VistA EHR system in favor of the off-the-shelf commercial EHR system. Oracle Health is one of the largest players in EHR and a direct competitor to Epic Systems. The intention behind the move was to align with the Department of Defense's past use of Cerner's electronic systems.

The swap out and rollout was a complete catastrophe.

The new EHR system has been directly linked to significant patient safety issues, a number of software errors, outages, and actual patient harm. Physicians were angry at the inability to retrieve records, the high number of missing orders, the poor usability, and the disruption of workflows compromising patient care and safety.

Several Congressional briefings starting in 2022 revealed that Oracle Health's software had resulted in thousands of unfilled and misdirected clinical orders, inaccurate pharmacy and allergy information, incorrect patient identifiers, the inability for physicians to access records, record numbers of outages, and a general lack of alerts directly resulting in four veterans' deaths and over 150 cases of direct patient harm.[47]

The federal government paused its implementation of Oracle Health into additional VA hospitals until software corrections were made. As of April 2025, only six VA facilities are using Oracle Health. Seven additional facilities will gain Oracle Health by 2026, with the rest of the 170 facilities following along by 2031.

It is strange that the U.S. government is sticking with Oracle Health. Conversations with those who had been involved in the original six centers have often mentioned how the physicians and nurses were never consulted about the electronic health record change or what was important to preserve.

Even in spring of 2024, the House Committee on Veterans' Affairs Chairman Mike Bost excoriated the current situation: "The VA medical centers that are using the Oracle Health electronic health record have been turned upside down. We've heard it in oversight hearings, during briefings, from veterans and VA's dedicated doctors and nurses across the country." Congress' focus has appropriately been on the disastrous rollout and the joint accountability of the VA leadership and Oracle Health.

However, there has been little discussion about what *else* has also been jettisoned. Many of the custom features of VistA were created specifically for issues that were directly related to the veteran population, something an off-the-shelf EHR product would not have. This means more workarounds, on top of the fact that the VA needs a working and functional EHR. Does this sound familiar?

According to its website, Oracle Health's EHR products are certified under ONC Health IT Certification Program and meet federal standards for interoperability, security, and functionality.

Oracle's 2022 acquisition of Cerner gave Oracle a large foothold in the EHR market. Cerner's growth was fueled by HITECH and Oracle Health continues to benefit from the entrenched market position afforded by HITECH. And its large position gives it a continued role in ONCHIT's efforts to push interoperability.

The Office of the National Coordinator's relentless focus on interoperability seems to have produced mixed results. While ONCHIT was not the impetus behind HITECH, its conferring of government-designated network status (QHIN) to parties such as Epic Systems further cemented an incumbent.

HITECH drove EHR adoption without directly focusing on interoperability or research and allowed large vendors to grow with government subsidies. Meanwhile, TEFCA, in trying to address interoperability and reduce barriers for smaller players, has had to involve the large vendors. For these large vendors, the goal is to maintain and enhance their market influence.

As evidenced by the situation at the VA, it is possible for large players to be certified and still roll out flawed software.

What is worrisome is that these same large vendors are in the position to define the universe of the next big thing: generative AI. Will they rush headlong into this as well?

Once again, there is NO marketplace incentive to develop better usability for physicians and patients and no place to have a discussion about the best way forward with development of these kinds of tools.

The continued marketplace distortion will almost certainly be more dangerous in the brave new world of generative AI and agentic AI*, and having interoperability being pushed by ONCHIT may make things worse. Already, it has not been very effective as a coordinator and has kept large players entrenched.

This naturally begs the question, what is the purpose of ONCHIT? Perhaps it is time for it to be abolished.

---

* AI that can act autonomously through AI agents to pursue goals and make decisions without constant human input

"There is an emerging bipartisan consensus in one vitally important area: that the challenges facing U.S. healthcare require major, transformative change… In a new system, innovations stimulated by information technology will improve care, lower costs, improve quality, and empower consumers."

~ Senators Bill Frist (R-TN) and Hillary Clinton (D-NY),
Washington Post, August 25, 2004

CHAPTER 9:

INTEROPERABILITY AND PAYERS

I remember, back in 2005, stepping into a large room in Washington, D.C. where a number of health IT executives were gathered. Janet Marchibroda was leading the eHealth Initiative (eHI), which was funded by a grant from the Markle Foundation and Robert Wood Johnson. We were supposed to "roundtable" our way to agreement over policies and best practices to enhance the goals of interoperability, including quality, safety, and efficiency of healthcare transactions. The stakeholders gathered included the largest payers, biopharma companies, the federal government (ONCHIT—both current and future leaders), electronic health record companies, and healthcare IT players involved in everything from ePrescribing to revenue cycle management.

What ensued was a long series of meetings over many more years, in which most participants congratulated themselves for supporting interoperability and the need for better policy. Unfortunately, the work performed at these meetings was often piecemeal and marked by grandstanding from standards groups and stakeholders. Most participants believed the federal government needed to be directly involved in healthcare IT, particularly in terms of creating mandates and incentives. Foremost among these issues was the central challenge that not only was there little interest in creating a national patient identifier, but there was also active hostility toward it, especially from privacy hawks. Conversations around interoperability thus remained focused on the primacy and the sacrosanctity of patient privacy as the overriding principle behind secure systems design.

I suspect this is one of the reasons why interoperability took so long: we were in a situation where cooperation among stakeholders was voluntary and slow. Because our healthcare system was, and still is, fragmented, a consensus started to develop around needing the federal government to be more involved, first as a coordinator in the form of ONCHIT, and later to provide mandates requiring that healthcare transactions be recorded electronically.

What we failed to recognize was that in trying to be all things to all people, we were simply designing rules of the road that favored pre-existing entities. We underestimated the deep suspicion people held about private entities collecting and sharing patient data. This wariness later became an excuse to prevent sharing health information at all. Our dogged determination not to provide "socialized medicine" meant that we had neither the appetite nor the ability to collectively push for a national patient identifier.

Instead, our healthcare information technology infrastructure grew up within the permanent economic battlefield that is the U.S. health system. Despite having multiple partnerships, health care providers and payers continue to be locked into a zero-sum game.

As a result, patients are unable to truly access their own complete data and physicians must experience continual devaluation of their professional judgment while also taking on more administrative burdens. These are all the byproducts of what started as a call for reform and a goal of making everything electronic.

ePrescribing: Who Determines the Rules of the Road?

In 2002, my team at Pfizer was approached by the National Association of Chain Drug Stores (NACDS) and the National Community Pharmacy Association (NCPA), who wanted to introduce us to a new electronic prescribing company called Surescripts. The company's founding CEO was Kevin Hutchinson, a true believer in how secure electronic prescribing could support patient safety.[48]

While most people won't recognize the name, Surescripts became an important "middleware" responsible for running prescriptions between clinic-based physicians and the pharmacies where their orders were filled. Surescripts became the nation's largest provider of electronic prescribing networking and certification services, making it essentially the backbone of ePrescribing transactions.

When NACDS and NCPA approached Pfizer, they were extremely worried about the rise of RxHub, an ePrescribing network created in 2001. RxHub was funded by the three largest pharmacy benefit managers (PBMs) at the time: Merck Medco, ExpressScripts, and AdvancePCS Inc.

Employers often contract PBMs to process pharmaceutical claims through a network of retail pharmacies. Many PBMs own their own online pharmacies that can dispense medications for chronic diseases and directly send these medications via mail order/home delivery.

The prevailing concern surrounding the emergence of RxHub was who would control the ePrescribing network. The three PBMs had together contributed $60 million to RxHub. If it was to become the dominant network for ePrescribing transactions, the pharmacies worried that the prescriptions could be routed to mail order houses and other distribution sites that were not necessarily selected by the physician or patient.

They also held concerns about potential prescription substitutions. If the prescription claims were routed to the PBMs' own clearinghouses, it was possible that a cheaper medication, such as a generic version of what had originally been prescribed by the physician, could be supplied to the patient by mail order. This approach effectively bypassed both the pharmacy and the physician's order.

The chain drug stores and the independent pharmacists did not want to be cut out. We at Pfizer also had a vested interest in physicians retaining prescribing authority. In the end, Pfizer, along with Johnson & Johnson, invested in Surescripts.

This investment was a clear reflection of the value we placed on network neutrality, the accuracy of physicians' prescriptions, and the patient's ability to access their medications at their choice of pharmacy. I also insisted that it show our refusal to allow advertisements or outside influences within the "pipes".

Most people were unaware of these networks and didn't realize that the design would determine the final infrastructure of electronic data transmission and whether decisions or intent would carry through.

After investing, we then went on to help educate policymakers. We testified in front of Congress to explain why we believed the "pipes" for ePrescribing were important not only to safeguard against errors but also to preserve the professional decisions of physicians and the choice of patients. We also lobbied against an ePrescribing mandate. While we believed the marketplace would ultimately prevail, we knew it was important to be transparent about preventing switching downstream.

I clearly remember sitting in one of those rooms with no windows, my boss standing in front of me reading a statement I had crafted. I remember feeling that we had advocated well, not only against an ePrescribing mandate but also in favor of free market ePrescribing solutions guided by decision-support as opposed to decision-control. An ePrescribing network free of advertising and an accompanying pipe without interference were the same guiding principle, which was the need to protect the patient-physician relationship and, by extension, to ensure that prescribing decisions could be transmitted and fulfilled without interference. The goal was to help keep the lanes of competition free. What happened later, however, ended up concentrating market power instead.

Six years later, SureScripts would enter into a merger with RxHub.[49] In 2008, the pipes were free of advertising, but fulfilling electronic prescriptions required more channels than the retail pharmacies. In fact, the volume was anemic across all channels. Electronic prescribing had not really taken off, and adoption rates were under 20 percent. The concerns about re-routing prescriptions and swapping out fulfillment were not being realized at such low volumes.

You can probably see where this is going. The parts of the 2009 HITECH and the ACA of the 2010s that were dedicated to ePrescribing relied on widespread EHR adoption by physicians. Mandating that physicians adopt EHR systems certified by HHS to comply with "meaningful use" criteria effectively also meant that those systems had to be able to provide electronic prescribing capabilities.

With a 50 percent ownership by the PBMs, combined with EHR meaningful use criteria, SureScripts eventually became an ePre-scribing monopoly and thus a *de facto* public utility.

Fifteen years later, in October 2024, the global asset management firm TPG made a majority investment in SureScripts. The expressed goals were to expand the company's ability to scale "intelligent prescribing", to focus on benefits and authorizations, and to promote "clinical interoperability."[50] In other words, the focus had shifted to the data—the data of coverage decisions.

PBMs (Pharmacy Benefit Managers)

Every decade, PBMs make it into the news on a new groundswell of outrage. Their role is that of the middlemen between drug manufac-turers (pharma), payers, pharmacies, and patients. PBMs administer the health insurance plan's prescription drug benefits and negotiate the drug prices with pharmaceutical companies.

In exchange for a lower price or rebate, they offer a place on the plan's formulary, in which is a list of drugs that will be partially covered by the health insurance plan. PBMs also negotiate directly with pharmacies by offering them a place on the health insurance plan's network, and thus a place for patients to fill their prescriptions.

PBMs process pharmacy claims as an administrative service and essentially manage which drugs are on a plan's formulary and which pharmacies are available on the plan.

The controversy lies in how PBMs make a profit. In negotiations with pharmaceutical drug manufacturers, a discounted price comes in the form of a rebate. In theory, manufacturers will pass on the majority of that rebate to the payers, who will then cost-share with the patients. The larger the rebate, the better the cost-share arrangement will be for patients.

However, PBMs are not required to disclose the rebate amounts, which they argue would violate their confidential negotiation and price protections. Since they aren't required to be transparent with the rebate amounts, no one truly knows how much they receive or what percentage is passed to the payers. The result is what we call pharmacy "spread" pricing.

Certification and Standards Settings

Standards-setting for the whole health ecosystem has felt at times like a Sisyphean endeavor.

Standards-setting has been underway since 2000. Numerous coalition meetings, multi-stakeholder roundtables, and task forces all focusing on rules of the road and technical standards are the hallmarks of this process, which results in countless hours spent trying to reach an agreement.

The technical standards are not the issue. Rather, it is the challenge of maintaining cooperation among all parties. Implementing standards means more time, more costs, and sometimes, slower speed. In addition, every company wants to sit at the table to make sure they aren't left out of discussions or decisions.

The technical standards are not the issue. Rather, it is the challenge of maintaining cooperation among all parties.

After twenty-five years, we have seen some significant advancements in interoperability standards, both via technology innovations and regulatory efforts. However, much of this progress has come about simply because the largest players have finally come to the table.

Given the difficulty of keeping track of the many acronyms and technical names of government and standard organizations, I thought it would be helpful to provide a quick timeline and divide the efforts over three distinct periods.

Early foundational standards (2000-2009)

➤ Health Level Seven International (HL7): An organization that became the dominant interoperability standards developer.

➤ Clinical Document Architecture (CDA): A framework for exchanging clinical documents.

➤ Continuity Care Record (CCR): a standard created by the American Academy of Family Physicians for exchanging clinical documents. CCR was later combined with CDA to create Continuity Care Document (CCD), which later morphed into C-CDA for EHR and would also become part of CMS' Blue Button initiative as a way for Medicare patients to access their data.

➤ Creation of ONCHIT to facilitate interoperability efforts.

Government Initiatives (2009-2019)

➤ HITECH Act of 2009: Required physicians and hospitals to demonstrate Meaningful Use by implementing EHRs that could connect to various network capabilities including ePrescribing

➤ Direct Standard: Developed in 2010 to ensure secure messaging among physicians.

➤ Fast Healthcare Interoperability Resources (FHIR): Established in 2012 by HL7 as a more flexible and modern standard for healthcare data exchange.

➤ ONCHIT in 2016 introduced a ten-year roadmap for achieving nationwide interoperability.

➤ The 2016 21st Century Cures Act pushed for the use of APIs for patient data access.

Frameworks and Exchanges (2020-present)

➤ CMS Interoperability and Patient Access Final Rule in 2020 pushed for the use of standardized APIs to facilitate seamless electronic health information data exchange.

➤ Trusted Exchange Framework and Common Agreement (TEFCA): Established in 2021 to establish a standardized framework for health information exchange by creating Qualified Health Information Networks (QHINs) and requiring FHIR adoption and United States Core Data for Interoperability (USCDI) standards for APIs to standardize data exchange.

➤ QHIN designation means participating in a broader health information exchange system beyond EHRs. Epic Systems and eClinicalWorks are the only two large EHRs officially designated, along with SureScripts network at the time of this writing.

Payers and Interoperability

Payers (sometimes written as "payors") are the organizations, government, commercial or non-profit, that finance healthcare services and manage the financial risk of healthcare. These are insurers of healthcare and their operations are highly complex, including billing, claims processing, approvals, care management, and regulatory compliance.

Highly dependent on sophisticated health IT systems that unify clinical, financial, and administrative data, payers rely on interoperability to exchange data and communicate with EHRs, physicians, other payers, and regulators. For physicians, hospitals, and health systems to get paid, not only do they have to ensure every bill is properly coded, but they also rely on payer's IT systems to be interoperable/interconnected in order to ensure seamless movement of transactions. In order to manage all the transactions, payers use large clearinghouses for processing authorizations and payments.

On February 21, 2024, the Russian ransomware group ALPHV Black-Cata launched a cyberattack on Change Healthcare, a clearinghouse owned by UnitedHealth Group, one of the largest private payers in the U.S. and responsible for processing billions of transactions annually. This breach exposed critical vulnerabilities in the U.S. healthcare system. Change Healthcare annually processes 15 billion healthcare transactions or close to one in every three patient records. The functions that were crippled included insurance eligibility verification and authorization, drug prescriptions, claims transmittals and payments.[51]

The fallout was wide reaching and operationally catastrophic; nearly every U.S. hospital, most clinics, and pharmacies felt the impact, with delays in patient care, steep financial losses, and prolonged operational disruptions for many months.

Change Healthcare had failed to secure one of its critical remote servers with multi factor authentication. The exposed data included names, contact information, social security numbers, claims, diagnoses, test results, health insurance member numbers and financial information. The total data exposure was for a record-breaking 190 million people, approximately half of the U.S. population, and is the single largest breach to date.

UnitedHealth Group was forced to take Change Healthcare's systems offline and spent many months restoring them. During that time, pharmacy transactions, claims processing, provider/physician reimbursement, prior authorizations, and other functions came to a halt. Various workarounds and alternate vendors stepped in, but Change Healthcare's main clearinghouse platform wasn't back up until November 2024 or nine months later.

This incident revealed just how dependent the entire healthcare ecosystem is on this digital financial backbone, how risky the reliance on a single vendor can be, and how cybersecurity has become critical for the digital infrastructure.

With healthcare payments, authorizations, and pharmacy functions halted, many health systems and physician offices were forced to pull from cash reserves, take out private loans—just to pay salaries, acquire supplies and medications, as well as critical services (security, dietary, waste management, etc.) for their organizations. Even a year after the incident, many physician offices and pharmacies have not yet been made whole.[52,53]

"THE HEALTH AND WELL-BEING OF MY PATIENT will be my first consideration;

I WILL RESPECT the autonomy and dignity of my patient;

I WILL SHARE my medical knowledge for the benefit of the patient and the advancement of healthcare."

excerpts from the Declaration of Geneva, adopted by the General Assembly of the World Medical Association, 2017 edition

CHAPTER 10

PHYSICIANS

Doctors and the Machine– Clicking to Care

Most physicians in the early 2000s were unable to afford, and would not have spent money on, electronic medical records.

The U.S. government's carrot-and-stick method, providing financial assistance to offset the cost of installation and exacting a penalty if the physician didn't adopt the technology created an EHR market where customers were guaranteed.

But physicians were not true customers.

Their needs were less important than meeting and adhering to the criteria laid out by the U.S. government about their EHR installation.

EHR product design therefore did not consider physicians' desire or ability to conduct research or even analyze their own patients' data to detect patterns. The valuable asset was not patient data, it was ensuring that the data was properly coded for efficient payments. And this required a great deal of documentation.

The problem is, someone has to be responsible for the documentation to make it all work. That "someone" is the physician.

Once you are on the hook for documentation, it begins to alter behavior. Physicians will find themselves spending many additional hours every evening—trying to get the documentation done. Because their patients need approval from insurance companies to pay for their care, the documentation burden is even higher as physicians are also tasked to appeal authorization denials for their patients.

Transformed into documentation-oriented service providers is bad enough, but physicians are also liable for the result. Add to that, the diminishing respect or authority as a professional have all contributed to physician dissatisfaction and burnout.

The most disheartening aspect is there hasn't been any meaningful effort to tap into the "scientist in every physician" by involving them in designing EHRs or building tools to visualize and conduct localized research. Instead of appealing to the professionalism and expertise of physicians, the health IT world has used them as nothing more than the scribes of clinical information.

The ramifications of this missed opportunity are still felt today.

Instead of appealing to the professionalism and expertise of physicians, the health IT world has used them as nothing more than the scribes of clinical information.

Tales of Frustration

Whenever I visit the physicians who care for me and my family, I am always regaled with new stories about the shortcomings of EHRs, which never seem to improve despite all these years.

I learn how the expectations, the environment, and even the new technologies being developed continue to force physicians to create new and different workarounds.

Time and again, I find myself sharing a wry laugh with them because there are no good solutions.

At the end of 2023, I found myself stepping into the role of interim CEO of Veradigm, one of the largest ambulatory EHR companies (the old Allscripts). As an interim CEO, I couldn't do anything to immediately alleviate their issues, and it truly pained me.

My dermatologist likes to remind me that "no one ever asked us what we wanted" when they designed the EHR. He talks about how physicians have to continuously experiment to create new workflows just to pay attention to their patients.

My endocrinologist laments that the electronic system is relentless at suggesting diagnosis to add.

My ob/gyn recently informed me that she is finally throwing in the towel and going electronic—because the cost of managing billing has now reached a tipping point in terms of becoming too expensive. After priding herself for being able to operate without electronic records for so long, she worries about what this will mean for her clinic's workflow and ability to provide the kind of meaningful care she has been doing for many decades. She also worries about what happens if this information is easily shared.

As a former physician, I find that other physicians are comfortable speaking with me about their frustrations with health IT. I am sympathetic, almost to a fault, largely because I know what each of them wants is to regain the agency to be able to care for their patients in a humanist way. The administrative demands wrought by technology and executives have made them feel insignificant, just cogs in a large machine.

As I have been working on this book, I have been having more in-depth conversations with physicians when they casually bring up their dissatisfaction with their EHR, health IT, and the pressures of modern medicine.

A highly sought after academic infectious disease specialist whom I spoke with recently told me she has chosen to turn off all the AI tools embedded in the Epic system because these tools were creating incomplete and often incorrect notes for her, causing her to worry about the error rate and what might be happening to her colleagues, fellows, and residents.

Then there is the ob/gyn physician in her early thirties who recently joined a private practice on the Upper East Side of Manhattan and was dismayed to discover the practice recently decided to adopt electronic records. For her, a millennial and someone who was in middle school when HITECH passed, even she could tell the difference. Care can actually be "better" without the use of an electronic record.

And there's the medical student I sat with at a dinner recently who was telling me all about his clinical research in a Boston-based academic medical center. Without any prompting, he began to list out all the shortcomings and issues with Epic Systems and how the data entry and retrieval aspects have made it impossible to study effects across populations, subpopulations, or to answer specific research questions.

As a former physician, I have the privilege of having access to incredible doctors, many who are practicing at the top of their field. But I am continually amazed and dismayed at the new stories I hear every year from these dedicated professionals.

Their stories about the indignities and the misses and the tone-deafness of these electronic systems, including those with the latest AI tools, never seem to end and the most plaintive and even resigned sentiment is that "no one bothers to ask us what we need or want to give better care."

Managed Care Supercharged

While it is sometimes convenient and appropriate to blame healthcare IT and the policies which pushed adoption and utilization of EHRs as a main driver for physicians losing professional agency and autonomy, the structural issues and devaluation of clinical professionalism actually began much earlier — with the rise of managed care.

Managed care existed in various incarnations throughout most of the twentieth century. It wasn't until the 1990s that managed care experienced rapid growth, substantial expansion, and subsequent challenges.

The growth of health maintenance organizations (HMOs) caused a dramatic shift in managed care. By the mid-1990s, most Americans with employer-based health insurance were enrolled in some form of managed care.[54]

Managed care plans relied heavily on selective provider networks, negotiated rates, gatekeepers, and reduction in hospital utilization. While overall costs did stabilize, there was a backlash from consumers and employees. Their complaints about the increasingly restrictive practices prompted many *state* laws to be designed to regulate managed care. Critics argued that most managed care plans were simply denying medically necessary service or providing lower-quality care.[55]

Under managed care models, physicians were held responsible for healthcare spending. They were expected to be equally sensitive to costs as well as concern for their patients. Many popular models relied on capitation, in which a fixed amount is paid to physicians for the care of an individual over a set period of time.

This structure puts physicians in a tough position, as they often have to weigh the cost of one course of action against the cost of another while also factoring in concerns about preventative care versus treatment. More often than not, they generally don't know the costs involved, which creates further headaches for the overworked physicians.[56]

While physicians struggled with having to determine rough cost-effectiveness calculations, patients were increasingly viewed as a revenue source on a per-unit basis. Frequently, physicians were asked to increase revenue by seeing more patients in a day.

Relative Value Units (RVUs)

In 1988, a team of researchers from the Department of Health Policy and Management at the Harvard School of Public Health and Department of Psychology at Harvard published a paper in the *New England*

Journal of Medicine introducing a resource-based relative value scale for measuring physician services.[57]

This measurement approach was deemed a more objective way to measure productivity of physician services, and in 1989, it became enshrined in federal law when the Medicare Physician Fee Schedule was introduced and later implemented in 1992.

RVUs are the basis for physician payment. Combining time, intensity, and the cost of care into one relative ranking scale called Resource-Based Relative Value Scale (RBRVS), the principle behind this calculation is that payments for physician services should correlate directly with all the resource costs for providing those services. This approach undergirds the physician payment system and uses adjustment factors to manage new procedures or as procedures modernize.

An RVU is calculated by adding the components of work (technical skill, effort to perform a service), practice expense (operational cost to maintain the practice), and liability protection (estimated cost of malpractice insurance). All components are adjusted by geography and multiplied by a health system wide conversion factor. RVUs are also adjusted along with updates in billing codes by regions.

I won't go into all the reasons why the RVU concept was controversial, but you can see how the downstream effects could be detrimental to progress. To calculate RVUs meant more documentation in terms of billing codes as well as a way for hospital and health systems administrators to determine relative value of various offered services and allocation of resources.

The RVU system has been adopted widescale across all payers and is updated every five years by the Centers for Medicare and Medicaid

Services (CMS). Only recently has the formula included the factor of time or medical decision-making as important.

The real tragedy of the RVU system is its effect on data needed for providing care and research. Efficiency is not the same as effectiveness. With systems geared heavily toward measuring efficiency and productivity, a commonly heard discussion between a physician and billing coder is: "It doesn't matter how much you wrote in the chart about the patient. If you do not use these two particular keywords, I cannot bill that code." [58]

Professional Sweatshop

My late and dear friend Dr. Wolffe Nadoolman[59] used to say that the industrial model of providing medical care was turning physicians into sweatshop workers. As physicians are often paid on a per visit basis, akin to working piecemeal, they face ever growing pressures to increase the number of patients seen in a set period of time. Essentially, the system goal was to determine the minimum amount of time needed to achieve a consistent result (a patient visit), and preferably at the lowest cost—not great for the patient, not great for the physician.[60]

The industrial model of providing medical care was turning physicians into sweatshop workers.

Under managed care, physicians' professional status first began to erode, and they were referred to as service *providers*, an unfortunate term that would stick. The rising documentation burden associated with electronic health information technology reinforced this. To this day, I still see physicians bristle when they are referred to as "providers".

To add insult to injury, electronic health systems also monitor behavior and require documentation for efficiency metrics, which is asking how much did you do in what period of time and still have an acceptable result? Today, payments to health systems require measuring both the *efficiency* of healthcare professionals and health systems. This concept of efficiency is the cornerstone of the latest rubric of managed care: "Value-Based Care".

Value Based Care

Value-based health care is a framework in which healthcare reimbursement or payment is based on patient outcomes and quality care versus activity or transactions. The "value" in value-based care (VBC) focuses on patient outcomes, provider performance, and patient experience; it is predicated on all these factors being measured objectively.

Herein lies the rub. This is almost akin to trying to figure out the "value" in education. Because it is difficult to measure, given that outcomes can vary based on time horizon or may not be directly related to the physician's performance, measurement ends up being focused on efficiency.

Patient outcomes are directly affected by care given and indirectly affected by the patient's health status, living, and working conditions, or what have come to be called social determinants of health (SDOH).

Provider performance can be measured in terms of efficiency, such as saving the system money, time spent per patient and ensuring that checklists of preventative care measures (e.g., mammograms, colonoscopies, eye checks, etc.) are discussed and ordered.

Patient experience can be determined by a physician's bedside manner, but equally if not more, by the entire healthcare experience.

What is interesting is that healthcare IT is supposed to support these kinds of measurements because it collects data. As to be expected, however, data management for health systems is all about making sure that health systems aren't missing out on the payments associated with value-based care.

Value-based care has been sold as a way to give physicians more flexibility to provide care. In reality, it is simply a way to define good care and good value in terms of a ratio such as efficiency versus straight payment for activity in fee-for-service-type metrics.

Let's not forget the impact of time. Interventions today can create better outcomes years in the future. It may be different for each person, so how does value slide along with time?

The focus on outcomes and accountability is understandable, but the movement feels again like another attempt to create payment reform, based on systems that simply collect binary information.

"We cannot manage what we can't measure," is the old Deming adage.

We measure activity because it is the easiest thing to measure. Measuring outcomes is much more difficult because not only is it multi-factorial, but the time scale of when one sees a good outcome varies from the immediate to years in the future. That means if we are measuring activity, we are back to measuring interventions, orders, and behavior.

Value-based care is simply the latest scheme to apply economic pressure to achieve these clinical ends. Great in theory, but in practice, efficiency and quality metrics just get built into the incumbent EHR systems. The physicians have their behavior tracked; and the whole game is still centered on saving the system money rather than focused on quality care.

PART II:
DATA AND RESEARCH

"We were collecting data on a new virus that nobody understood at a time [when] there was not a single web page dedicated to COVID-19 case count."[61]

~ Dr. Lauren Gardner, co-founder of the CoVID-19 dashboard which became the leading source of centralized data on the COVID pandemic in 2020– allowing governments, media, and the public to visualize and combat the virus' rapid spread

CHAPTER 11

DATA IS THE NEW OIL *

The year was 2013 and I was in the office with Context Matters' head of Data, Emily Rubinstein. We had just gained an old and obsolete dataset of public FDA information, curated by our client Pfizer, and were now discussing a change in our overall data curation and linking processes based on a suggestion from another client, the French pharmaceutical company, Sanofi.

Context Matters was a data analytics software-as-a-service company I founded in 2010. Our primary goal was to help biopharmaceutical companies understand how different governments around the world used clinical evidence and clinical trials to determine the cost-effectiveness (and ultimately pricing) of newly developed drugs for each country's population.

---

* "Data is the New Oil" was the title of a talk by British mathematician Clive Humby in 2006 at the Association of National Advertisers.

As we primarily focused on pharmaceutical products, we had a very collaborative approach with all our pharmaceutical customers. In fact, we had built our software and data curation methods with the direct feedback of their global health economics, outcomes research, and market access teams. Our customers were often our uncredited co-developers, giving us suggestions along the way as they used our software and showed us how to discern which of the curated information truly mattered. Our product had been built by the industry for the industry.

That day, we kept circling back to the question of which trial endpoints really matter. After all, an endpoint can get a drug through the regulatory door, but it also sets the stage for how that drug stacks up against competitors when people later ask, "Is this treatment worth the cost?"

Emily pointed out that the pivotal trials were where we should be paying attention. These are the big, high-stakes studies in any drug program—the ones that directly shape FDA or EMA approval. The endpoints from those trials usually have the most weight, not just for getting a green light, but for shaping the clinical outcomes we'll eventually use in cost-effectiveness comparisons.

For example, imagine a drug that improves performance on a six-minute walk test. That result might be enough to support approval. But what happens after that? Better walk test scores could translate into steadier gait in daily life, fewer falls, and less need for mobility aids or special monitoring. Each of those has a real dollar value attached—costs avoided for both patients and the healthcare system. So in the end, the same endpoint that drives regulatory approval can also become the start point for showing whether the drug delivers value beyond just clinical benefit.

I had just returned from Pfizer's research headquarters in New London, CT, where we had received an unexpected gift—a copy of an old Access database that had been put together by a few former Pfizer colleagues as a labor of love. The database was simply a listing of all the FDA drug approvals for the past twenty-seven years, but it also contained some commentary about which endpoints were the most interesting. All the data was public information, but the format was inconsistent and it was clear someone had read and entered each piece of information manually. The real value was that the only trials included in the database were the pivotal trials– indicating that the group of drug development researchers who had put the database together only cared about the endpoints associated with pivotal trials. Emily was right.

Their prioritization of the measured endpoints ranged from educated hunches to measurement challenges. But at the time of database construction– there simply weren't the technology tools or connections to link databases, do easy annotation, or even download information from the FDA in an easy-to-use way.

In 2013, however, we could do it, at least within Context Matters' tech environment. We could create a relational database. We already had built one database from curating comparative effectiveness outcomes from various agencies. Now we had the design of a regulatory decision database. The old database we were given was not easy to use, but we could recreate it by directly scraping the data from the FDA website, tagging what was useful, and then later linking it with our other database from different sources.

If we could connect this information together, our customers would gain the ability to determine (with high probability) which endpoints in a clinical trial had the highest impact many years down the road when their drug's outcomes would be compared head-to-head in a future assessment.

We got started immediately.

Data Takes the Spotlight

The early decades of healthcare IT were focused almost exclusively on building an electronic infrastructure and interoperability. Most of the action had been focused on trying to regulate the power dynamic of healthcare IT organizations and the dominance around rights, sharing, and integrations.

Concerned more as to who owned what and who controlled which part of the infrastructure, these players often ignored the value of the data flowing within their systems and networks. Because the building of the infrastructure never included physicians or their user preferences, few companies recognized the inherent value in the data itself.

Physician-scientists and healthcare researchers knew that the data was the real treasure, but it was locked, incomplete, inconsistent, and inaccessible. While the clinical data coursed through the electronic system, only certain pieces of information were considered useful for financial tracking, such as identification, diagnosis, interventions, and treatments. Any coordination and management of care came from medical professionals accessing and *reading* the records.

Systems shape how we behave, and in turn, we design systems with the intention of guiding behavior. As electronic health records (EHRs) had evolved to serve a payment-driven model, their primary focus became documenting care as transactions—captured through billing codes rather than clinical context.

This transactional system in healthcare demands heavy and constant documentation. All this gets funneled into electronic systems, which are then used to track efficiency, productivity, and costs. But the metrics captured are inherently designed to manage the overall system (within a hospital or a clinic or an institution), and not to directly benefit individual patients. Because transactional systems reward efficiency, the quality of the clinical data itself becomes an afterthought. As long as the data is accurate, that is all that matters. Accuracy and meaningful aren't equivalent.

> **Systems shape how we behave, and in turn, we design systems with the intention of guiding behavior.**

If we can treat clinical data as more than a billing artifact and more as a resource for research, we open the door to learning directly from care itself. That shift allows us to see what is missing, what could be improved, and how the data can be enriched to better reflect patient experience.

But how do you do that, especially being mindful of patient privacy?

De-identification is a first step, but we also need to aggregate clinical data into curated datasets in order to perform any kind of statistical analysis. In doing so, we create a powerful tool for discovery: revealing insights to guide individual patient treatment and highlighting patterns across others with similar conditions.

Curating the clinical data is only a start point. To make it valuable, we also have to determine all the events that happened in a patient's journey and the context of their care. Much of the data has been converted into billing codes, necessitating us to read through the record to understand what actually happened to the patient.

If you can do this across a cohort of patients, you can start seeing patterns in treatment effects. More importantly, you can imagine that perhaps one day it will be possible to develop a feedback loop where the more information we gain from every day patient care, the faster we might understand the progression of disease and which treatments are most effective.

In fact, 2012 marked the beginning of a convergence of true interest from various stakeholders regarding this "real world" data. This interest did not originate from the existing healthcare IT players. Rather, it came from within the epidemiology researchers in both academia and pharma companies. What developed was sophisticated, complex, and expensive workarounds to turn the clinical data into meaningful research datasets.

"Science replaces private prejudice with public, verifiable evidence."

~ Carl Sagan

CHAPTER 12

EVIDENCE-BASED MEDICINE

In November 1992, when I was a first-year medical student, a seminal article was published in the *Journal of the American Medical Association* (JAMA) about a new paradigm for teaching medicine: evidence-based medicine (EBM).[62] The opening line was astounding.

"Evidence-based medicine de-emphasizes intuition, unsystematic clinical experience, and pathophysiologic rationale as sufficient grounds for clinical decision-making and stresses the examination of evidence from clinical research."

The article essentially posited that care to date had been less focused on systematic evidence and more focused on intuition and experience. Looking back, it seems medicine was having its "Moneyball"[63] moment.

Unfortunately, misconceptions began almost immediately. The idea of systematic use of evidence got misconstrued as "one-size-fits-all" and "cookie cutter medicine". In fact, a second paper was published shortly after in the *British Medical Journal*, with lead author Dr. David Sackett, entitled "Evidence Based Medicine: What It Is and What It Isn't."[64] This definition became the one that would be the most widely used:

"Evidence based medicine is the conscientious, explicit, and judicious use of current best evidence in making decisions about the care of individual patients."

Evidence based medicine is the conscientious, explicit, and judicious use of current best evidence in making decisions about the care of individual patients.

Journal clubs started gaining greater popularity while medical educators started emphasizing the ability to understand new research. Evidence-based medicine (EBM) was having a moment.

However, the rapid increase in the sheer number of peer-reviewed articles, along with the time pressures associated with clinical practice, were also making it difficult for physicians to keep up with new developments and research.

In response, the medical and specialty associations began to develop guidelines that would provide practice recommendations based on the best evidence to date and accompanied with recommendations from panels of relevant experts. It was a systematic approach with the goal of giving physicians the ability to determine the individual circumstances in which to apply these practice guidelines.[65]

A few years later, in 1996, the first national report was published from the *Dartmouth Atlas of Health Care Project*[66] (Dartmouth Atlas). This was the shot heard around the healthcare policy world.

Jack Wennberg (1934-2024) was a highly influential American healthcare researcher and the founder of The Dartmouth Institute for Health Policy & Practice. In 1996 and for the next few decades under his leadership and beyond, the Dartmouth Atlas of Health Care Project would publish reports using extensive Medicare data to show and track the striking variations in how medical resources are distributed and used across different regions of the United States.

That first national report was a shocker. With meticulous documentation and analysis, Dr. Wennberg demonstrated that the kind or amount of care a patient would receive varied dramatically based on *where they lived*. In regions with more healthcare resources, patients often received more care simply because those services were available. Yet this greater intensity of care did not translate into better health outcomes or higher patient satisfaction. The concept of "small-area variation" challenged the prevailing assumption that healthcare decisions were based solely on scientific evidence and patient need.[67]

Dr. Wennberg's work and the *Dartmouth Atlas* consistently showed significant regional differences among the rates of surgeries, hospitalizations, and procedures for patients with similar conditions. At the same time, their research highlighted that the availability of medical resources (e.g., specialists or capacity) influenced the intensity of care delivered (supply-sensitive care).

Dr. Wennberg became a strong advocate for patients having access to objective treatment option information and a say in the decision-making process. He would later help establish the Informed Medical Decisions Foundation and his work would greatly influence U.S. healthcare policymakers as he pushed for national healthcare reform. His research would become the basis for establishing HHS's Agency for Healthcare Research and Quality (AHRQ).

The federal government, through AHRQ, began to fund regional evidence-based practice centers (EPCs). The hope was to smooth out variations in care across physicians, institutions, and geographical regions. The larger hope would be to reduce the overall cost of healthcare delivery, particularly if variations could be made smaller.

Interestingly, the Dartmouth Atlas also examined patterns of end-of-life care, inequities in Medicare reimbursement, and the underuse of preventive care, which would later lead to a series of "pay-for-performance" programs. During the 2006-2010 time period, these programs gained popularity among private payers and insurers. They later morphed into various schemas for payment of care, including today's value-based care.

In 2005, I coordinated efforts across Pfizer to better understand how EBM was being reoriented to support comparative effectiveness (if one drug works better than another) and cost-effectiveness (if one drug is more cost-effective than another) policies.

In June of 2006, my colleagues, Drs. Newell McElwee, Kimberly McGuigan, Mark Horn, and I penned a piece published in *Health Affairs* entitled "Evidence-Based Coverage Decisions? *Primum Non Nocere*."[68] Our perspective was that the leap from evidence-based medicine to evidence-based coverage decisions was a leap too far. We were a group of physicians and outcomes research experts who felt that while evidence-based medicine was designed to support physicians in their care with patients, evidence-based coverage was a different matter altogether.

At the time, the fields of health economics and outcomes research were still relatively young, but methods known as systematic review* and the use of meta-analysis** had been gaining favor, particularly outside the U.S., as a means of determining whether new therapeutics (or new technology) were better than existing therapies when it came to outcomes and cost. In the U.S., there was a growing desire to experiment with the concept of cost-effectiveness in the policy sphere.

In 2003, Oregon Health and Science University (OHSU), one of the federal government's evidence-based practice centers (EPCs), developed a program to incorporate systematic review to help determine what therapies would be covered under state Medicaid programs. In fact, they invited other ones from other states to share in their analysis and approach. The program was called the Drug

---

* A systematic review for health outcomes rigorously identifies, evaluates, and synthesizes all relevant studies on a specific health question in a transparent, reproducible way.

** A meta-analysis statistically combines results from multiple independent studies on the same question to provide a more precise overall estimate of effect or outcome.

Effectiveness Review Project (DERP).[69] These were still early days in determining the best criteria to measure and calculate comparative cost-effectiveness in a way that all parties found acceptable.

The main concern for biopharma companies was whether DERP's initial intentions would involve cutting costs and therefore bias the cost-effectiveness analysis. The central question was whether you could really use the concept of evidence-based medicine as the basis of coverage decisions, both in practice and politically.

Intention frames analysis. Evidence-based medicine, an approach philosophically similar to but not the same as a systematic review, was geared toward individual care. Evidence-based medicine in practice took into account individual patient preferences and was meant to be a data analytical approach to supporting physicians in their decision-making with patients. Equating this approach to systematic review felt inappropriate, since systematic review was designed to determine what may be appropriate for a *population* or a state policy, rather than an individual patient.

Intention frames analysis.

Evidence-Based Coverage Decisions and Systematic Review

As described earlier, outside the U.S, there are Health Technology Assessment (HTA) agencies that are tasked to perform systematic reviews and meta-analyses on new therapies as they become available for prescribing. These analyses result in assessments that help governments manage their healthcare spending and budget. Many governments use the assessments themselves to directly negotiate price and access with pharma and medical device companies.

In the U.S., the Agency for Healthcare Research and Quality (AHRQ), through their evidence practice centers (EPCs), promoted a similar type of assessment. However, without an enforcement mechanism, they could only publish their recommendations. Not until twenty years later, in 2022, when the Inflation Reduction Act under then-President Biden was passed, did the federal government gain the ability to negotiate (in a limited fashion) directly with pharma and med device companies. For most of the history of AHRQ, there has been no ability to enforce any recommendations made about one drug being deemed cost-effective, more cost-effective, or simply better comparatively.

This was what made OHSU so interesting. The state of Oregon, through the DERP project, was launching *its own version* of an HTA and forming a loose coalition with other state Medicaid programs. Building upon past experimentations in keeping Medicaid budgets affordable, Oregon was now marrying the systematic review process with putting a dollar figure on cost and quality of life.

Until then, the quality-adjusted life year (QALY), a concept that had long existed within health economics circles and been used as a measure in other countries (e.g., Canada, UK, Australia), had never been introduced by a state government as a methodology to determine affordability.

The QALY is a calculated measure of disease burden, which takes into account both the quality and quantity of life lived. Used to assess the value of a medical intervention, including drugs and devices, one QALY equates one year in perfect health, less the reduction in quality of life attributable to the disease and treatment.

A QALY tries to calculate how much longer a treatment helps someone to live and how good those extra years are in terms of health and well-being. Take, for example, paying for dialysis in a diabetic patient with kidney failure. Suppose this patient can live five more years with dialysis, but because of side effects, their quality of life is rated as a 0.5 (on a scale of 0 = dead to 1 = perfect health). Without dialysis, they may only live one more year, but the quality of life is even worse, say 0.3. What happens next is a calculation.

➤ With dialysis: 5 years × 0.5 = 2.5 QALYs

➤ Without dialysis: 1 year × 0.3 = 0.3 QALYs

➤ QALYs gained from dialysis: 2.5 – 0.3 = 2.2 QALYs

However, dialysis is expensive. Let's say it costs $400,000 over those five years. To determine if it is "worth it" the cost of $400,000 is divided by the QALYs gained from dialysis:

$$\$400,000 \div 2.2 \text{ QALYs} \approx \$182,000 \text{ per QALY.}$$

The health system can set a "threshold" for how much they are willing to pay for one QALY. Let's say the QALY threshold is $100,000. Since the cost per QALY is above the threshold ($182,000), it is not considered a good value and therefore is less likely to be funded, unless there are special circumstances.

For a state Medicaid program or any government payer, a methodology like this could provide a common measurement for all different treatments as you could measure and compare QALYs for any new drug or surgery or device. This calculation could allow a decision-maker to allocate limited healthcare resources (e.g., Medicaid budget) in a manner that tries to maximize the health benefits for the most number of people (state population).

It isn't difficult to see why using this approach would be controversial.

First of all, QALYs may not capture everything that matters to an individual patient, such as their personal values or what they themselves consider "worth it" in life. This kind of calculated comparison could undervalue treatments for people with chronic illnesses or disabilities because their quality of life scores (which are also subjective) could be designated as lower. Sometimes there simply isn't enough time and experience with a new therapeutic to understand its effect on quality of life.

The issue we raised in our *Health Affairs* piece was that evidence-based medicine was meant to support a decision made between a physician and a patient in the context of providing the medical care best suited for that patient. Using evidence to support coverage decisions was completely different because the evidence and calculations involved were for a population and primarily furnished a method to allocate resources.

Evidence-based medicine centers on physicians and patients using clinical evidence to make personalized care decisions, whereas evidence-based coverage decisions use evidence to determine which therapies should be funded or are cost-effective for populations. The former is about individualized care; the latter about population-level reimbursement.

"The PCORI (Patient-Centered Outcomes Research Institute)... shall not develop or employ a dollars-per-quality adjusted life year (or similar measure that discounts the value of a life because of an individual's disability) as a threshold to establish what type of health care is cost effective or recommended. The Secretary shall not utilize such an adjusted life year (or such a similar measure) as a threshold to determine coverage, reimbursement, or incentive programs."

Section 1182e, Affordable Care Act of 2010

CHAPTER 13

HOW DO I COMPARE THEE?

Comparative & Cost Effectiveness

Comparative Effectiveness Research is not a new concept. Comparative effectiveness" refers to how well a therapy works and what its benefits and harms are when *compared directly* to other existing treatments (drugs, procedures, etc.) for the same condition. The goal is to provide evidence to help patients, clinicians, and policymakers make informed decisions about the most effective and appropriate treatment options.

The worry back in 2005 (pre-ACA) was that comparative effectiveness might get corrupted by baking cost into the comparison too early.

For the biopharma or life sciences industry, this meant there were three things to consider and prove when developing a product:

A. the drug works at all (efficacy)

B. the drug works well in the real-world setting (effectiveness)

C. it works better than its competitors under similar conditions (comparative effectiveness)

When you factor in the price of the product and compare it again, you get an assessment (cost-effectiveness) that becomes harder to control and predict but easier to manipulate after the fact.

The state of Oregon decided to take a stand and considered using *both* comparative and cost-effectiveness as a possible path to managing Medicaid spending. Biopharma companies' concern was that without a more robust discussion about how to calculate the comparisons, the evaluation might overly rely on cost and not fully consider the comparative differences in impact among different subgroups of patients.

To implement this in a wide-scale manner meant public acceptance about these methodologies AND the political capital to fund these kinds of appraisals in an independent manner.

How do you manage the cost-value determination? What do you do with a drug which may be highly effective for one subpopulation but costs much more than the standard of care? Is that enough to justify Medicaid dollars? Or what happens if a drug that works marginally better for a wider group of patients, but costs just slightly more than the standard of care? Is this the one that gets approval for those Medicaid dollars?

It is difficult to make these determinations without thinking about cost when you are trying to balance a budget, but the bias of including cost in a comparative evaluation may not be valid either.

The Affordable Care Act tried to encourage more study of comparative effectiveness by funding an institute called Patient-Centered Outcomes Research Institute (PCORI) at the price tag of $1.1 billion. The goal was to provide grants to support comparative effectiveness research, but the institute was strictly prohibited from making any comparisons of cost or cost-effectiveness among different therapies.[70]

Aside from simply determining whether one drug works better than another or one drug is more cost-effective than another, there are also other levers to save the system money. Discouraging utilization is the most common approach, but how do you do this fairly?

We as Americans are used to being able to access every new innovation as soon as it is available. How do we balance the desire to access new and improved therapies immediately while also slowing down rapid growth healthcare spending as a country?

As medical science continues to improve, we are continually gaining a better understanding of individual variability to different treatments. In the long run, it can effectively decrease utilization, but only if we can determine targeted effectiveness and comparative effectiveness of various therapies.

Not all individuals experience the same outcomes. Not all therapies work equally well across individuals, subpopulations, or even by different indications (e.g., one type of cancer versus another). This is where data and analytics help to parse out which therapies will work and for whom. This is known as the Heterogeneity of Treatment Effect (HTE).

Health Technology Assessments Explained

In 2010, everyone loved the name of my company, Context Matters Inc. Despite having a broad conceptual name, we were actually a company focused on a specific and complex problem. We were comparing various countries' Health Technology Assessments (HTA) or how different countries were determining comparative and cost-effectiveness of therapies.[*]

Because countries outside the U.S. had been developing these methodologies, it seemed rather strange for us, an American company, to be focused on this issue when we had no equivalent in the U.S. at the federal or even a state level. Although Oregon's DERP was doing effectiveness assessments, the impact was limited to a handful of states and affected only Medicaid state formularies. Even PCORI had limited effect.

But these methodologies were still being developed. And we realized that if the methodologies were grounded in easy to understand criteria, there was a reasonable probability that some variation might make it into the U.S. one day.

Even if that scenario never came to pass, the biopharma companies were still selling into these global markets and we saw the opportunity to relate specifically defined clinical and economic criteria. Once you understood the criteria, you could better understand the relative financial value assigned by the country's government based on their population makeup. Understanding the priorities for a government healthcare budget meant better negotiations.

---

[*] HTA Agencies include U.K.'s National Institute for Health and Care Excellence (NICE), Germany's Federal Joint Committee (G-BA), Germany's Institute for Quality and Efficiency in Health Care (IQWiG), Brazil's National Committee for Health Technology Incorporation (CONITEC), and South Korea's Health Insurance Review and Assessment Service (HIRA)

There is no "one size fits all" analysis on a global scale. In showcasing the world's assessments in one application, we would make it easier for biopharma companies to plan better negotiations and even better outcomes research by country. Having a common understanding about relative value might shorten price negotiations and guide future outcomes research. This could only benefit everyone's understanding about the differential effects of drugs on different subpopulations.

The HTA agencies had developed health economics criteria based on extensive meta-analysis of clinical trial results and then applied these criteria to determine the comparative effectiveness and cost-effectiveness of a new therapeutic across a variety of contexts.

Their remit was only for their country's population and the prevalence of specific diseases across subpopulations. Because the timing of the analysis was frequently based on the entry of new therapeutics, many of these agencies had to determine their schedule of review– particularly when a large number of new therapeutics hit the market.

As such, these agencies would need to both evaluate and periodically reevaluate new technologies against whatever treatments are currently already on the market. The guiding question at all times was whether the benefits were worth making the treatment available to patients and if so, for *which* patients.

In the most general sense, HTAs simply ask if new therapeutics are "better than what we already have." A new therapeutic could provide excellent outcomes for a particular subpopulation, like many cancer drugs. However, if the price is too high for that particular country's budget to justify making it widely available, the conditions for access would become more exacting.

What happens when a therapy's effect is only slightly better, but for a larger population? Should funds be spent to make a new therapy available that affects a broader population but is only slightly better than what is used today?

Alzheimer's therapeutics are a great example. Most Alzheimer's drugs work only marginally better than one another. However, for some subpopulations, you can see a delay of cognitive decline. Economically, we can quantify delay in terms of time gained before patients were placed into a nursing home by simply calculating the cost of outlay by the number of days delayed.

What is that delay worth? And to whom? These kinds of questions are complex, evidence-based, and require clinically minded and economically conscious evaluation processes.

HTA in Action

In 2013, Gilead developed and launched Sovaldi, the first cure for Hepatitis C.[71] It was a breakthrough drug and gained a lot of fanfare. The price point was considered very high, but it was a cure. How does one consider the comparative and cost-effectiveness of this type of drug?

In Germany, the HTA agency (G-BA) came up with an interesting start point. They reviewed the clinical data and noticed that there was a slight difference in outcomes across six different genotypes of patients. They then came up with an approach to stack rank the genotypes and the purported benefits. This allowed the German government to make the drug available, with certain restrictions based on the genotype of the patient.

They could point to the clinical trial data supporting the drug's effectiveness as a fair way to rationalize segmenting their population suffering from Hepatitis C. It was based on the probability of success related to a certain marker. Over time, as the drug was used, new data would be collected, and the assessment could eventually broaden or narrow.

Context Matters Inc.

At Context Matters, although we were collecting the assessments across multiple countries, we structured the data and made it viewable and comparable (apples to apples) on our software platform. Within our platform, users could drill down and understand how the assessments were made and the various clinical outcomes and economic factors which contributed to the final recommendations.

Our customers could *compare* the assessments across various HTA agencies from multiple countries along several dimensions, including time and the emergence of new comparators. Hence the company name, because *context does matter*.

When these various recommendations are placed side-by-side in context, a change in the filters and parameters reveals new layers of meaning.

When people discovered how the name of the company aligned with this concept, it became the easiest sell of all. It was possible for our biopharma customers to compare, understand context, and determine a strategy based on a country.

By 2014, although our customers were biopharma companies, we found ourselves with an interesting situation. We had multiple countries' HTA agencies themselves (including Germany and

Egypt) calling us about these cross-country comparisons we were showing.

For countries with HTAs, there was a fascination as to how their own assessments stacked up or evolved over time. For countries without HTAs and who wanted to establish this process, the idea of benchmarking with other established agencies was intriguing. Understanding how others were doing it mattered. Benchmarking is powerful.

In 2017, I sold Context Matters to Decision Resource Group [72], who later sold the technology to Clarivate Analytics to combine with their clinical trial tracking software. While the customer base for these companies was solely focused on biopharmaceutical companies, I have often wondered what would have happened if we had pivoted as a company to make our comparisons available to those various country governments who had shown such interest.

HTA in the U.S.?

It has been more than two decades since the State of Oregon came out with its experiment to use HTA-like analysis to manage Medicaid budgets.

So it is particularly interesting to watch independent U.S. organizations emerge and evolve, such as the Institute for Clinical and Economic Review (ICER), whose aim was to create an American version of health technology assessment (HTA).[73] Organizations like these face inherent limitations, chiefly their lack of enforcement power since they are not government entities.

That said, if a critical mass of private payers begins to rely on these analyses, could their behaviors influence public payers in the U.S.?

When evaluations are conducted outside government authority, they can raise legitimate questions about the rigor of outcomes research and the credibility of the price negotiations that follow. Just as importantly, the timeframe for judging both outcomes and "cost-effectiveness" varies tremendously between private and public payers.

Private payers often make short-term decisions tied to the one-year cycle of enrollment and plan selection. In contrast, only Medicare and the VA maintain stable patient populations, allowing them to benefit from long-term cost-effectiveness assessments. Most private payers face churn, patients switching plans annually, which undermines the incentive to prioritize interventions with long-term benefits.

Private payers often make short-term decisions tied to the one-year cycle of enrollment and plan selection.

This dynamic makes outcomes-based analysis in the U.S. especially challenging. A private payer operating on a one-year cycle has little reason to invest in treatments whose payoffs extend far into the future. For instance, a payer covering the cost of an expensive Hepatitis C cure may see the health benefits accrue over the patient's lifetime, yet that patient could leave the plan before those benefits translate into savings. In such cases, the long-term gains do not necessarily accrue to the payer who paid the initial bill.

"In the realm of ideas, everything depends on enthusiasm; in the real-world, all rests on perseverance."

~ Johann Wolfgang von Goethe

CHAPTER 14

"REAL WORLD" EVIDENCE

In the mid-2010s, biopharmaceutical companies and clinical researchers began to focus on gaining access to more granular and representative data at an individual, subpopulation, and indication level to support health economics and outcomes research analysis. There was a quiet curiosity and acknowledgement that this data could help position therapeutics appropriately for the right populations and indications.

To make this determination in the traditional way would have required running multiple clinical trials to assess all the different variations in patients and their conditions. This would have been prohibitively expensive and limited by the strict inclusion and exclusion criteria that apply in a clinical trial setting. The question then became: what if the data was not from clinical trials, but from actual clinical care in the real world?

Real-world data (RWD) is defined as data related to a patient's health status that is routinely collected from a variety of sources that are not clinical trials. Common sources include EHRs, insurance claims, disease registries, and patient-generated or collected data.

RWD can complement clinical trial data and provide a more comprehensive and more granular understanding of how a healthcare technology, intervention, or therapy works in a real-world setting. In other words, it makes it possible to determine more than whether the drug works (efficacy, which is usually determined when you can control the environment) by also allowing you to determine if it also works in the real-world or uncontrolled settings (effectiveness).

Real-world data alone can't determine effectiveness. The data has to be analyzed, and, more importantly, put into context.

Efficacy is whether the drug works at all. We determine this by conducting clinical trials in controlled settings to isolate any variability or confounding factors.

Effectiveness is a broader measure. It is about whether a drug actually works outside the controlled setting and in the real-world with patients. These patients may have more than one disease condition (which would have made them ineligible for some clinical trials) or individual variability in their conditions. However, real-world data alone can't determine effectiveness. The data has to be analyzed, and, more importantly, put into context.

Real-world evidence (RWE) is the analysis of real-world data (RWD) to provide the clinical evidence that determines the benefits and risks of a health technology, intervention, or therapy.

When dealing with the nuances of RWD, you have to consider the study question, create cohorts of similar patients, and apply appropriate methodologies. The aim is to develop the evidence from the real-world data to determine how a drug or device is working within a specific subpopulation or within selected parameters.

In essence, the goal of creating RWE is to determine cause and effect in a statistically rigorous way. The results and findings can supplement clinical trial results and, at times, substitute for clinical trials, particularly if the trial is difficult to run (e.g., rare diseases).

Once you can use RWE to help segment populations and determine new uses, policymakers and payers can then make data-driven determinations about which therapeutics should be made available to whom while also defining additional uses. Biopharma companies can determine how to design future trials and explore new indications.

It all depends on the quality of the data. To generate rigorous, repeatable, and high-grade real-world evidence, the real-world data sources need to be available, organized, curated, validated, and abstracted for quality and relevance. After all, the data was originally collected during the course of normal care—care that tends to be coded for optimal billing.

The Cures Act

With the 21st Century Cures Act of 2016, RWD and RWE were ready for prime time.

The scientific and statistical acceptance of using data collected in routine care to help determine how new therapies would work with greater precision was a real game changer. We could now analyze routine care data to determine if certain therapies worked better for some groups or individuals than others.

The Cures Act was designed to accelerate medical product development and bring new innovations faster and more efficiently to patients. The FDA as a whole was initially reluctant to adopt real-world evidence, given the primacy of the randomized clinical trial. But the Cures Act made a push for real-world data to help speed up product development and approval for therapies, initially targeting rare diseases, which affect very small populations and are notoriously difficult to test in traditional clinical trial settings. The chance to use real-world data to help speed up development was too good to pass up.

In 2018, the FDA created a framework for using RWE in regulatory deliberations.[74] While clinical trials remain the gold standard used by the FDA for approval of new therapies, there is now room for RWE to support additional indications or supplement primary research.

The rare disease push to include real-world evidence also highlighted how difficult and time-consuming it was to obtain clinical trial data. It showcased the impracticality of running a trial for every new indication prescribed by physicians for approved therapies.

Subsequent discussions moved beyond debating whether to use real-world evidence, focusing instead on how to apply it to support a wide range of purposes, from gaining approval for new indications to meeting post-approval study requirements.

In 2018, I joined Aetion, first as an advisor and later as the Chief Strategy and Product Officer. Aetion was one of the first companies to bet on real-world data and evidence as the viable path forward for FDA approvals. They are responsible for having coined the terms "fit-for-purpose" data and "regulatory-grade" analysis.

Using newly developed methodologies applied to claims data, the most abundant data available about healthcare intervention and delivery, Aetion and others shaped how pharmaceutical companies and the FDA would view the evidence derived from real-world sources.

Very early on, Aetion ran FDA demonstration projects showcasing how closely RWD analysis could replicate clinical trial results. In addition, they led the wave of creating synthetic control arms[*] derived from patients' real-world data.

Today, there are many companies involved in RWE and a growing appetite to include more novel and multi-modal data sources, including radiology, pathology, and genomics, as well as a growing list of disease registries and patient-collected information.

Interestingly enough, one rich source remains fully untapped and often unavailable: the unstructured clinical notes within the electronic health records.

Claims and Tokenization

Insurance or payment claims are the most abundant type of data available that could give you a sense of what clinical care and treatments had been provided to patients.

This should not be a surprise, given that the health IT systems focused on billing and payment had generated so many insurance claims.

---

[*] A synthetic control arm uses external data (clinical data or clinical data proxies) to create a virtual control group in clinical trials, allowing all participants to get the treatment while providing a comparator, reducing patient burden and speeding up studies when randomization is impractical or unethical.

Using these claims as a proxy for understanding what care was given made a lot of sense. As expected, this data is not standardized and often incomplete. It is the equivalent of figuring out someone's shopping patterns based on reviewing some of their receipts.

Aside from the task of having to interpret meaning from them, it was equally important to determine if you could define the time period when certain events may have happened. You had to be confident that nothing else could have caused an outcome or effect in order to know that an intervention and an outcome were related. How could you do that?

There are two kinds of claims: open claims and closed claims.

Open claims reflect what a doctor sees, the interventions or actions that are prescribed by her and others and sometimes the test results from those orders. Other activities could have (and probably did) happen but aren't necessarily reflected within these claims.

Closed claims, on the other hand, reflect the perspective of the patient, everything that happened to them. It is called "closed" because it is basically a closed system around the patient, and all the claims are tied to that specific patient.

When working with claims data, the goal is to understand the patient's journey, what happened to them, and then triangulate to determine causality. Repeat that for multiple patients in a cohort to gain statistical significance. It is no surprise the value of these data sources is also reflected in the price, with closed claims being less available and therefore more expensive and coveted.

What about someone's identity? To do research and to be compliant with HIPAA, a patient's identification has to be stripped and the cohort must be blinded. This means the claims and any other data source would first require de-identification before the data could be aggregated to perform analysis.

To do that, the process used is tokenization or privacy tokenization. It is a pretty straightforward concept. You basically convert identifiable information into unique codes known as "tokens" and each token represents an individual with encrypted information about that patient such as name or date of birth. Using these tokens, you can track the same patient from different sources such as clinical trials, electronic health records, insurance claims, and pharmacy records—in a secure way without revealing their identity or compromising privacy.

This approach enables researchers to capture the full range of ways a patient interacts with the U.S. healthcare system. However, it is costly, as linking data requires aggregating many different types, such as clinical notes, lab results, test results, and evaluations. In the absence of a national patient identifier, tokenization is used to determine whether records belong to the same patient. Because these tokens exclude any personally identifiable information (PII) and are difficult to reverse-engineer, they preserve patient privacy while allowing data from multiple sources to be securely linked.

An analogy is like a player ID in a video game, allowing all your game data to be linked without showing your real name and keeping your identity private but your information connected. Even in the gaming world, it is possible to aggregate the gameplay experience of multiple players.

"Without the gift of participation in clinical trials, medicine and public health would be reduced to folklore."[75]

~ Dr. Ken Getz, Founder of CISCRP,
a resource for patients and clinical trials

CHAPTER 15:

CLINICAL TRIALS AND PATIENTS

In 2003, Ken Getz, the serial entrepreneur, executive director of Tufts Center for Drug Development, and a well-known authority on clinical trials, launched the Center for Information and Study on Clinical Research Participation (CISCRP). This was his reaction to a controversial cover article in the April 22, 2002 edition of *TIME* magazine showing a patient inside an animal cage with a feeding bottle hung on the side with the title, "How Medical Testing Has Turned Millions of Us into Human Guinea Pigs." [76]

For the clinical trial research community, this article, and similar articles within, surprised many professionals and institutions involved in ethically conducted clinical trials and put them immediately on the defensive. For weeks after, they could not escape the hostile questioning at talks, trade associations, or other media coverage. Several professionals took the opportunity to explain how clinical trials worked.

These were people who had bravely chosen to put their bodies on the line to help advance medical and scientific knowledge for all of us.

But for Ken, the real tragedy was how they had depicted patients and how no one had stood up for the clinical trial volunteer, the woman in the cage. He felt that portraying them as helpless subjects of scientific experiments was insulting. Rather, these were people who had bravely chosen to put their bodies on the line to help advance medical and scientific knowledge for all of us. In founding CISCRP, Ken's goal, and the organization's mission, was to change the way the world would view and recognize the generosity of the clinical trial volunteers. He wanted to help educate and engage patients as partners in clinical research.

Back in 2001, when Pfizer launched Amicore, the electronic medical record company with Microsoft and IBM to support the small independent physician practice, we were also exploring another idea. We wondered whether these small independent physician practices could become new and more effective sites for clinical trials. Could our electronic medical record technology create a bridge to clinical research? Would it be possible to "integrate," or at least connect, the electronic data capture (EDC) systems used for clinical trial documentation into our new electronic medical record?

This was exciting in theory but ultimately proved not possible in practice.

The workflow and the roles were simply too different. Clinical trial roles were more defined, and the data captured had more structure than the free text typed into electronic health records, both then and now. However, the seduction was not merely electronic data collection, but the idea of having physician practices as *new* clinical trial sites. They and their patients could provide a new source of clinical data for research and increase participation in trials.

Later that year, I launched a pilot program called SiteFocus with Tracy Blumenfeld, the CEO of RapidTrials, a company dedicated to making clinical trial sites successful. The program goal was two-fold: first, we wanted to help interested physician practices using Amicore's EHR to become clinical trial sites. Second, we also wanted to demonstrate that practices with sufficient numbers of eligible patients, given the training, support for a new workflow, plus the right economic alignment, could become *high-performing* trial sites.

The pilot program was a partial success. It was not a technology success, but it did create a path to develop community physician practices into high-performing clinical trial sites. We had succeeded simply because we had identified what defined a high-potential site and then provided the right training and support. The critical success factor was educating the physicians about the economics of clinical trials and then providing their sites with the training and teaching them a *workflow* to conduct trials efficiently. Not only are the economics of clinical trials unfavorable to physician practices, but the workflow to run a trial is a separate, and often conflicting, one from the routine of healthcare delivery to patients.

From a technology and data integration point of view, it was a failure. We may have been too early in terms of technology integration, but we also couldn't combine the different workflows. EHRs with all the large unstructured text fields versus EDC with defined fields with specific criteria couldn't be easily bridged. Even then, we would have needed some kind of abstraction capability to bridge the data.

The workflow difference was the real impediment.

EHRs were still mimicking paper records as a place to record and store information for easy retrieval. EHRs provided an electronic "place" to read notes and provide care, not create a data repository for doing research. As such, the workflow in a clinic viewed EHRs as a replacement for their paper record and continued to schedule and care for patients within the general flow and rhythm of a practice. If one clinical or administrative activity took too long, something else would get delayed. It didn't really matter in the course of a day.

EDCs, however, were used to record the information collected in a clinical trial: specific timed activities, observations and tests, and data collection accounted for different roles in conducting a trial. EDC also followed a series of well-established steps from initial screenings of patients and close-out of a study and site. Because EDC data entry and processes are organized by roles, when data is collected, reviewed, entered, and signed off, it is done in a defined and predictable manner.

How would you add this kind of methodical workflow to a busy practice? It is not one that can easily function within a natural flow and rhythm of clinical activities in a physician practice, at least not without some dedicated staff, space and well-defined rules and standard operating procedures.

Electronic Data Capture (EDC)

Similar to EMRs and EHRs, data capture for clinical trials began in the 1970s and 1980s with the help of mainframe computers at academic medical centers involved in clinical trials. Most workstations were data entry terminals, which later proved to be very limiting. With the advent of the personal computer, the concept of remote data entry (RDE) was introduced by the pharmaceutical industry, which had been long experimenting with ways to remove the inefficiencies of data entry.

The ability to remotely enter data allowed investigators to collect and submit information directly to sponsors in an electronic format. This was an attractive option to investigators and physicians, but in the 1980s and early 2000s, this was accomplished by saving the data to floppy disks, computer disks, and later thumb drives to pass to the sponsor. The data portability and elimination of transferring large volumes of paper forms, however, was welcome.

The first RDE computer programs included programmatic checks on the data that was entered. These programs could flag problems with dates and range values before saving the data. In the 1990s, the term RDE gave way to electronic data capture (EDC), and these systems were built on client-server architecture. Still, sharing data was still technically difficult.

In March of 1997, the FDA issued final 21 CRF Part 11 regulations that provide criteria for acceptance by the FDA for electronic records, electronic signatures, and handwritten signatures executed to electronic records as equivalent to paper records and handwritten signatures executed on paper. These regulations were intended to permit the use of electronic technology.

This paved the way for more vendors to develop EDC systems. The earliest versions of EDC were supplied by pharmaceutical companies with IT departments that built their own custom applications or home-grown EDC capabilities in academic centers. By the late 1990s and early 2000s, commercial vendors emerged, both small and large. Oracle Clinical, Phase Forward, and later Medidata were the largest entities. Eventually, Phase Forward was acquired by Oracle Clinical, and Medidata was acquired by Dassault Systems.

Software development in clinical trials rapidly improved and expanded data capture by integrating other key activities in the clinical trial data process, including how data was defined, handled, and transferred from one site to another, as well as trial planning and regulatory submission. In the late 1990s, a consortium of pharma companies collaborated to define the global standards for streamlining clinical research, known as the Clinical Data Interchange Standards Consortium (CDISC).

During this long history, the marketplace for clinical trial data software, unlike EHRs, never involved government incentives. Software applications continued to improve, and systems often prioritized user experience and user preferences to compete. In addition, further integration along the trial-planning chain of events was popular and well-received.

In 2008, I left Pfizer to join a rising star clinical trial software company called Medidata. Medidata was unusual in that it cared enormously about user experience and user preferences, at a time when few organizations and almost no one in healthcare IT or clinical trial software did. In fact, the roots of the company began with two of the three founders working in an academic research lab, trying to enter data into an old system for the lab's clinical trials. It was a frustrating process and one of the founders, the late Glen deVries, felt the entire process not only could be improved but should just *feel* better.

I can still remember my first day in January 2008 when I walked into a packed room with desks formed in daisy wheel formation and the only free desk was next to Joe Rugilio, the head of user experience. Joe was approaching what seemed like just a random set of data collection software and I was fascinated by how he was thinking about creating a delightful experience for each of the different roles.

Medidata invested in making their product easy to use, which was no small task given that collecting clinical trial data is not an intuitive process. The company would be rewarded in the most unusual way: the biopharma users and customers, on their own accord, suggested, sponsored, and *paid* for the first ten years of user conferences for Medidata, their EDC vendor.

Data validation, the ability to correct data, and data lock-down are hallmarks of the information collected within an EDC system. While the primary goal is to capture high-quality data right from the beginning, it is equally important that users can collect, correct, and manage the data before it is then validated and locked down. The "quality assurance" aspect of EDC is a shared goal of all the participants in a trial. This data is used for submissions to the FDA and other regulatory bodies to approve new therapeutics and gain new uses or indications. Mistakes will set a new drug application back months and can cost tens of millions of dollars in market capitalization for the sponsoring life-science company.

Although quality data capture and management has continued to be a high priority, the clinical trials enterprise still faces other long-term and intractable challenges– many which have little to do with the electronic data systems. Instead, the problems that continue to bedevil this industry include site performance, patient recruitment, and clinical trial design; all which remain unsolved issues.

Clinical trial sites tend to be concentrated in urban areas near academic medical centers, which limits population representation. Sites should align with where care is delivered; without this, recruitment will remain constrained.

Despite the obviousness of the statement above, it seems no one is able to solve this. The economics for sites remains unpredictable and unfavorable. Trial sponsors (biopharmaceutical companies) can't find enough patients quickly, and patients are still on their own in trying to find suitable trials.

In 2001, in our EMR adventure, my team at Pfizer wanted to train and *convert* community physician practices into high-performing clinical trial sites. We targeted physician practices who had electively adopted electronic records because it was a sign of an innovative practice, willing to figure out the workflow.

To prepare them for clinical trials meant investing in them. Payments for clinical trial work needed to align with the indirect costs of retraining of staff as well as the opportunity costs of acquiring a separate trial workflow. A pipeline of trials would have to be available to the new sites and the EHR data required easy sifting to help pre-screen potential patients and possibly track post-trial outcomes.

Twenty years later, in 2021, only 3 percent of U.S. physician practices have been involved in clinical trials[77] and only 5 percent of the eligible U.S. adult population participates in clinical trials. EHR adoption, however, was at 78 percent of physician practices.

This is a telling example of how improving data collection in clinical trials requires more than just new technology. It requires an upfront investment in the human infrastructure and workflow, in addition to thinking about what key issues prevent integration across systems.

The Systemic Cost of Outsourcing

Biopharma sponsors tend to outsource clinical trials to contract research organizations or CROs.

CROs create efficiencies for their own internal operations and not necessarily on behalf of the larger universe of sites. Investing to develop physician practices into clinical trial sites is not a compelling business case for most stakeholders in clinical trials. The CRO business model is one that is primarily paid based on time and materials.

Investing in physician practices would involve time, training, workflow, additional staff and there is no immediate incentive for any one CRO or stakeholder to pay for this professional development when the benefits will not necessarily accrue to any one particular CRO. It is a "tragedy of the anticommons" problem–no one has sufficient incentive to invest in or maintain a common good, even though it would benefit everyone collectively.

Contrast this to what happened in the healthcare delivery universe of EHRs and interoperability efforts. Massive incentives for EHR adoption entrenched large players, but voluntary interoperability could go only so far.

In clinical trials, clinical trial software companies developed electronic systems to meet the data needs and preferences of clinical trial sponsors and the various roles in clinical trials. But the systemic challenges were based on a *lack of qualified capacity*, lack of investment in community-based trial sites, and expecting an outsourced model to somehow make the system changes needed to improve clinical trial participation.

What are CROs?

Contract Research Organizations, or CROs, are companies that provide outsourced research services to the biopharma and medical device industries. CROs are made up of professionals who help manage clinical trials by performing many of the roles of oversight and staffing to ensure clinical trials are run effectively and ethically to achieve the goals of the companies (or sponsors) whose assets they are testing and meet regulatory requirements.

Some of the services offered by CROs are trial planning, site selection, patient recruitment, data management, regulatory compliance, and project management. The CRO market is global, and in the U.S., the landscape is dominated by a handful of large players and a long tail of smaller, more specialized vendors.

CROs are paid like contractors, on a time and materials basis. While there is occasionally a contract that may be paid in a shared risk model, most contracts are tied to single trials or a small bundle of them.

The time and materials payment model means there is no real systemic incentive for a single CRO to improve the overall environment of clinical trials.

In the late 1990s, pharma companies started outsourcing more of their clinical trial activity to CROs. By the mid-2000s, CROs were the main engine for conducting clinical research and development in the pharmaceutical industry. The shift was due to increased trial complexity, globalization of research, pressure within pharma companies to cut internal costs and shift the personnel burden to contractors, and the need for rapid enrollment and specialized expertise that CROs were building up.[78]

The irony is that outsourcing is one of the major reasons why physician participation in clinical trials is low.

The ecosystem challenge as described earlier is a *capacity* challenge. There are simply not enough qualified *and enrolling* clinical trial sites distributed around the country. At active sites (such as academic centers), there aren't enough patients as they tend to be located in places not easy for many patients to travel to, and certainly not for multiple visits during a clinical trial program. Most community physicians are either unaware of the existence of a nearby trial at another site or unwilling to refer their patient. As an overall ecosystem, there has been no system-wide investment to increase the number of sites.

> **Outsourcing is one of the major reasons why physician participation in clinical trials is low.**

The whole situation boils down to a problem of misaligned incentives in a three-way deal. A pharma company hires a CRO to run a clinical trial, and the CRO's main goal is to do that one trial as efficiently as possible. Even if they succeed, it doesn't really make the overall clinical trials environment more efficient because each trial is bid upon separately. This means every time the pharma company outsources another trial, they will continue to hit the same roadblocks.

This persistent lack of overall system process improvement or investing in greater capacity is why, despite so many years of improvements to technology and information sharing, it remains difficult for physician practices and patients to participate in clinical trials. The process is not designed to ease finding or participating in a trial.

Where are the Patients?

Estimates of patients participating in clinical trials have historically been low and most statistics have only focused only on enrollment-to-treat trials.

Biorepositories, registries, genetic, and diagnostic studies do not tend to be included in estimates, which means the number of patients involved in a clinical study should be higher than reported. In April 2024, *The Journal of Clinical Oncology* decided to expand their estimates to include these kinds of studies and in doing so, the authors determined that the overall estimate of clinical trial participation for adults with cancer was higher than the historic estimate of 5 percent.

Looking at the period from 2013 to 2017, the overall estimate of adult participation in cancer treatment trials was 7.1 percent and registry participation raising the estimate to 7.3 percent.[79] But even with this inclusion, the numbers are still low.

While cancer trials may be the most sought-after trials, government surveys estimate that only approximately 9 percent of adults are invited to participate in a clinical trial, and the prevalence of cancer is much higher.

Multiple surveys have repeatedly shown that patients remain generally unaware of trials, particularly trials from biopharmaceutical sponsors which tend to be the more popular trials because their trials involve new drugs in development.

Patients expect their physician to be the one to raise the possibility of participating in a trial. Internet research is frustrating. There are a number of structural barriers, including transportation, which continue to discourage participation.

And there is the problem of patients dropping out of trials. Many trial designs are so complex, it is difficult for patients to maintain compliance with the protocol requirements.[80] So, on top of having a hard time finding a trial, getting to a trial, now staying in a trial is a hardship.

Everyone seems to know this, but there are few solutions to help patients take a more proactive role.

Not surprising, the largest number of patients enrolled in cancer trials are at accredited cancer centers, programs, and academic or integrated networks. Fewer than 5 percent (of those patients in a clinical trial) were at community programs.

Aside from uneven distribution, the most troubling aspect of all this is that despite all the subsidies and government money that pushed for EHR adoption and interoperability, we did NOT build an infrastructure that could do double duty: data collection and support patients, particularly with research efforts.

Rather, our healthcare delivery infrastructure is designed to manage and track transactions flowing from care to billing without considering what it would take to create better routes either for patients to be invited into clinical trials or for clinical data to be easily included in real world evidence studies.

Today, most physicians are still not aware of relevant trials, nor do their practices have the time, necessary training, or workflow modifications to help screen and facilitate trial participation for their patients.

Patients themselves face challenges in determining their own eligibility for clinical trials due to limited access to clear information and a lack of straightforward enrollment pathways. Privacy regulations and complex, financially driven systems have created barriers that restrict patients' access to their complete medical records, even for routine care.

Moreover, as CROs are engaged on a per-trial basis, they lack a system-wide incentive to develop broader infrastructural solutions that could integrate more physicians and patients into the clinical trial ecosystem. And while pharmaceutical sponsors pay for specific trial activities, they are prohibited from investing more broadly in physician practices and trial sites due to conflict-of-interest laws and regulation.

*"Medicine is a science of uncertainty
and an art of probability."*

~ Sir William Osler

CHAPTER 16

PHYSICIAN-INVESTIGATORS

Community Practices and Academic Medical Centers

There is a great paradox about academic medical centers. While they represent a huge concentration of resources and the nexus of many innovations cements their role as an important node in the healthcare system, they are *not* the full backbone of the healthcare infrastructure, even for clinical trials.

Community practices, on the other hand, are run like small businesses, and the economic pressures they face to stay solvent prevent them from making large investments into capital-intensive capabilities. Nonetheless, these independent practices actually do make up more of the backbone of the healthcare infrastructure because the widest variety and highest volume of patients receive care from their local community practices.

So while conventional wisdom may favor the concept that physicians at academic medical centers are best suited to conduct clinical trials, the majority of patients are actually being cared for in community practices and arguably, in more "real-world" settings.

When electronic medical records were originally designed and later expanded to include practice management, the predominant workflow was the measurement of activities from the time a patient checked in to their follow-up results, and many of the observations were documented in unstructured notes.

When electronic data capture was originally designed and later expanded to include aspects of the trial planning (i.e., clinical data management or randomization), the predominant workflow was maximized to manage both the conduct and the data of multiple clinical trial protocols. As each protocol was different, physician-investigators and their staff required additional support from the clinical monitors, CROs, and biopharma sponsors, particularly in ensuring data quality.

These two very different workflows, converging within a physicians' practice, have made it difficult for a practice to do both care and clinical trials well.

Over the past twenty-plus years, I have heard countless health IT investors and entrepreneurs discuss similar versions of the same ideas, using EHRs to identify patients eligible for clinical trials and then using analytics on patient populations to identify possible sites. Few, if any, have considered how this will work economically for all parties or the investment required to manage competing workflows. Nor have many thought logistically about what it all would mean for the patients.

The discussions usually end up settling on the idea of having physician practices simply refer patients to a dedicated site, or there is some venture who decides to roll up dedicated clinical trial sites and manage the operational back-office demands of clinical trials. These ideas have rarely moved the needle over the years; clinical trials are still concentrated in sites that represent a tiny minority of the clinical practices, and the protocols remain managed by the CROs.

Site Economics Aren't Worth It

The economics of clinical trials are unfavorable to community physician practices or to a new site participating in a single trial.

Sites are compensated for every *enrolled* patient, which means all the burden and financial cost of pre-screening falls to the site without necessarily a commensurate reimbursement. And to run trials, sites often need to hire additional staff such as a trial coordinator to manage the clinical trial workflow. To justify the additional cost, each site must contract multiple trials simultaneously to ensure their additional staff are fully utilized.

Keep in mind that because the cadence and workflows of a clinical trial versus clinical care are quite different, the ability to switch between workflows is near impossible. The end result is that each staff member ends up having to be designated to do a specific job, eliminating any scale effects.

The math also quickly plays itself out. If a site is contracted to enroll five patients, then it must do quite a bit of work to recruit and then enroll those patients and follow through. If it recruits a single patient, it must remain open until the end of the trial, even if the site fails to recruit another patient. If it recruits no patients, it will get shut down as a site by the trial sponsor and will not be reimbursed for having prepared and screened patients.[81]

For a site to generate a profit or even break-even to conduct trials, it must take on four-to-five trials on average and also meet the enrollment targets for each trial.[82] It doesn't take long to see how this becomes a losing proposition for the physician practice if it fails to recruit and enroll a set number of patients, and it should not be a surprise that most community sites lose money and quietly drop out.

Workflow and Tech Discordance

When I look back at the early 2000s and our efforts to introduce a new EMR/EHR and clinical trials to community physician practices, I can see how simplistic our assumptions were.

We needed to consider the workflow changes our EHR was creating, but we also needed our EHR to be capable of identifying patients who could be eligible for clinical trials. We also had to consider that the EDC was a separate data entry system which couldn't easily integrate into the EHR. We also had to invest in training the practice not only to use a new technology but also about clinical trials, how to adopt an additional workflow, and how to manage both a practice and a site without it becoming a financial drain.

To date, no one has successfully bridged the two. I am unsure the bridge is possible, at least not without more attention paid toward workflow and user experience. There remains this stubborn, even magical thinking that if physicians and their staff simply use and trust the technology provided, their performance will improve.

The theoretical benefits have always emphasized, and the specifics around usability have not. Physicians are expected to trust the technology, but vendors and CROs are not willing to invest the time into understanding the physician practice's workflows or economic risk.

The technology design has also not moved in the direction to support either workflow. EHR products are designed without the end user's needs in mind and, therefore, require workarounds to access research-worthy data. Many EHR products do not allow the physician to easily do analysis on their patients' data within the EHR and are not set up to support research efforts.

EDC technology may be better for capturing data, but it can only handle clinical trial data entry by roles and by trial protocol. Most EDC technology was originally designed to support dedicated investigators and sites, not part-time sites (e.g., physician practice also doing clinical trials).

Clinical care and clinical research have been and are continuing to run on parallel tracks.

The data from EHRs is largely unstructured whereas the data within an EDC is highly structured and validated by a clinical monitor who will cross-reference from the electronic record.

Clinical care and clinical research have been and are continuing to run on parallel tracks: two different workflows, collection methods, different protocols, and different risks to manage. There is no feedback loop between them.

"Given the information intensity of medicine, the quality problems associated with inadequate IT, the magnitude of U.S. health spending, and the large federal share of that spending, this market failure requires aggressive governmental intervention."

~ J.D. Kleinke,
Health Affairs, September 2005

CHAPTER 17

THE HEALTHCARE IT ECOSYSTEM - LOOKING BACK

In 2005, an important paper was published in the journal *Health Affairs* called "Dot-Gov: Market Failure And The Creation Of A National Health Information Technology System." [83]

Health technology economist J.D. Kleinke made the argument that if we allow the market to do its own job, the incentives for healthcare are so maligned that no one would ever take on the cost of developing the infrastructure without essentially having everybody else join rent-free. He laid out an economic and marketing case for federal government intervention in investing in Healthcare IT infrastructure.

He wasn't entirely wrong. His reasoning became the basis for much of the subsequent legislation related to HITECH and the patient data access provisions of the Affordable Care Act; he offered a clear-eyed rationale as to why the government must step in and create the appropriate incentives for the adoption of this technology. If we didn't have a modern Health IT infrastructure, he argued, we weren't going to make any progress on broader health system goals.

The Promise and the Reality of Health IT

When the internet became widely available, it coincided with a renaissance in consumer-oriented technology in which many industries developed new and novel ways to reach their customers and to provide them with tools that gave them the ability to self-manage in a way not possible before. Prominent examples include banking and travel. While Medscape had made medical knowledge and information widely available, the ability to manage your own health and your interactions with the healthcare system remained opaque and without consumer-oriented tools.

> **Big Tech failed because they simply didn't understand the bizarre and labyrinthine world of healthcare and its many competing interests.**

Big Tech, along with many of us, found this unfathomable. Many jumped into the fray thinking they could easily connect all the various stakeholders because they believed it was only about connecting patients and physicians within a hospital or clinic setting and managing payments that would come from a typical insurance company. What none of them expected was how the U.S. healthcare system was a mess of competing interests and highly regulated with legislation and policies around patient privacy, exchange of information, and with no national ID number to link everything together. As a result, Big Tech failed because they simply didn't understand the bizarre and labyrinthine world of healthcare and its many competing interests.

Top-Down Design: Tyranny of Efficiency

In 2005, there were two leading policy arguments for advancing health IT: cut wasteful spending in healthcare and reduce medical errors.[84] Better data would reveal inefficiencies, like duplicate tests, and promote smarter spending, while improved information exchange would enhance care coordination and outcomes.

When the goal is to identify waste and enforce efficiency, systems tend to focus on easy measurable transactions rather than the less quantifiable quality of care, or they equate efficiency with quality. They were designed to prioritize certain metrics or capture the outputs that would allow easy calculations.

Again, how a system is designed inevitably shapes the behaviors it produces.

One of the central selling points around adoption of EHR was about being smarter about resource allocation and better utilization. To help physicians be more aware of when they might be spending too much or selecting an expensive drug or possibly making a mistake, the health IT system was designed with flags, alerts, and reminders.

While alerts tend to lose their effect when they become commonplace, they also lead to a more insidious and subtle behavioral change.

Physicians now pause before making a selection of therapy in an EHR. While there may be a choice of therapies to select, some therapies — particularly the more expensive ones — often require additional administrative steps (extra clicks, extra screens, additional permissioning) that it can sometimes be less of a hassle to just select from the menu of presented options rather than order something "special" based on clinical judgment. Even if the decision support tools are meant to help a physician, these tools can produce a behavior where the end result is the same as decision control. As for alerts, alert fatigue can set in quickly and alerts become easily ignored.

What if you as a physician are hoping to learn from your patients and have some tools to study the effects of certain decisions — to do your own data analysis on your patient population. Well, you are a little out of luck. More times than not, you are manually compiling your own data and creating your own workaround to access data to study. The EHR you are using hasn't prioritized your ability to investigate nor given you the kind of tools to easily analyze data.

Looking back, it feels almost quaint to review past articles talking about how a big goal of healthcare IT was to prevent medical professionals from making the worst errors. To have achieved that would have meant giving professionals better access to clinical data, the tools to analyze this data without competing agendas, and treating them as professionals with judgement rooted in the art and science of medicine.

Physician-Informaticians as Bridge and Battleground

Medical informatics is a field that can trace its roots back to the 1950s. This multidisciplinary, but not *interdisciplinary* field is at the intersection of engineering and medicine and is credited with many of the technology advances within large hospital and health system IT systems, including the famous Regenstrief* and the invention of the electronic medical record.

Medical or clinical informaticians are often physicians with a deep interest in computer systems and have a passion to effectively use data and information science to help streamline healthcare operations to improve patient care, healthcare delivery, and support research.

The realities of implementing complex systems that include electronic records, decision-support, telemedicine, remote monitoring, and health information exchanges is difficult, especially getting those systems to reduce redundancy, prevent medical errors, and improve care coordination. These are lengthy and costly implementations and are viewed as investments toward efficient, error-free care, thereby creating a strong emphasis on economic return.

Medical informaticians, equal parts idealists and evangelists, were often the ones involved in implementing these systems. Many hoped that the emphasis on interoperability from ONCHIT would help realize an ecosystem more akin to an interconnected rail network that promoted exchange of information. Instead, the reality was that the largest health IT systems were centralized within large hospital systems, favoring the control and efficiency of delivering seamless transactions within a closed network. Integrated delivery systems like Kaiser Permanente expanded these models, and interoperability faltered outside network boundaries.

---

* The Regenstrief Institute, founded in 1969 by Sam and Myrtie Regenstrief, is a nonprofit dedicated to improving care, efficiency, and patient safety. It pioneered integrated electronic medical records, enabling system-wide data access long before most U.S. healthcare, and continues innovating in health IT, care models, and population health.

Some of these informaticians will go on to become the CIOs of these large health systems and hospitals and will lead the installation and deployment of large-scale EHR/health IT systems such as Epic and Oracle Health (formerly Cerner). They will also encounter the limited flexibility to adapt software by these large systems. This will unfortunately put these CIO-informaticians in the uncomfortable position of having to mediate between the aspirations of improved patient care and the realities of institutional priorities.

Instead of empowering other physicians to act as scientist-practitioners, these CIOs will be fighting for only incremental changes negotiated with major vendors. They will have to create workarounds and become advocates for new processes and capabilities as the systems they now oversee continue to prioritize efficiency, documentation, and billing. The "art" of medicine will disappear in a quixotic quest to ensure the "science" is hardcoded into the system.

There was once a time when clinicians would provide a patient with a set of choices and their best recommendations, based on a humanist perspective of healthcare.

Today, they begin the conversation by laying out which choices are covered by the patients' insurance first before they give them the full menu of treatments or recommended interventions. When their patients run into financial problems with insurance company denials, physicians will find themselves in the role of managing financial toxicity by coding various interventions in a particular way—in a manner that will get covered for their patient.

Consumer Behavior

During the mid-2000s, we thought consumers would take charge of their healthcare. Everywhere you looked, there were stories about consumer-directed healthcare and how new information and tools would soon be available to consumers/patients to manage their care.

With the passage of the ACA (ObamaCare) exchanges, an insurance purchasing platform was made available to consumers and patients who were underinsured or uninsured. Despite an initially botched rollout and many political attempts to end the program, it has proved to be enduring and has changed the way some consumers have begun to shop for their care.

The challenge with electing private insurance is the difficulty in how to make an optimal choice. There are many to choose from and consumers still have to weigh their own expected health needs, the premium differential, and their desire to stay with their physicians.

The CMS Blue Button, launched in 2010, provided a way for Medicare patients to log into their Medicare.gov account information and then select providers to share their data with, review all their health records in one place, and submit their health information to clinical research studies.[85] At launch, the functionality was quite limited. Today, the button has been rebranded BlueButton 2.0, and it now allows Medicare patients to access their claims and share with other third parties via APIs. It is unclear how many Medicare patients use this service or how complete it is. As for submitting information to clinical research studies, there is little said about this initial benefit anymore.

Social media and mobile devices have made it easier for patients to find each other. Advocacy groups have become more powerful at disseminating information, but clinical trials still remain elusive to most patients looking to participate.

Large hospital systems started creating patient portals, though their functionality was initially limited to communication and a few information pages. Today, these portals allow access to test results, scheduling of appointments, and provide access to a limited summary of clinical notes. Since 2021, there has been an increase in hospitals posting their negotiated prices with commercial insurers, but there isn't much consistency.

Dozens of startups have tried to provide information about prices of pharmaceuticals, procedures, and hospital stays, but most have had mixed business results. They all continue to be hamstrung by incomplete and sometimes outdated information.

The language in government mandates has often been vague, leaving many hospitals and their representatives unsure how to interpret regulations about what prices need to be shown. As a result, prices for healthcare intervention can vary widely and are not known beforehand.

Large Retailers See Opportunities

Amazon and other large retailers have begun to operate marketplaces for pharmacy, medical equipment, and supplies with reasonable success.

During and following the pandemic, COVID vaccination distribution took place primarily through retail pharmacies.[86]

The largest distributors (CVS and Walgreens)' vaccine distribution success was due largely because they were closer in geography to and had a simpler check-in process for patients than most clinics. Getting a vaccine from a local pharmacy was just easier.

Buoyed by this success, these pharmacy chains made the leap to get into conducting clinical trials, thinking the reasons for clinical trial low enrollment was due to sites not being close enough to patients.[87,88] While partially correct, the results were more mixed. Deciding how much to get involved in clinical trials meant understanding workflow, regulations, patient privacy, representation, and the level of investment and facilities needed to conduct specialized trials.

The end result: CVS exited out of clinical trials in under three years after making a failed bet on running trials in their facilities.[89] Walgreens instead focused on building trial awareness and educating participants, particularly by increasing outreach to underrepresented populations and addressing the broader educational challenges that limit overall clinical trial enrollment.[90]

Personal Health Records (PHR) Redux

Patients' health data today is widely recognized as valuable across healthcare IT. But patients themselves struggle to gather their own data or find guidance, second opinions, and clinical trials without first seeking help from healthcare professionals or their personal networks.

Despite better interoperability, the rise of standards around data extraction and exchange (e.g., FHIR*), and the rise of data from wearables, most patients are still dealing with a frustratingly opaque healthcare system where they are still navigating on their own.

Those same improvements in standards and new tools have also inspired a new generation of enterprising PHR startups.

---

* FHIR (Fast Healthcare Interoperability Resources) is a healthcare data standard and API created by HL7 International to allow secure, patient-controlled data exchange between medical systems.

While the PHRs of Microsoft, Google, and (to some extent) Apple have either failed or languished, these new startups are tapping into a growing consumer desire to gain access to one's own information, a true business-to-consumer (B2C) moment.

The COVID pandemic, along with the rise of telemedicine, has expanded the number of people seeking to manage their own or their loved ones' health information.

But not everyone knows how to or truly wants to actively manage their health data. They still need a dynamic organizing "template" to house the information and an application that will update the data automatically. They also need to know how to start.

Suppose you knew what to search for, you could start pulling *some* of your data together. I can recall the excitement several years ago from a number of tech-savvy physicians who had figured out how to tap into the hospital health IT systems, download their own data, and then store it into their own home-grown personal health record (which was usually just a document). They had the benefit of understanding the context of what they were looking for and the knowledge to assemble their findings. One physician I know scheduled visits with each of her doctors so she could directly download her records from their EHRs and compile them into her own portable PHR.

Today, health systems do offer patient portals for patients to schedule their appointments, access their lab and radiology findings, read a summary of a clinical note, and make payments. But putting together a full health picture is a complicated process, and the data available in the patient portal is still only a subset.

A comprehensive personal health record must be dynamic, easy to update, accept additional data from other sources, give the user the ability to record observations, and provide context and narrative. Even today, patients are still forced to locate where their medical information may be stored and ensure ancillary service reports are also included, and that is across all the health systems they may have interacted with.

Downloading information from systems isn't always easy. From an "ownership" standpoint, while patient data belongs to the patient, health system security systems around this data create an additional layer of complexity and navigational challenge.

If you download a copy of your information and bring it into your own private possession, you are responsible for protecting that information. By leaving your data within the health system, you are trusting that the system will have the right security measures and protocols to protect your information.

Personal health records are still fundamentally different from electronic health records. Although both document aspects of a patient's health, EHRs also represent the physician's work product, comprised of notes, observations, diagnoses, orders, results, and clinical reasoning. This information can be considered proprietary and shared only with the physician's authorization, typically through the systems managed by EHR vendors.

The end result is that patients generally only have access to a subset of their electronic record.

Creating your own PHR

The ability to create your own PHRs can be laborious and requires significant navigation and shoe leather. Amassing information from paper records and faxes, manually inputting images and tests, recording symptoms and health statuses, and using tools to pull information from existing electronic systems is challenging for anyone. This is even more difficult when the person lacks a template or even a directory of contents to help them organize.

Although patients have the right to all their data, it is difficult to pull it all together. First, they need to remember where they were cared for; second, they have no "table of contents" to let them know what pieces may or may not be contained in a health record; third, if there is any multi-modal information (labs, radiology), they have to access each piece separately. In many cases, they are also the ones physically picking up each item (think print outs and DVDs of images) and assembling it together into a physical box.

Imagine if the process could be facilitated and the patient could annotate or provide additional information to the compilation. In fact, an individual's own aggregation efforts of their health care data, coupled with their *own personal narrative* has the potential to create a more useful record, one which could provide a more holistic and comprehensive perspective on individual health.

Could this be a path toward a better representation of health information to both manage your care with your physician and also benefit from sharing with a variety of research projects?

Today's new PHR companies are creating tools, using standards like FHIR and APIs, to access patient records and any associated documentation. These companies are also supporting patients by providing organizational support, community, and a purposeful mindset around how to access and enhance data for both patients and others. Although the uptake is not widespread and tends to be concentrated within certain disease conditions and specific populations, the tools could support more patients. If the patient is directing the access, they are exercising their data rights, and these patients could also be directing the use of their patient data for research.

*"Tell me and I forget,
teach me and I may remember,
involve me and I learn."*

~ Benjamin Franklin

CHAPTER 18:

ESSENCE OF DATA, DISTILLED

I vividly remember a particular conversation I had in 2012 with Travis Donia, my Chief Technology Officer at Context Matters.

We were trying to find a solution to manage a surging demand for more data from non-English language documents.

"Have you ever heard of the mechanical turk concept?" Travis asked.

"Yes, isn't that when you break up work into small pieces and then job shop it out?" I replied.

"Yes, and I think we could apply it to our language translation problem," Travis said with enthusiasm.

"How?"

"If we can find translators for hire around the world but first test them with our own data analysts about their ability to do a high-fidelity translation of the technical text that we are extracting, we may be able to translate at scale, or at least much faster and in a cost-effective manner."

"And then our folks take the translated text and start to abstract the meaning into structured fields for our application," I added.

"Yes, and by breaking the translation task into smaller parts, we can continue to test and spot check to ensure the translations remain high quality."

"How are we going to find these translators?" I asked.

He replied calmly: "With freelancers through ODesk."*

Clinical Abstraction

The richest sources of information today are actually the clinician narrative within the physician's clinical note, the patient's narrative of their journey, and any longitudinal or supplementary data.

Accessing this data is challenging.

For many people, the term "electronic health record" implies that all information contained is easily searchable. That is far from the case. Most information contained in an electronic record is simply digitized documentation, meaning paper files converted into digital format. This includes faxes, paper reports, and related media simply scanned and attached within electronic files. The data contained on

---

* ODesk was the original name of a company today known as Upwork, connecting freelancers with clients looking for additional help.

any additional document is not automatically added to the record in searchable fields.

This data status has become even more significant today: as the value of real-world evidence has grown, so too has the demand for more — and higher-quality — sources of real-world data.

In 2016, and even today in 2025, insurance claims data is still the most abundant real-world data available.

As claims are processed by clearinghouses, this data is easy to collect and aggregate. It represents all the transactions, including procedures, prescriptions and activities, that happen to a patient during a visit or a hospital stay. It can serve as proxy data for routine clinical care.

In theory, if you can create a timeline with claims data and then gain access to the patient outcomes, you can begin to create a longitudinal record of a patient's journey, which can be used in a cohort of records to study real-world effects of treatments.

BUT remember: the representative nature of claims data is limited.

Here's an example.

ICD-10 codes are part of the International Classification of Diseases, 10th Revision, a standardized system developed by the World Health Organization for classifying and reporting diseases globally. In the U.S., ICD-10 includes ICD-10-CM for diagnoses and ICD-10-PCS for inpatient procedures. These codes are used for documenting medical conditions, procedures, and supporting billing and insurance claims.

The ICD-10 code for lung cancer is the *same* for both non-small cell and small cell lung cancer, two very different cancers. This is because the ICD-10 codes for cancer are built based on where the cancer is *located* on the body. Today, we know that location is only part of the picture and even incidental. The code definition doesn't include any histology or biomarkers.

This means that even though a claim could be generated to pay for the services related to care of someone with lung cancer, we are now facing two terrible outcomes: (1) certain diagnostic tests are denied payment and generate a raft of back-and-forth documentation and stress, and (2) the need to do time-consuming clinical abstraction to even conduct real-world research. .

For a researcher trying to pull together a cohort of patients with non-small cell lung cancer, they will need to go read the unstructured clinical note, the pathology reports, and other documentation to figure out exactly which kind of lung cancer this patient has.

Earlier in the book, I discussed the difference between open and closed claims, but in either case, claims data does not include clinical rationale nor the clinical hypothesis. Analysis of this data is still looking retrospectively at events that have happened and trying to determine or isolate the effects of a therapy. Very often there are specific reasons why a patient may have one diagnosis, but the selected codes don't match. One reason worth noting, and that is recognized and understood by physicians, is that physicians may be trying to avoid financial toxicity for the patient because they know that using a certain code is more likely to get a particular insurer to cover a treatment.

The narrative in the clinical note is what your doctors write about the visit and about what they noticed. It can include the conversation your doctor had with you, various answers to questions, and sometimes the voice of the writer. The note follows a structure or template but is written in a prose format. Consider trying to analyze thousands of these notes to find patterns.

> **Physicians may be trying to avoid financial toxicity for the patient because they know that using a certain code is more likely to get a particular insurer to cover a treatment.**

The narrative may be unstructured (information not recorded in specific fields on a form), but it does contain the clinical thought process and important data. For example, if the physician is looking for unsteadiness in gait, what they observe may simply be captured in a few lines in a clinical note, or perhaps the infusion rate of a new drug is captured in the nurse's log. These can be important data points, not just for analysis but also for context. The data is not easily accessible because the meaning needs to be abstracted from the note.

Meaning is often based on the question or what information may be sought. If you are looking for clues around gait being affected, you would need to figure out if the note contained some description of a walking test that might have been performed. This would involve more than simple extraction or search by keywords. It would require interpretation or abstraction. What one person could be describing as a sign of progression of a cancer could also be classified as a sign of metastasis.

Distinguishing between what is a description and what is a marker requires reading the note, abstracting the meaning, validating it, and then determining whether the text is a description irrelevant to the study question or a shorthand for something significant.

Manual Abstraction

Converting unstructured data into structured data, with all the variations in the practice of medicine and the idiosyncrasies in documentation, is a very tall order. It requires abstraction by clinically trained professionals who can discern the meaning written and what additional pieces of information may be needed to validate an assumption. The process is heavily manual and usually requires two readers to verify and validate.

Because it is so expensive and difficult to abstract quality clinical data from electronic records, biopharma companies became excited when efforts to abstract data became more widely available and novel new datasets were created to support real-world analysis and research.

In 2012, Flatiron Health emerged onto the scene. Their business model was to sell oncology-specific EHR software and analytics to community-based oncologists. From the software, they could then abstract the data, aggregate it into new structured datasets, and subsequently sell it to research teams at pharmaceutical companies developing oncology therapeutics.

To achieve high quality data abstraction, the company hired an army of clinicians and clinically trained abstractors to *manually* abstract data from the clinical notes within these oncology EHRs.

The research teams in pharma used this structured real-world data to help answer questions about drug effectiveness and impact on subpopulations as well as understand potential new indications.

Flatiron recognized that the most important cancer data and information in health records wasn't stored within the structured data fields, but rather in the unstructured text of pathology reports and clinical notes. Even within the clinical note, there could be a critical, if not lifesaving mention of a tumor grading, a symptom, a narrative about progression, or some random remark about an unusual finding.

Dr. Amy Abernethy, then Chief Medical and Scientific Officer for Flatiron, understood that to truly elevate the quality of the data in the EHR, the context needed to be understood. She estimated that the majority of the critical data points needed for research existed in these free text fields and that only with abstraction could the context be taken fully into consideration.

The price for these high-quality oncology datasets was high but in great demand. The high price point was due to the high-cost labor involved in validated, quality expert abstraction.

Six years later, in 2018, Roche acquired the company for $2.1 billion based on a vision that the ease of obtaining regulatory grade data in near real time from oncologists would save the clinical studies significant time and cost.[91]

High Price of Abstraction Doesn't Scale

The economics of the model using high-cost clinical abstractors, however, was not scalable and could not easily be applied to other disease conditions and therapeutic areas.

Oncology products tended to be priced high (six figures per patient) and, therefore, it was easier to justify the high cost of abstracting oncology data. But for many other conditions, such as hypertension or even diabetes, the cost of specialized abstraction labor was simply not worth it.

This has left us with an understanding that while clinical abstraction is useful, it is not scalable with manual abstraction. Even with hybrid processes, the supply of clinical professionals to engage in abstraction is constrained.

This means that a lot of unstructured and useful clinical information remains trapped in EHRs, and it perhaps represents the single greatest target for applying generative AI capabilities.

PART III:
A GENERATIONAL
OPPORTUNITY

"The fact that the twelve most commonly occurring letters in the English language are e-t-a-o-i-n-s-h-r-d-l-u (from most to least), along with other letter-frequency lists, are used by the guessing player to increase the odds when it is their turn to guess."

Wikipedia strategies
for the game Hangman

CHAPTER 19

GENERATIVE AI

The 2024 Nobel Prize for Physics was awarded to two of the godfathers of AI: Geoffrey Hinton and John Hopfield. Their work on neural networks led to the development of AI. Both have admitted that they are incredibly scared about the future directions that AI might take. They think AI will wreak havoc on humanity.

When interviewed by *The Wall Street Journal* shortly after receiving the award, Hopfield stated, "The worry I have is not AI quite directly, but AI combined with information flow around the globe."

He noted that he feels "unnerved" about adding a simple algorithm in a neural network, which might then have the capacity to control a very big system of information and make the resulting network difficult to fully understand.

His fear is shared by others: we may lack the capacity to detect harm simply by not understanding how a system works or propagates content through a large information system. Before acting, we must pause to consider what role we, as humans, should play and what vigilance we should require as we experiment.

We may lack the capacity to detect harm simply by not understanding how a system works.

By contrast, in chemistry, the Nobel Prize that same year was awarded to three scientists: Dr. David Baker, Dr. Demis Hassabis and Dr. John M. Jumper. Dr. Baker received the award for his work on computational protein design using AI. This work allows us to design proteins, even proteins that don't exist in nature.

Dr. Hassabis and Dr. Jumper's work showed how we could also predict protein structures. They used AI models to address the structural biology problem of predicting complex three-dimensional structures of proteins from their linear amino acid sequences.

Interestingly, Baker, Hassabis and Jumper's work on proteins is a great example of using AI as a *support* tool under the control of human experts to accelerate the ability to create new proteins. In essence, we can also use AI to *augment* human understanding of proteins.

We are presented with the great AI paradox in healthcare. While the existential risk of combining simple algorithms into large systems of information is real and requires vigilance, developing AI tools and decision-assists in the lab can help us be more productive or allow us to support our research instincts and intuition.

Fundamentals of Generative AI

Before we discuss how to apply AI to solve healthcare challenges, specifically data gaps, let's first take a step back and talk about the fundamentals of how generative AI works as well as the importance of large language models (LLMs) and other learning models.

Generative AI is a type of artificial intelligence that creates original content, such as text, images and videos, by learning patterns from large datasets. Large language models (LLMs) are models using a neural network and machine learning techniques to acquire knowledge and improve their performance over time without having to be explicitly programmed for each scenario. The "learning" process is about finding the best set of parameters or conditions that allow the model to accurately perform a task.

Before finding the best set of parameters, the model has to be trained from vast amounts of data and from there, starts to detect patterns with relationships within language.

Consider the LLM ability to predict the next word.

If I asked the LLM to write a definition for generative AI that a 5th grader can understand,

> **Write an explanation of LLMs that a 5th grader can understand.**

The text or prompt* is first broken down word-by-word for the model to process. Write-an-explanation-of-LLMs-that-a-5th-grader-can-understand. We call this "tokenization" (not to be confused with privacy tokenization).

---

* ChatGPT-4o prompt

These tokens are then converted into a mathematical string which represents meaning. Each string has been assigned to a particular word. For example, using the decimal system, a string for the word could be created from simply each letter getting assigned a number and produce a sequence like: [119, 114, 105, 116, 101] where w=119, r=114, i=105, t=116, and e=101.

The model then uses a transformer to focus on the most relevant parts of the input text (which is now strings of numbers). The LLM determines how important a word is by "understanding" every other word in the command. To do that, it needs to first classify the word. Is the word a query or declarative? Is the word a label or a key? Does the word contain a value? These representations allow the model to then determine how much attention has existed in these words across all the representations it can review. Then it can assign a relative weight to that word. When it puts all the weights together for the command, it can now determine the relationship between the words and the context.

It then predicts the next word based on prior context. That's it.

Finally, the model comes up with all the possible word possibilities and uses the patterns of what it has consumed to continue to predict. It is an iterative process.

While this simple scenario shows the iterative nature of how these models can work, the astounding part about Generative AI is the sheer size of the datasets these models have been trained on.

Learning Models

LLMs are a prominent type of foundational model. A foundational model (base model) is a large AI model, usually a deep learning neural network trained on a very large and (hopefully) diverse dataset using self-supervised learning.

What do we mean by self-supervised learning? It comes down to whether the data is labeled or not. For supervised learning, we use labeled data. Basically, it is for tasks where we know the correct answer for each input (e.g., translating English to French). The model learns by trying to predict the label and comparing its prediction to the true label.

When the data has no explicit labels, we call this "unsupervised learning" because the model has to piece together the inherent structures or relationships within the unlabeled data.

What is used in developing LLMs and foundational models is a form of unsupervised learning in which the model creates its own "labels" from the input data (such as predicting the next word in a sentence) and then learns to predict these self-generated labels.

This extensive pre-training allows the model to learn a broad range of general patterns, structures and representations, enabling it to be adapted to a wide variety of downstream tasks and applications across different domains rather than being designed for a single, narrow purpose.

The most well-known LLMs commercially available today include Open AI (Chat GPT series), Google (Gemini series), Anthropic (Claude series), Meta (Llama series), Mistral AI, IBM (Granite series), Amazon (Titan series), xAI (Grok series), and DeepSeek (Coder series).

Keep in mind that as impressive as generative AI models may be, these models are only as good as the training datasets. In healthcare, this means how well the data is labeled.

When we think about generative AI, we have to remember that while new models can mimic reasoning, the reasoning is still based on training data. We have to be very careful about all the particulars that come with that notion.

Models are only as good as the training datasets. In healthcare, this means how well the data is labeled.

The concept of learning is more than merely training. Rather, it also involves being taught, which is something humans do. Human experts, and humans in general, can course-correct a specious jump in logic, an incorrect result, or detect a hallucination.

For example, AI might get the words wrong, write a sentence in a strange way, or misspell someone's name in a transcription. If it is something simple of that nature, we can quickly figure out the mistake and fix it most of the time.

When the errors are more subtle or detectable only by an expert who recognizes that the logic is spurious and the data may be flawed or mislabeled, that is when it can become worrisome. It can be even more concerning when these models start stringing together a series of steps in a multi-step sequence.

The possibility of incorporating erroneous assumptions and the distribution of bias are all areas where we need humans to help guide and correct.

Dr. Amil Smith, a British neuroscientist and University of Sussex professor, calls hallucinations "confabulations." His term is actually more accurate and scarier because it means generative AI can "make up stuff". We have already seen this happen when a recent case of a legal brief was used in a court case that cited a number of "made up" references.[92]

The difference between humans and generative AI when it comes to "making up stuff" is that for humans, there is intention. The end result, even without intention, is nevertheless just as frightening.

Vigilance in teaching and trying to ensure an expert is in the loop may be one way to begin to mitigate this tendency. Given that generative AI simply makes a 'best guess' when confronted with a question, it behooves us to ensure that the data quality is high and that we remain attentive while removing biases. AI engineers call this "alignment" with a value system, and alignment needs constant reinforcement.

If we return to our possible "perfect application" of generative AI in which the data we are looking to abstract from clinical notes could be done more automatically, we need to realize that we not only have to train models to help us accurately infer what is being written in these notes, but we also need to ensure that the classification and labeling of the data is correct.

Training Around Bias

We do not teach bias to a machine. Rather, bias occurs when we feed learning models data from the past.

For example, historically, there were more men in clinical trials than women. Even in terms of overall clinical data, there is more data for men than women. In the early days of AI models, asking AI to determine a person's profession based on their name would yield what felt like sexist results. For a traditionally male name, it would assume the person was the doctor. For a traditionally female name, it would assume the person was either the nurse or a patient.

These biases reflect a number of issues with data: in particular, a lack of representation, past social mores and biases, and insufficient volume of quality data.

For many situations, this kind of bias may not have much of an effect. Gender and race don't matter when AI is prompted to write in the style of Hemingway or paint in the style of Matisse.

But if bias is baked into the model, we may face much bigger problems, such as erroneous and harmful care recommendations or poor clinical trial design. This is a real risk if the data used for training is of lower quality and contains less diversity of people, outcomes, and context.

There are two ways to manage this. One way is to improve the quality of the data with greater representation of the population it serves or rebalance the dataset with an oversampling of underrepresented groups. In some cases, we can use synthetic data to help mitigate social bias. Another way is to apply alignment to remove bias.

"Alignment" is the process of ensuring that AI models behave in accordance with human intentions, values, and goals. It often involves designing systems not only to achieve objectives but also to align with broader ethical and societal standards with the goal of preventing unintended consequences derived from bias.

There are many alignment techniques, and several truly resemble teaching. One is giving contrasting examples of "what not to do," something we actually do when we teach children. Other techniques involve using synthetic preference data to control how the model reacts, using fairness constraints within the algorithms, adding cultural specifics, and continuously monitoring and correcting outputs.

In healthcare, while we may be able to remove some of the more obvious biases, the unconventional and uneven nature of healthcare data makes some biases harder to detect. Further complicating this are patients who are often quite different from one another—in ways we may not always understand from the outset.

Our knowledge may not be complete as to why there are differences. Consider if these differences are related to phenotype, genotype, disease prevalence by subpopulation, individual context, living conditions, access to care, or even different physicians. Multiple hypotheses are hard to incorporate simultaneously because our understanding tends to be retrospective and after-the-fact.

Going back to the example around having more data for white males in clinical trials than any other subgroup, what is the result of this disproportion of training data? Most likely, it will be not realizing there could be "missing" symptoms experienced

Because we are learning in real-time, it may be more difficult to simultaneously course correct a model.

by other groups. The problem is that we are often unsure what the search criteria should be *a priori*, as our understanding is only as good as the data we have already collected and our knowledge to date. There is a role for real-world data from women or other groups to supplement the training data. Because we are learning in real-time, it may be more difficult to simultaneously course correct a model. While continuous monitoring and feedback loops will be essential, the concept of curation may matter even more.

"Models are opinions embedded in math."

~ Dr. Cathy O'Neil,
Weapons of Math Destruction

CHAPTER 20

MODELS AND ALGORITHMS

Generative AI model development is moving at a breakneck speed. More than $45 billion was invested in generative AI in 2024 alone, with projections that it will reach $644 billion worldwide in 2025.[93,94] Models have become more sophisticated, and we are now confronting reasoning models, world models, and more recently, "persuasive" models. The pace may be breathtaking, but the fundamental issues within a human world remain.

I first encountered neural networks when I was in high school in Oak Ridge, Tennessee, where neural networks were being studied and built at Oak Ridge National Labs. The earliest neural networks were from the 1950s and focused on computation, weights, and thresholds to produce output. These neural networks served as the architecture of the artificial "brain". By the 1980s (when I was in high school), it became possible to design algorithms to manage weights and thresholds to allow for more than one layer of a multi-layer artificial brain.

Almost forty years later, with deeper, multi-layer neural networks underpinning AI, we face far different questions than simply generating an output with pre-determined weights and thresholds.

Advances in computational power and availability of large datasets in the 2000s led to a deep learning revival and generative models emerged in the mid 2010s. However, it was not until the introduction of transformer architectures around 2017 when the power of these models was boosted by significantly improving upon natural language processing around context and sequence analysis.

In 2020, we saw the emergence of LLMs like ChatGPT, which could generate text, summarize, and be conversational. LLMs could perform multiple tasks with less fine tuning than in the past.

In 2022, the landscape erupted with multiple foundational models. It is important to understand that the data these models were originally trained upon have often been scraped from the internet and comprise any and all available public information. At times, the training data has also included intellectual property infringement.

It is important to recognize that while large language models (LLMs) for general tasks may need little additional training, the same is not true for specialized applications, especially in healthcare. As new use cases emerge that challenge our sense of human judgment and its role in decision-making, we must consider what this means for professions like medicine, where judgment is an essential part of both the art and practice of care.

Although powerful and impressive, LLMs require training, teaching, and sometimes perform in unusual ways. We don't fully understand how LLMs make particular leaps of logic, which gives them a "black box" feel. We also don't fully understand why generative AI produces hallucinations or confabulations at a high and unpredictable rate, particularly with highly-specialized subjects.

To develop accurate models, or at least models that behave the way we think they should, we have to think about data quality and representation. We also need to contemplate what happens when we scale the model or application.

Despite the great excitement with LLMs, there is not a clear approach to determining or ensuring the quality of the data used for training. Improving an LLM to manage a specialized kind of query or task may not even be possible without an enormous amount of data. Even then, adding more data and more parameters

Adding more data and more parameters doesn't necessarily enhance accuracy.

doesn't necessarily enhance accuracy. In fact, more data and parameters may add to a higher likelihood of hallucinations and an inflated *confidence* associated with these confabulations.

The most disturbing part of hallucinations is that as generative AI uses text and human-like speech, the outputs can sometimes be imbued with the perception of confidence that can lead to easy acceptance and undetected errors.

It takes an expert, someone with subject-matter knowledge or strong critical thinking skills, to recognize when a confidently stated LLM output is actually a hallucination. In medicine, judgement or expertise tends to be stronger among experienced physicians than those just beginning their careers.

When LLMs are used to help solve general problems like writing a letter or finding all technical options for rebooting a system, we can work around errors or poor suggestions. We are able to accept answers with some wiggle room because we can usually make up the difference. But what happens when we try to use general models to solve more specific, specialized problems in which the ability to detect errors, or confabulations, is so much more difficult? How about when a patient's life is at risk?

Size Matters

Healthcare data needs its own specialized models. Data labeling is dependent on context and can be peculiar in this industry.

Small language models (SLM) and retrieval-augmented generation (RAG) are designed to handle specialized information efficiently, but each approach is different.

SLMs are notable for their compact design and size. Using fewer parameters to enhance efficiency and domain specialization to offer more precision, the beauty of an SLM is that the source training data can be highly specialized and the course correction is not affected by additional irrelevant information.

If you can better understand the response, you can easily align, remove bias, and make modifications. The small model size makes this more manageable, and the iterations are better for ensuring higher quality training data. SLMs can also run on edge applications and "on premise" without the need to use cloud-based servers, which enhances their security for data leaks and require far less energy than LLMs.[95]

Retrieval-augmented generation (RAG) approaches specialized information differently. It combines information, enhancing the quality and relevance of its generated outcome by grounding or comparing its output with outside external knowledge or references.

The main benefit is that it can scale easier by allowing models to query an external knowledge base for updated information and reduce the need for retraining. It is commonly used in science and other fast-moving fields and is particularly helpful in summarizing information such as medical research. The decrease in computational power for RAG is the avoidance of retraining and the ability to use external data sources for verification.

SLMs can be optimized for healthcare with a focus on efficiency and privacy, which is ideal for iterative development of applications. Meanwhile, RAG enhances accuracy and scalability by leveraging external knowledge bases, which is ideal for trying to keep up with new research developments or the need to provide the most current information.

Decision-Support versus Control

With EHRs and insurance coverage decisions, there is the hope that systems will steer physicians to make cost-effective decisions, but there is also the concern that they may find themselves having to do additional work just to exercise independent professional judgment in the care of their patients. We have worried over the years about the tipping point of when decision-support becomes decision control.

What happens when the system is generating options via a model versus a programmed output from a human process? Would you trust the output more? Or would you be worried about the model not taking into account your values?

Let's take, for example, a woman who is diagnosed with Stage 3 ovarian cancer and faces a terrible prognosis. The range of treatment choices this patient is eligible for is a tradeoff between toxicity and time.

One treatment may buy more time, say fifteen months, but with greater toxicity. However, the other treatment may provide only nine months but is gentler on her system. The choice is deeply personal.

An AI model may be able to provide the most up-to-date information and summarize medical findings to help support her choice of treatment. What is ultimately selected will likely conform with a patient's values and preferences. Certainly the model could provide probabilistic outcomes, but in the end, would you want AI to provide a recommendation?

For most people, there probably would be a fair bit of discomfort from taking a recommendation from an artificial intelligence. Most of us wouldn't want an AI ranking of the options either because the prioritization may not be weighted to what matters most to us. If the model is designed to maximize survival time, then the option of more time (fifteen months) will always get selected. If quality of life is more important to us, then we may weigh that factor higher. Having the ability to determine our own preferences, our own weights, is part of having personal agency and what makes us human.

A recent interview with Dr. Rebecca Weintraub Brendel, the director of Harvard Medical School's Center for Bioethics[96] summarizes this even better. Brendel notes that AI models are built into the decision-support tools within our electronic health systems. She uses end-of-life as an illustration to show its limitations.

For someone competent, decisions are made respecting the patient's wishes. However, what happens when someone is incapacitated and suffers from dementia? How does one determine what someone *would have* wanted? In our current world, we rely on family members or written directives, but more often than not, these are not adequate either.

Suppose we decide to rely on an AI tool to help us with the decision. Dr. Brendel points out that if an AI tool could tell you that there is a less than 5 percent chance of survival, that fact alone may be insufficient to make a decision because not only would it lack context, it would also lack a particular patient's wishes.

What AI is unable to do is determine what matters within the rules, norms, and values around human behavior. She points out that even if our decisions are based on data, the responsibility to center human meaning and human consequences is not something we can assign over to an artificial intelligence.

Data for Training AI Models

Today, in 2025, we live in a world in which generative AI is the dominant transformative technology that will affect all industries. Generative AI platforms, despite their apparent complexity, are powered by models and are only as good as the training data on which they are taught.

LLMs make up the bulk of foundational models. These models tend to learn from information in the public domain and on other internet sources. Training for these models draws from collections of random, publicly accessible information, as well as all the data it gains from users (the public) interacting with the LLMs.

There has also been a fair amount of, and at times, flagrant copyright infringement from libraries, newspapers, journals, and the work of writers and artists. Only in the past year has accessing proprietary databases become part of the training.

The concern for these models is that the crowdsourced data used to train generally lacks the benefit that comes with being taught by curators or experts. There also tends to be an absence of systematic efforts to align these models against errors, values, and biases, except when they are being used in specific cases by individual companies.

Many of these models have run out of quality, easily available data. Arguably, the processes and models will continue to degrade if less "curated" data is used over time. Realizing this, large tech companies are now starting to purchase access to proprietary datasets specifically created and curated for training their models. How this will square with intellectual property infringement remains legally contentious and without clear guidelines.[97]

Algorithms

One of my favorite books on algorithms is Cathy O'Neil's *Weapons of Math Destruction*[98] In it, she has a definition I love, the definition of a model: "Models are opinions embedded in math." She makes the argument that models are not neutral but instead reflect ideology and goals.

Computerized risk models and algorithms have dominated many institutional, organizational and personal decisions as well as our behavior for the past several years. She demonstrates that these risk models have been used for predicting recidivism in criminals, sorting between successful and failing teachers, and determining an individual's creditworthiness.

While the models she discusses were pre-generative AI, our behavior and reaction is a cautionary tale. Many times, recommendations from these risk models were simply accepted by humans without any question, costing individuals their liberty and sometimes their life. Dr. O'Neil posits that our fear and shame of "not understanding the math" behind the models led to our willful ignorance of asking the critical questions about how these models even worked. In the end, we accepted the output. What subsequently emerged were careless risk model development, less rigorous training data, and the passive acceptance of unvalidated conclusions.

This begs the question: if we weren't vigilant around risk-model development pre-LLMs, how will we develop, trust, and validate AI models when the speed and scale of these models make it even harder to determine where errors begin and end? Worse, how fast will we accept the output without question?

In January 2024, I invited the co-founder and CEO of ScienceIO, Will Manidis, to share the J.P. Morgan healthcare conference stage with me to talk about the promise of generative AI small language models (SLMs) and the prospect of training the model only on a specific set of EHR data.

We discussed some of the concerns around bias and how to course-correct by training SLMs specific to healthcare rather than depending on large language models (LLMs) and their more generalized training data.

Will used an example that I still believe best illustrates the concerns of an LLM exhibiting a medical cultural bias. The results between the prompt, "John suffers from S.A.D." and "Jamal suffers from S.A.D." were staggeringly different for the diagnosis and treatment. In John's case, the LLM had assumed the young man suffered from seasonal affective disorder. However, for Jamal, S.A.D. was assumed to be a substance abuse disorder.

In healthcare, the process of integrating LLMs into clinical decision support should be a cause of serious concern. Flawed systems could potentially lead to inaccurate diagnoses and, more importantly, misguided clinical reasoning based on outdated and incorrect stereotypes. There is a difference between decision-support and decision-control, and we haven't always shown ourselves to be discerning between the two.

There is a difference between decision-support and decision-control, and we haven't always shown ourselves to be discerning between the two.

LLMs reflect the biases of their training data, and if we accept the outputs without question, we run the risk of perpetuating stereotypes we have about various ethnic groups[99], not just into clinical records and training models but also further downstream into our research. The care these individuals may receive could be subpar and indifferent to their needs.

How and where do we embed expertise, critical thinking, and professional judgment both into the models and our application of the output?

We can control factors such as inputs, processes and course correction. We can also create processes to validate and create iterative learning (feedback loops). We can commit to constant alignment and realignment to remove bias and incorporate new data and knowledge, but we also have to recognize that even fine-tuning performed by humans can add bias.

How did we end up assuming the role of teachers of AI models? Collectively, we are now responsible for the quality of the training data, the curation of data, and the course-correcting at all steps of development. How will we validate the outputs? Where will we find the time?

"Sometimes when we look at innovation, we make the mistake of thinking that innovation is specific to an individual invention or a device. The greatest transformation brought about by technology is when you bring the various pieces and have them work together in combination. It's the synergies that bring about the greatest changes in the world.[100]

~ Malcolm Gladwell,
HIMSS speech. Feb 1, 2014

CHAPTER 21

HEALTHCARE AI: DISRUPTION OR DEEPER ROOTS FOR INCUMBENTS?

Healthcare IT in the late 1990s was supposed to solve an information asymmetry* problem by increasing patients and physicians' access to health information and medical data. We believed that making information more available would empower everyone to make better healthcare decisions. We assumed that experts would provide the context to understand it.

In the 2000s, the rapid increase in data and a greater emphasis on evidence-supported decisions gave rise to power algorithms. These

---

* Information asymmetry occurs when one party in a relationship possesses more or better information than the other, creating an imbalance that can lead to unequal power, inefficiency, or unfair outcomes.

mathematical models could be tweaked to help support diagnoses and treatments, assist in preventative interventions, test research hypotheses, and streamline operational tasks. The underlying assumption was humans would be the designers and operators of the algorithms and, thus, the ones adjusting, making changes, and incorporating new data, information and knowledge.

We operated with a belief in guardrails, that our information and analysis would be bound by adherence to scientific discovery and a scientific method mindset. We relied on validation, transparency, peer reviews, shared discussions, and a shared set of values around new discoveries.

AI has the potential to disrupt the marketplace but also to strengthen the dominance of incumbent firms.

Today, we face something much murkier. We are trying to train AI models with past and present data to elevate these machines to a status where they can make us more efficient. We can teach various rules and use different weights and validation methods, but there is little discussion about curation or the reliability of source data.

While generative AI has the ability to decrease repetitive administrative tasks and increase our productivity, most models appear to have been developed without robust discussion. Concepts such as the inherent variability, nuance, and heterogeneity in medicine may not be adequately represented. Furthermore, many AI applications seem to be geared more toward increasing automation rather than augmenting the capabilities of our physicians and experts.

Disruption?

AI has the potential to disrupt the marketplace but also to strengthen the dominance of incumbent firms.

The classic strategy to galvanize dominant market position would be to start by leveraging the existing customer base, bundle in AI features, take advantage of existing scale, create preferential ecosystem dealings, and use their data advantage and compliance barriers as well as continue to exploit regulatory capture.

At the same time, it is also possible for a different path to open up: there could be new AI solutions specialized in a manner to support a reimagined feature set, better workflow capture and feedback loops, as well as include new data sources.

The current healthcare IT infrastructure doesn't favor a change from a billing-oriented system to a research-oriented ecosystem; there is no incentive to make this change, nor would it necessarily be cost-effective.

The current healthcare IT infrastructure doesn't favor a change from a billing-oriented system to a research-oriented ecosystem.

The economics could be different if new companies using generative AI could support this shift or at least make it possible and plausible.

Still, even if generative AI technologies can change the healthcare marketplace, the ability to change market buying behavior is not straightforward.

Already, the largest health systems and EHR players are partnering with well-funded generative AI companies. They are running many pilots utilizing their scale and established customer base. Will they take advantage of the moment to try to meet real workflow and user experience needs? It may be easier to take advantage of the administrative gains from bundled-in, embedded AI tools to solidify the hold on current customers and create a new ability to increase price.

This is the path of least resistance, and it also happens to be the classic strategy of maintaining a hold on customers who have little choice to leave their current EHR vendor.

But the concern goes further. The incumbent EHRs have access to a lot of data and are also data originators. Their partnerships and experimentation with generative AI will take advantage of their scale. They will not be willing to share their data with other companies, nor will they likely create proprietary small language models when it is easier to rely on partnerships with technology companies offering LLMs and AI tools.

This is a real shame because true leaps in harnessing generative AI will be the result of experimentation and development within smaller language models or proprietary models, giving us a better sense of how to create customized use cases to support physicians and patients; but, again, no systemic incentive to act in favor of physician preferences. After all, few physicians will ever quit a health system because of their choice of EHR.

Regulatory capture remains a real and long-lasting issue. At the pace things are going, it won't be long before there will be a call to certify healthcare AI tools and uses. This, too, will put the incumbents in yet another advantaged position to benefit from complying with new regulations. They will likely have a hand in contributing to the regulations' language (as they have before with previous regulations), and the new certifications will create an additional cost hurdle for new companies.

In fact, the entire ecosystem of healthcare IT may end up exactly where we are now: in a zero-sum stalemate. On one side are the dominant EHR players, ePrescribing monopolies, consolidated and vertically integrated payers, and large entities involved in doing clinical research. On the other side will be physicians, patients, health systems, independent hospitals, and community practices. Alongside will be new generative AI startups focusing on various data problems and information transparency issues, many trying to create new ways to empower physicians, patients, and research.

These startups will still need access to healthcare and patient data, just as much as the technology partners working with the large incumbent health IT companies with most of the patient data.

If we are expecting startups to replace or supplant EHRs and large systems, that will take time and is likely a losing proposition.

If we are expecting startups to tackle the data issues, turning the data from clinical care to be fit for purpose for research, then these startups will also need to work with a number of midsize data analytics companies that are also hungry for clinical data.

The midsize data analytics companies and data aggregators, all which emerged in the mid-2010s, are also dealing with both the scarcity and expense of top generative AI talent. None can easily incorporate AI into their platforms without significant investment and better access to data, especially new data.

This is a healthcare data interoperability and innovation bottleneck problem, which includes issues of technical capability, market dynamics, talent scarcity, and regulatory requirements. Startups and medium-sized firms will struggle to both access the data they need and leverage new technologies like generative AI due to these combined hurdles.

Agency

For healthcare IT, we can already see how ruthless the efficiency game will become between the billing mentality and the advent of new tools. Physicians and patients will increasingly be viewed as the testers of new AI algorithms embedded in their EHRs; it will be their use of tools (some voluntary) which will teach everyone else how to create potentially greater efficiency from health IT.

For physicians to regain agency and for patients to gain and control their own data, simply creating better analytical tools designed for them will be insufficient. An actual transformative reordering would have to happen.

Physicians would need to gain the independence to do their own data tracking and analysis, and not just because it is mandated by their health system's billing and collection needs.

Patients would need to learn how to organize their information and understand how this data interacts within the healthcare system.

Think of how difficult it is today to pull together your own healthcare information, even with products like Apple Health which provide a place to use tools to extract, store, and add data. The process likely begins with downloading information from a patient portal of which you have to renew permissions through multiple screens. This portal will give you access to your test results, appointments and possibly an abbreviated set of notes and codes, and then you have to do this at every place you have ever been cared for— particularly if they are using a different electronic record system. Plus how many of us have had to stand inside some sub-basement of a hospital waiting for a DVD to be burned with our radiology images? Now consider what happens when we need access to help a family member, such as obtaining an elderly parent's records as their caregiver or a college-age child who may need our help.

This is where it gets tricky. Generative AI may seem like a transformative technology, but structural power dynamics aren't easily disrupted.

Commercial LLMs

To complicate matters, generative AI models also carry their own risks. In fact, it isn't hard to imagine how some of these risks (hallucinations, medical cultural bias, decision recommendations) can propagate.

From a systems point of view, the partnerships of large EHR vendors and generative AI tool companies means there may be a reliance on commercial LLMs without fully understanding the implications. These LLMs are not fully within the control of the EHR vendors nor the generative AI companies. The amount of data they are gaining from their users (clinical staff)—sometimes with context, though often without full context—means the way these LLMs are trained may result in some unintended consequences downstream.

There is a real risk that we will effectively blindly trust models and algorithms, or maybe we simply won't have a choice. Few people today are asking (or able to ask) whether we should be relying on off-the-shelf LLMs or what is happening with the data generated from their experimentation with new AI-enabled tools.

Our health systems may be trying to grapple with AI governance, but I wonder if there are any real discussions about developing and maintaining proprietary models designed for healthcare.

Current experimentation with AI in health systems largely occurs within controlled sandbox environments designed to manage risk and ensure compliance. However, the underlying models being tested are typically adapted versions of commercially available LLMs or proprietary AI tools integrated through their EHR vendors rather than novel or independently developed models.

Presently, it feels a little dangerous, given we haven't fully figured out how to mitigate unintended errors that can rapidly propagate.

What if we rely on or have no choice about which AI tools are integrated within the systems used by these large entities who hold our data? What happens when physicians using faulty AI tools are led down the path of medical malpractice? Who gets sued—the AI vendor or the physician?

Can you imagine a scenario in which a false clinical value gets attached to a person's record and there is no way to erase, correct or even appeal it?

Data Exhaust

There is another kind of data that is generated within the health IT system called the "data exhaust."

Data exhaust refers to the large volume of secondary data generated passively as a byproduct of all the interactions with digital health systems, medical devices, and electronic health records. This data stream includes log files, usage patterns, device outputs and sensor information that may not be purposefully created or immediately analyzed but can hold future value for predictive analytics, quality control, and research. It too is unstructured raw data and can be used to track user behavior.

Given the vast amount of clinical data generated within electronic health records (EHRs) that is already unstructured and the claims data produced through healthcare transactions, the exhaust trail is easy to ignore.

But this data has inherent or latent value. It is inaccessible, largely because it is in the background and generally not as well protected. Because user behavior data is included, there are additional rights, responsibilities and compliance obligations that may need to be addressed, both legally and ethically. Even with generative AI tools capable of structuring and analyzing this data, access challenges would likely persist.

Missing Data

For physicians, the electronic health record is a cumbersome documentation tool designed for billing, requiring hunting through disconnected tabs to piece together a clinical narrative. In addition, any past history for a patient, particularly if it is in another electronic system from a previously visited but different healthcare system, is simply not available.

For patients, the ability to have "fill in the blanks" is also not straight-forward. Consider how many records actually contain accurate or detailed family history or the patients' own narratives or reported outcomes.

For researchers, understanding a patient's journey requires triangulating across multiple and separated data sources. It is often with data that has been optimally coded for expedient billing and payment but not reflective of what happened clinically.

Useful access and reliable data would require cooperation among the originators of data, physicians, patients and researchers. Those who control and manage documentation would need to keep in mind that the data cannot be corrupted by the inherent risks of generative AI and LLMs.

Compounding Quality Problems

Generative AI in healthcare and in clinical research should be a collective experiment. All professionals need to be actively involved and not consider AI as the sole purview of engineers, informaticians or specific companies.

If we can develop AI from the perspective where human dignity and agency are paramount, we may be able to ward off the worst of its effects. This means keeping humans in charge and developing AI as tools to supplement or enhance our capabilities.

The pace of development and the urge to drive efficiency is far faster than our ability to be deliberate and thoughtful. This is compounded with the rise of AI agents. It is a problem we have never faced before.

In the early days, the focus was on getting healthcare organizations to cooperate and adopt health IT systems, followed by standards and the capability to exchange information effectively. Instead of creating a competitive marketplace, policy mistakes led to an ecosystem dominated by large incumbents and closed-off, centralized organizations.

Although centralized structures can drive efficiency, they are not always conducive to innovation. The efforts to accelerate the pace of health IT development only resulted in a fragmented healthcare system in which interoperability alone is no longer the right solution.

Today, we face a completely different problem.

Even if we can connect systems together and remove the friction from data flow, we are still allowing unsupervised AI learning to occur. Generative AI can create content, and our digital world is embedded with algorithms that we cannot easily challenge.

In healthcare, many years of compartmentalized health information and data has led to inconsistent quality issues in our healthcare data. Now we have to worry about how our models may incorporate bias and make incorrect inferences from this poor quality or missing data.

As major players continue to advance AI tool adoption with a narrow focus on efficiency, we risk deepening our reliance on increasingly degraded data and outputs, sacrificing long-term data integrity for transactional smoothness. We will make it harder to develop high-fidelity, well-governed data and the models, in turn, will also be less trustworthy.

Veradigm and Science IO

In February 2024, as the interim CEO of Veradigm (the old Allscripts), I led a $140 million acquisition of a young generative AI company, Science IO.[101, 102]

The acquisition wasn't simply about gaining the talents of nineteen top notch AI and Machine Learning (ML) engineers; it was also a strategic investment in Science IO's healthcare-specialized AI, small language models (SLMs) trained on the complexities of clinical data. The goal was to further train these models and develop capabilities to transform the clinical data in our EHRs into a new and powerful resource for clinical research.

Prior to the acquisition, Science IO had a clear strategy: raise capital to acquire a small EHR company to further train proprietary models. At the time, the rapidly inflating valuations for generative AI companies presented a favorable environment for them to secure that funding.

But I flipped the script. Instead of Science IO becoming an acquirer, I convinced them to sell to Veradigm. The acquisition would give them immediate access to the extensive data within our EHRs to train their models while simultaneously bringing in-house generative AI capabilities that we could use to improve our EHR software. We were doing it before generative AI capabilities became prohibitively expensive for the healthcare IT and healthcare industries.

An in-depth *Forbes* article came out shortly after the acquisition and highlighted the potential of this bold move and the promise of having proprietary models to train and fine-tune, and a chance to peek into those unstructured clinical notes and potentially abstract some meaning, thereby turning it into a valuable dataset to support real-world evidence questions.[103]

While the article presented the acquisition in the context of the company's history and recent challenges, it also highlighted the excitement surrounding the vast potential for data and research as well as the opportunity to influence how future models are developed and trained. However, the journalist also acknowledged the huge challenges of operating in an industry known for technology disappointments.

"Why are we so good at accumulating more information and power, but far less successful at acquiring wisdom?"

~ Yuval Noah Harari's 2024 book, *Nexus: A Brief History of Information Networks from the Stone Age to AI*

CHAPTER 22

NEXT LEVEL CAPABILITY?

"Lisa, you are a great diagnostician. I'm curious what you think of the new AI-scribe pilot?"

I asked this of my friend Dr. Lisa Sanders, head of the Yale Long COVID clinic and the author of the popular column "Diagnosis" in *The New York Times*.

Her answer was unexpected, but not surprising. She talked about how the new AI scribe pilot didn't really capture her process or workflow and had a tendency to summarize details she felt were unimportant or not what she wanted to focus on. In essence, it wasn't paying attention to what was important and limiting its usefulness as a tool.

I had been curious about her perspective largely because so much of the art of diagnosis is not too dissimilar to being a detective, and this was one aspect that had not received as much attention in the rapid adoption of AI-scribing tools. The context was that a pilot project had just been offered by Epic and Abridge (an AI/ambient scribe company) and was receiving positive reviews for the time saved for clinicians.

Needless to say, her answer surprised me when time wasn't even mentioned. My next question was: "How so? I hear it's a real time saver. A game changer even."

She then went on to describe to me that when she speaks to a patient, she is looking for clues. In fact, the line of inquiry isn't necessarily obvious to anyone (or anything) listening. How a patient reacts often says much more than what the patient is actually saying. There is no easy way to capture this with a recording device converting sound into written text. While it made intuitive sense that a recording device wouldn't be able to detect body language nor would an AI scribe be aware of the intentionality of the questioner, her next point showed how a feature of the tool was based on a casual assumption around usefulness.

AI scribes create summaries of conversations. If you have ever used a LLM like ChatGPT, you will know that you usually have to dictate the style of the summary, and it often misses key details. In an AI scribe setting, there is no ability to attenuate intentionality or even to explain it adequately. If your goal is to document a series of observations in a particular order, the summary is not only less useful but potentially misleading. The summary has to first make an assumption of what is important to emphasize.

What she was describing was a real limitation in design and reminded me of the importance of who designs the specs. Having an AI scribe make assumptions around intention, followed by an LLM "fitting in" the most plausible information, or in this case, the order of information, meant there was no ability to predict the kind of summary that would be generated. Worse though, those same summaries could be used to continue to train the model for future summaries.

The bottom line is if you are having to correct the AI-generated note, it is probably not you saving much time.

Ambient Scribe

My earliest favorite use-case example of generative AI is AI Scribe or Ambient Scribe, which can auto-generate a clinical note from a patient-physician visit. It seems to meet all the criteria of how AI could help support physicians by saving time during the visit and allowing them to better focus on their patients while an AI recording device is recording the conversation and then auto-generating a note. The time savings should improve a physician's quality of life, allowing them more time to spend thinking, reading, living, and empathizing with their patients professionally.

Or does it?

Ambient scribing has been available since 2020. Among partnerships forming between EHR vendors and a growing group of ambient scribe vendors, one of the larger partnerships was formed by Epic and Abridge to pilot this capability in several academic hospitals and health systems.

The early results are mixed as described in the exchange I had with my friend and esteemed physician. Her perspective isn't unique. Over the past six months, I have learned of and spoken to other physicians who have found the drawbacks are too great to continue.

The concern is around how will this capability continue to evolve and improve.

Some physicians are delighted with the speed of ambient scribe while others are upset about the amount of *time* they are spending correcting the notes.

Ambient scribe-generated notes which should be technical records with precise terminology and a thoughtful narrative too often are either filled out forms or generic prose designed for a non-clinical person to read. This is an example of how the technology has pulled from the language syntax contained in the LLMs that are predominantly non-clinical and weren't exclusively trained on clinical data.

Aside from getting better at recognizing clinical words, physicians and other healthcare professionals have also noticed errors and nonsensical logic along with hallucinations. The sheer "confidence" with which models exhibit in providing information further worries many professionals to take more time to review the model's work.

A survey in spring 2025, conducted by the University of Pennsylvania, showed that while most physicians surveyed found time savings from the technology, it was much more of a mixed picture when asked about the *quality* of the notes, with several physicians citing multiple errors.[104]

Of course, there is the question of cut and paste and how PHI (protected health information) is indeed protected. In order to clean up notes or just fill in fields, it is not uncommon to see clinicians cut and paste whole blocks of text as they reorient the information in a manner that is more indicative of medical workflow. In the process, generative AI reshuffles the text for better reading, and PHI becomes just like any other text.

The ease of generating a note can be a slippery slope. Where you sit can be where you stand.

For one group of physicians who may be managing a busy Emergency Department, the quick note may be truly helpful in speeding up the workflow. For the specialist who was requested for a deeper dive consultation, the perspective may be quite different. One example is when an expert has been asked to review a head injury. There have been reports that the AI generated note contained subtle errors that required an expert to pick up. These physicians have also reported feeling greater anxiety and the additional cognitive load of having to double check AI output, unsure if there are "missed signs" from other preliminary notes.

After all, the physician is still the one who has to do the final review and sign off before the note becomes the record. The physician is still the accountable entity.

It raises the question of how we should value generative AI tools and development. Maybe the value of a tool is not that it cuts down on tasks and saves time. Perhaps we should be emphasizing how technology makes a job less stressful and enhances and *augments* the abilities of experts and professionals.

In the case of generative AI, we probably want to understand what data it learns from and what the model it is using. If we think in terms of a research-oriented ecosystem, then accuracy, ability to learn, and validation become the driving aspects of developing tools.

Unfortunately, the large EHR vendors are not in the habit of viewing physicians as expert user-designers. Their software is not developed with or for their design input. Most EHRs are still designed to meet the needs of the health system.

Which leads to another possibility. If ambient scribe technology can "reduce" the time required to write notes, then doesn't that mean there is just a little more room in the day for a physician to see yet another patient?

Triage

What about an example where a generative AI tool actually augments a physician's capabilities and provides room for their intuition?

One great example is how generative AI seems to be improving diagnostic capabilities at scale. In 2019, the Radiological Society of North America published a short piece[105] about how generative AI could be used to "learn" what normal chest x-rays looked like and support a triage system in which the non-normal x-rays were sent directly to the radiologists to spend a little more time reviewing. Given that about 40 percent of all x-rays taken tend to be chest x-rays— to rule out many diseases—this was a way to better focus radiologists' time while also creating some efficiency at clearing normal chest x-rays.

Fast forward to 2023, when HIMSS* reported that Yale New Haven Hospital's radiology department was starting to use AI to boost clearing non-contrast head CT scans in the emergency department.[106] Similar to chest x-rays, non-contrast head CT scans are a frequently ordered scan for rapid diagnostic rule out in an emergent situation, often involving head trauma after a fall. It was logical to try to decrease the review time similar to the chest x-ray triage use case.

Again, staff in the emergency department felt there was a gain in time and reported less stress, but one neuroradiologist reported that AI

---

* HIMSS- Healthcare Information and Management Systems Society

was slowing her down and forcing her to look at a scan more closely, particularly if she disagreed with the AI assessment.

The takeaway for physicians, hospitals, and health systems is to carefully evaluate AI technology vendors' algorithms, ease of integration with existing systems, ongoing support and updates, AND consider the cognitive load as well as time-savings effect on physicians and clinical staff. Keep in mind that one-time efficiency could translate into a greater burden elsewhere.

While AI can augment our capabilities, we may be framing the gain incorrectly. Are we looking for efficiency, time saving, or more time to think?

If we must continually check the work of AI, are we really making things better for the physician or expert? Or are they about to bear another cost for new technology?

If we must continually check the work of AI, are we really making things better for the physician or expert?

If we are relying on experts to do the final check on an AI-generated output, what happens when we start running out of experts? What happens to the new physicians who have not had time to hone their clinical instincts? How do we train new physicians and foster their expertise while we are experimenting with generative AI tools?

"The greatest victory is that which requires no battle."

~ Sun Tzu,
The Art of War

CHAPTER 23

BATTLE ROYALE

Prior Authorization

Prior authorization is an area that has gained much recent press, largely because insurers, especially large ones such as UnitedHealth Group and Cigna– have been highly criticized for using automation to manage and deny claims. The American Hospital Association has cited that the number of denials has increased, particularly for Medicare Advantage claims denials.[107] Insurers are facing lawsuits contending that they are using AI tools and algorithms to deny care.[108] Physicians and health systems are starting to turn to AI tools to fight back.

Prior authorization is one of several ways that insurers keep costs down. By demanding advanced permission to pay for a certain treatment, prior authorization is a means to determine whether a procedure or therapy is warranted or paid for, but the judgment comes from the insurer. Coupled with the ability to deny claims after the fact, payers can ration what care they will pay for.

Physicians spend countless hours on the phone or in written correspondence trying to advocate for their patients to gain coverage for treatments they deem necessary for their patients.

UnitedHealthcare has been cited for already using AI tools to auto-deny claims at scale, particularly for Medicare Advantage and most recently with physical therapy claims for seniors.[109]

As AI tools are being rapidly developed and more readily available, physicians have been fighting back by using AI tools to structure their appeals with specific language to get past the AI-enabled denials. You can see how this would lead to the beginning of an arms race around AI tools.

It would be even easier to deploy AI and agentic AI for one of these multi-round appeals cycles. After all, why not set one agentic AI to battle another one and save everyone some time and hassle. The problem, however, is there wouldn't be any resolution.

Revenue Cycle Management

The hottest area today for applying AI in healthcare should not come as any surprise; it is for revenue cycle management (RCM).

Revenue cycle management (RCM) tracks payments from patient scheduling to reimbursement but is complicated by insurance rules, contracts, coding, compliance, and changing rates. Many physicians lack RCM training, struggle with its administrative demands, and delegate it or accept reduced payments, resulting in significant lost revenue. It is the most commonly asked software product by ambulatory physician practices. Needless to say, it is also a big part of larger healthcare systems.

The inefficiency of getting paid on time and accurately is both a logical and easy place to apply efficiencies gained by AI tools. Consider the prior authorization problem of claims getting denied and then having to deal with a correct-and-resubmit game.

Applying AI-supported predictive analytics would allow practices and hospitals to pre-identify denials and their causes and enable proactive prevention. This could include automating coding, billing, and using AI tools to reduce errors and manage the intricacies of complex claims. It also could be applied to support value-based care metrics and accelerate billing and payment.

Needless to say, with all these tools, if you can understand where revenue might leak, you could also create more reliable revenue forecasting. It would lead you to use AI tools to help with streamlining payment optimization methods and clerical tasks such as scheduling and payment methods.

The market revenue cycle management was estimated at $172 billion in 2024[110] and expected to grow to $292 billion by 2033[111], largely driven by AI tools. It is noteworthy to point out that the first ROI-positive use case remains squarely within the billing and payments realm.

The pursuit of automating these functionalities at the speed and scale of AI also means that a cybersecurity attack or takeover of an AI-run system (think Change Healthcare in 2024) could be all the more crippling with more unintended consequences.

But perhaps the most troubling aspect of revenue cycle management being an attractive area to deploy AI automation is that we are repeating the mistakes of the past and the start of an AI arms race.[112] Providers, hospitals, and EHR systems are using AI to boost claim approvals, while payers and insurers deploy their own AI to find reasons to delay payments.

The quality of the clinical data will continue to degrade.

"Never let the future disturb you. You will meet it, if you have to, with the same weapons of reason which today arm you against the present."

~ Marcus Aurelius

CHAPTER 24

INVALIDATING FUTURE OPTIONS

There are no warning labels on generative AI.

The risks are real, but so are the potential benefits. The possibility of righting the structural balance among healthcare entities and, more importantly, restoring agency to physicians and giving it to patients would be a worthwhile marketplace to play in.

When I speak to medical professionals, I raise the point that the overall profession needs to get more involved and spend more time understanding how AI works and what is behind the models. Physicians and health systems should always ask vendors: "show me your model."

I can't emphasize enough how physicians were cut out of all the discussions about insurance reform and healthcare reform in the

1990s, forced to adopt electronic health records in the 2000s, become subjected to the administrative burden of entering billing data for most of the 2010s, and then deal with payers who would sometimes deny care to patients for reasons that seemed, at times, unfathomable.

I think about how the entire profession was never at the table to discuss how healthcare information technology innovation or business models might affect them. I vividly remember when they became service providers without realizing it. The result? The needs of physicians have perpetually been given lower priority than the needs of the system.

This time around, in the new world of AI tools where expertise is needed to help detect and correct errors as well as come up with innovative ways to expand *quality* care, physicians need to take the lead.

They need to become AI-proficient and speak up. They must demand that healthcare companies, vendors, and technology meet not only their needs from a systems point of view but also their needs as physicians, researchers, and as the people responsible for their patients' care.

The marketplace itself also needs to support new companies coming in to offer these applications in a less centralized way and not merely through the entrenched players. This means the government may need to get out of the way or at least reduce the regulatory capture and requirements that favor the large incumbents.

AI Humanism

It has been popular to talk about how AI development requires a human in the loop, but the other essential reason for why the medical profession needs to be profoundly involved is that these tools need professional guidance in their development to ensure that medical professionals are supported without sacrificing humanism and able to operate ethically.

Medical professionals are teachers. While their own experience and wisdom may be used to guide AI development, what about future generations of residents and medical students? How will they develop judgment based on experience learned through observation? How will their critical thinking and clinical instincts be nurtured? In essence, how will they be able to become experts and practice humanism?

Humanism has been at the core of medicine since the beginning of the profession. The Webster dictionary defines it as "any system or mode of thought or action in which human interests, values, and dignity predominate."

Essentially, humanism in an AI world will mean the broader ethical responsibility to preserve human dignity and agency by ensuring that AI development is a human-centered approach rather than a neverending focus on optimization and risk management. This new responsibility will need its stewards. It seems appropriate that it begins with physicians and researchers.

Agentic AI

The ability to leap across multiple ideas and disciplines to focus specifically on one hypothesis or many or to stumble into an "a-ha" moment is uniquely human. It is not something AI itself can do. The same goes for the ability to create solutions to solve human problems.

Take the endeavor to solve the public health issue of preventable blindness. The deployment and training involved has been a purely human undertaking; we use AI tools mainly to increase the accuracy of picking up earlier signs of disease. Because we can use AI to screen for diabetic retinopathy and detect changes in eye images earlier and on a larger scale, this can be a gamechanger when operating in the field with fewer resources.

Given the allure of creating efficiency and supporting a redeployment of human expertise resources, the larger question is what happens when we trust AI to be our agents? Will the tools still support our professionals' ability and expertise to "scale" without compromising quality, ingenuity and critical thinking?

Agentic AI is the use of AI agents, or autonomous systems that can independently carry out multistep tasks toward a set goal, for making decisions, adapting to new information, and coordinating different tools with minimal human input. Unlike generative AI which relies on user prompts to create new content such as text, image, and code, agentic AI connects a series of steps to automate complex workflow and can be easily integrated into external systems. The scary part is that it can act autonomously.

This of course raises the question to us humans: just how much agency do we still want to have in the decisions that have a real impact on our lives?

We might allow an AI agent to make one set of decisions that seem innocuous; but what if it leads to another set of decisions that we aren't as comfortable ceding to a machine?

Systems are built to support small and immediate decisions, but we don't always daisy chain our decisions within a single system without first ensuring we have the opportunity to make a judgment call or modify an intermediate decision in the process.

Judgement in decision-making, if there is a tradeoff to consider, easily enters into a moral quandary. How does AI deal with two similarly valued and weighted options when the consequences could be quite dramatic, either beneficial or devastating?

Ceding decision-making is not a theoretical concern. We already see how easy it is to hand over small decisions to others. The bioethics involved in healthcare decisions are not trivial nor academic. Think about end-of-life decisions. Would you cede control to an AI agent?

Algorithms 2.0

Algorithms created by generative AI may be more dangerous than the current healthcare ones built using traditional methods. Algorithms created by agentic AI may be treacherous.

In the past, you could trace back the data and assumptions used to create them. If there was bias in the data, then the algorithm was generally limited to an outcome using only those statistical assumptions. For example, if the data says one race is more prone to crime than another race, that data is perpetuated, regardless of its accuracy. Algorithms in the pre-generative AI time were more static, and we could more easily discern the underlying assumptions.

What about now?

Generative AI is powered by learning models which work off large datasets that can be continually refreshed. While the dynamic nature of the learning model allows for what seem like advances, it is difficult to trace back the work: we can't really see why a generative AI tool made a certain recommendation. We do not fully understand why AI sometimes makes it up. Even if we did understand completely, it does not mean that we would always be able to catch an error.

We only understand that the machine and neural network are trying to make sense of one another's patterns. The computation is trying to draw a line from one pattern to the next. When it doesn't know something, generative AI simply fills in the blank.

When it doesn't know something, AI simply fills in the blank.

In some strange way, AI behaves a bit like us because humans also fill in the gaps, sometimes not even intentionally. The way we look at an image is a good example of this phenomenon. If we can only see the initial outline, our mind will fill in the rest of the details. The difference is generative AI never has to explain how it reached a conclusion.

Many researchers hope that generative AI and agentic AI will save time by processing enough information to eliminate the lowest-level probability solutions and either problem-solve seamlessly OR allow researchers themselves to focus only on the solutions that may have real promise.

By contrast, human beings take a long time to catalog anything. The classification system can involve many years and many people. Information is also constantly being added, integrated, and can sometimes change our minds.

When humans try to understand an observation, we generate a hypothesis about what is happening and develop test data to help us prove that hypothesis. Sometimes we build models and create synthetic data to make the model more robust.

With the rapid speed of generative AI models, the key question is will we be able to distinguish between a synthetic versus an observed value over time? Going back to an earlier example, what happens when a patient has an erroneous value attached to their health record and it continues to propagate in their record going forward?

The disconnect seems to be around not giving enough value to the roles of intention and hypothesis generation.

Speed makes it harder for us to thoughtfully curate and piece together what we think is happening. If we humans can keep a query-based, research-oriented, hypothesis-driven approach with these powerful tools, we should be able to use them to enhance our capabilities. But more likely, will we simply get lazy and revert to asking the tech to fill in the blanks?

Will we be able to distinguish between a synthetic versus an observed value over time?

Automation Complacency

Many health systems today have patient portals (e.g., Epic's MyChart, Oracle's MyHealthHome) for patients to access scheduling and test results. These portals also serve as a messaging conduit between patients and their physicians.

A recent experiment in the Baltimore-D.C. area involved twenty primary care physicians using a simulated Oracle patient portal.[113]

Eighteen test messages, based on a review of over 2,000 real patient messages, were used to evaluate how well the generative AI could draft appropriate responses and how physicians would respond to them.

Given the risk of LLMs introducing inaccuracies, the study also assessed whether physicians could identify and correct any errors in the AI-generated drafts.

From those eighteen messages, four AI responses were known to contain errors that included inaccurate information, the kind that could create potential harm.

For each error, 75 percent of the physicians did not sufficiently address the error, and 35-45 percent of the erroneous drafts were submitted entirely unedited. What was even more surprising was that 70 percent of the participating physicians agreed with the statement "I found that the AI drafts were accurate," and 90 percent agreed with the statement "I trust the performance of this AI tool."

While workload and confirmation bias may have played a role, the real issue could also be "automation complacency," our tendency to assume automated systems are reliable and trust their output without performing a critical review.

Under heavy workloads, this tendency could easily become more pronounced. The physician would still be liable for the veracity of the message. Talk about an unexpected additional cognitive burden and stressor.

Changing the Way We Think

My dermatologist is very involved in supporting his institution's many AI initiatives. In the fall of 2024, he expressed a concern to me about how AI might affect his own behavior. He described himself as "old school" in that he has a "trust, but verify" approach to medicine.

Despite AI solutions possibly saving time by zeroing in on specific problem areas, his preference was still to do a full body review. The true question he was grappling with was whether simply having AI tools would actually cause him to "pay less attention" to a specific area of the body if it wasn't highlighted for a closer look by an AI tool. This is an interesting concern.

As described earlier, when using ambient scribe, physicians need to worry that the tool may generate some level of error-filled text that the physician will have to catch and correct. What if they miss an error?

For those who understand the gruesome realities of medical malpractice, it is an important, if not the most important, question. If physicians rely on AI tools to point out what to pay attention to, will they—as a consequence—become less vigilant overall at paying attention to other areas of the body? Sometimes an unusual mark may give a clue about a non-obvious or larger underlying condition. Will their observation skills atrophy?

This is not a theoretical risk. Studies are starting to show up evaluating if AI is actively "de-skilling" clinicians. In August 2025, *The Lancet* published a multi-center retrospective European observational study from 2021-2022 of gastroenterologists using AI tools for polyp detection. After introducing AI for polyp detection, researchers compared colonoscopies before and after AI exposure. They found that, for procedures done without AI after its introduction, doctors detected fewer adenomas (precancerous polyps): the adenoma detection rate (ADR) dropped from 28.4 percent to 22.4 percent. While preliminary, there is the suggestion that regular exposure to AI might reduce doctors' detection skills during standard (non-AI-assisted) colonoscopies.

Today, medical schools around the country are grappling with varying degrees of how much AI should be used in medical education. There is no uniformity, and many are taking various bets. All are developing policies around the appropriateness of incorpora-tion; some veer more toward limiting use and relying on simulations without AI to teach while others are wholeheartedly embracing AI directly into training and focusing on teaching soft skills to students. What if the concern of deskilling starts to turn into "never skilling?"

How do we gain professional judgment? Isn't it through trial and error, exposure, experience, and discussion? Isn't medicine more than just having the "right answers"? How much of medicine is detec-tive work? The best practitioners are the ones who spend a fair bit of time trying to piece together what is happening, and this usually involves thought and time.

What happens when the less experienced physician is the one teaching the AI models? From a data point of view, will these new physicians even gain the same level of expertise or awareness to correct and teach models? Could we see a slow followed by a rapid degradation of not just clinician skill but also the AI models as training data becomes outdated?

With that as context, are we truly comfortable with an AI agent taking steps on our behalf?

"Human centeredness for the individual recognizes that this technology [AI] can empower or harm human dignity, can enhance or take away human jobs and opportunity, and can enhance or replace human creativity."[114]

~ Dr. Fei Fei Li,
Sequoia Professor of Computer Science at Stanford University;
Co-founder and Director of the Institute for Human-Centered AI

CHAPTER 25

RESPONSIBLE AI

Begin With The Data

How do we use this generational opportunity to create a new world order within the healthcare ecosystem? How do we begin to use generative AI in a manner that supports both clinical care and clinical research?

Start with the data. Make the hard pivot.

Data collected in the electronic health record is messy, mainly unstructured, and not easily usable for research and analysis, at least not without some serious effort. Human abstractors often spend time reading, triangulating, matching, and inferring meaning from the various pieces of healthcare information stored in this electronic filing cabinet.

While we have data managers and data scientists as new professions that have developed over the past two decades, there is a difference between managing data and understanding it. To date, we have relied much more on forms, extracting keywords, and tagging specific terms as a way to filter and then analyze data. An extraction approach versus an *abstraction* approach will yield different results.

Abstraction is more sophisticated and requires both a level of clinical expertise and knowledge as well as a high sense of responsibility. Extraction is more mechanical and can be easily automated whereas abstraction requires clinically trained personnel who have experience with ascribing meaning across multiple documents containing possibly related information. It requires an understanding of syntax, validation, concurrence, aligning data, and reasoning for specific research questions.

Abstraction involves creating validated assumptions as to what is actually happening. For example, a medical note might describe a patient with localized HER-2 positive breast cancer who started an infusion treatment two weeks ago and is complaining of progressive shortness of breath over the past three days.

Simple extraction or keyword search might miss that the patient is still on the infusion treatment because the documented date may have only been at the start of treatment. The progressive shortness of breath may also include a normal chest x-ray. The question is whether this patient's symptoms are a consequence of progression of disease (e.g., metastasis) or a later-presenting side effect of the infusion therapy.

The study question determines the assumption. The abstraction process requires reasoning to determine what relevant data is available to map out a patient journey. To go further, you may wish to view this patient within the context of a cohort of patients with similar profiles and maybe similar reactions.

Extracting key terms would likely cause you to miss something. If a note states there is progression of disease based on tumor growth, you would then need to understand if tumor size was even recorded. If not, you would have to document progression of disease based on another factor or impute the data.

Abstracting key clinical concepts from notes is a difficult task. It can take a long time to train a clinical person how to do it consistently. There is time spent on achieving baseline reliability as well as iterating around various interpretations of a note. It is a customized process to have to glean what is happening from a note, particularly as most clinical notes are written in a narrative form.

Developing AI-enabled abstraction processes could drastically simplify, speed up, and scale this approach so it could be applied more broadly and to more disease conditions.

Earlier, I discussed how the economics of human abstraction only made sense for oncology therapeutics and, therefore, why there has not been any widespread abstraction applied to more prevalent or common disease conditions.

Today, there are several companies trying to create AI-abstraction capabilities, but the care and methods used to train their models are still variable. The market for quality AI-enabled abstraction is still nascent.

This is one of those moments where reliable and predictable methods created responsibly for an AI-enabled abstraction methodology could unlock meaning across larger volumes of data and patient records, allowing researchers to ask more precise questions.

You could even imagine that we might develop the ability to partially structure data we collect upfront or shortly after. Over time, it may even speed up the care-research feedback loop.

Better data collection design could be informed by the physician's natural ability to glean information. Better applications could pre-structure the note for future abstraction.

Imagine if we developed and taught specialized models, as in small language models, to become more discerning, more predictable and, in essence, shorten the time from data collected in routine care to data used to analyze patterns around disease and treatment.

If AI-enabled clinical abstraction becomes a real capability, you could begin to see how the marketplace would welcome newer, more specialized research-oriented players and new products.

Change the Focus

The old-world order of data aggregators, CROs, and EHRs could consider investing in AI tools to focus more on designing, collecting, and analyzing in tandem with life science research. In a world where value-based care is measured more by efficiency metrics, there is an opportunity to change this to be more about effectiveness. We could close the loop from care informing research and care being measured in more meaningful ways.

While interoperability allows systems to exchange data easily, it may actually become less important over time. Instead, faster abstraction may create a new data economy and an infrastructure that favors players both small and large. New business models could emerge that focus on the completeness and research utility of the data as well as new definitions of value.

Faster abstraction may create a new data economy and an infrastructure that favors players both small and large.

Today, new companies are able to take advantage of interoperability standards, in particular FHIR. As more companies are able to pull data from EHRs, the demand to filter and assemble for relevant information into specialized and summarized formats for patients, physicians, and health systems will grow.

At the time of this writing, Stanford Medicine has begun experimenting with a homegrown technology called Chat EHR[115] which allows voice-based queries to gather data from the EHR about a patient's longitudinal record and answer questions about their health history. Embedding LLM capabilities directly into the workflow will make the EHR more user friendly and change the way clinicians interact with the EHR.

The attention to clinician workflow is promising because it indicates *direct* clinician design involvement. But these are still early days, and most improvements are still within a closed system.

The Role of Friction and Redundancy

Thirty years ago, those of us in the nascent healthcare information technology space spoke of many goals.

We cared about streamlining but paid little attention to redundancy. In fact, the idea was to eliminate redundancy and friction. But redundancy has its merits, particularly as a security philosophy at a time when data breaches remain a constant threat.

As for friction, it depends on what created the friction in the first place and whether it is simply the unhelpful remnants of an uneasy compromise among stakeholders or the potentially helpful friction created from the exploration and push-pull of determining what might be the right course of treatment.

Redundancy has its merits, particularly as a security philosophy at a time when data breaches remain a constant threat.

In the world of health IT, the predominant friction is largely the administrative type between providers of care and providers of payment. There is an entire industry of software and tools that developed just to remove this.

The focus on streamlining initially was about making it easier for people to access their data from anywhere. We wanted to make sure it was possible to move around the country and not worry about our data being physically stuck in one place. We hoped we could tie it to insurance portability. We thought by increasing awareness and education around healthcare, we would have more empowered patients to direct their own care. We thought the sheer volume of data we were collecting would help us learn more about disease and how therapeutics worked.

Collectively, we wanted to improve healthcare AND slow down unnecessary spending. We thought it would be revolutionary if we could simply make information flow easier, be more consumable, and convince companies and systems to become more interoperable.

However, we got *stuck in the U.S. healthcare system* and how the dollars flow. We ended up fostering entrenched and incumbent players and allowed the healthcare ecosystem to become zero sum.

Had we primarily focused on the inherent value and potential of the clinical data itself, we might have built the infrastructure to be more geared toward supporting research. We may have redirected incentives to encourage better clinical workflow for better data.

The U.S. healthcare system today is heavily transactional, and the health IT infrastructure is all about facilitating these transactions and removing the friction in the process, particularly within the conflict of care and payment.

AI offers us a chance to shift healthcare toward research by simplifying the collection and analysis of meaningful clinical data. However, this reorientation may be a bit of a pipe dream, especially with established players prioritizing administrative efficiency and revenue cycle improvements.

For a responsible approach to applying AI, patient and physician involvement is crucial.

Most scalable AI solutions are controlled by major tech and healthcare IT companies. Our past efforts to drive strict certification and interoperability standards risk repeating our past mistakes, driving more regulatory capture and further entrenching an ecosystem where the largest players prevent competition without changing their behavior.

To use AI as a way to rebalance the healthcare experience for patients and clinicians, we need to consider what friction we should try to remove and what kind we may want to engender.

For patients and physicians, we would likely want to tackle the friction that impedes their ability to assemble their own data in a practical way or the data of their patients in a way conducive to analysis across their own practice.

For clinicians, we may also wish to engender a little bit of friction in decision-making in order to prevent AI from eroding skills and critical thinking.

AI Meets the Healthcare Machine

EHR vendor contracts are multi-year in implementation and length, and extremely difficult to switch out.

With the excitement and large investments in generative and agentic AI, we are witnessing a gold rush of new and existing health IT vendors developing and integrating AI tools (often untested) into clinical workflows as a way to maintain or capture the market share of U.S. health systems.

In fact, many new AI partners are eager to piggyback onto the existing market share and systems of the EHR incumbents and, in turn, are touting the benefits of never leaving a particular EHR's universe.

Old marketplace behavior patterns continue, with smaller, sub-scale AI firms defining innovative use-cases, large healthcare players galvanizing their hegemony, and Big Tech repeating past mistakes by treating health care as a vertical.

But remember, we have two health IT ecosystems: one for care and one for research. While there is a growing interest in bridging the two, the thinking is still preliminary, given that each ecosystem has its own peculiarities and workflow; neither system truly understands the complexity of the other, and each has opportunities to apply AI to their existing activities.

Prioritizing an infrastructure to facilitate the movement of data between the two ecosystems is complex, hard, and likely not the first thing anyone will want to apply AI to when there are easier (and more lucrative) efficiencies to be gained by applying AI to current activities.

For new health IT companies, the ability to access clinical data, particularly the clinical notes from the large incumbent health IT vendor, remains difficult.

Old battle lines tend to stay the same. We are witnessing hand-to-hand combat between the AI agents of EHR companies against the AI agents of the payers. Specifically, EHR companies are providing AI claims "optimization" tools for payment maximization versus payers' AI claims "adjudication" tools designed to reduce or deny those same payments. The same back and forth occurs before care is rendered, but now within an AI-enabled version of the old phone tag between payers and providers over prior authorization.

Lawsuits are increasing against insurers who are allegedly denying claims en masse instead of case-by-case. In the wake of those lawsuits are the inevitable Congressional hearings, and most recently a criminal investigation into the largest insurer, United HealthGroup.[116,117]

On the positive side, there are many pilots and experiments that are trying to address both legacy software problems and system gaps. Many AI pilots in healthcare aim to reduce alert fatigue, address staffing gaps (like providing elder care companions), help doctors write appeal letters, and assist patients in preparing records for clinical trial eligibility.

In the research ecosystem, there is greater and better use of privacy-related tokenization, AI supported annotations, and improvement in new multi-modal data sources (e.g., radiology images, pathology, video, microscope, genomics) for both for real-world evidence research and clinical trials.[118] We are also starting to see the emergence of AI-native engines in which health and pharma domain expertise is getting encoded in models.

A Responsible Direction

The main and even existential challenge is deciding how to use AI in healthcare responsibly, especially since most clinical research potential depends on data generated during clinical care. Despite new innovations, incumbents still control operations because the sheer volume of healthcare transactions favors established systems, like new cars forced to navigate an outdated city road network.

The number of large hospital or acute-based EHR vendors has shrunk over the years with Epic and Oracle holding the largest market share. There simply aren't many viable choices to meet the complex transactional and industrial needs of a large health system. The cost is in the billions of dollars, requiring several years to implement a comprehensive EHR system to maintain pace with the business. When asked about these multi-year installations, management and the boards of large health systems and hospitals give the heartbreaking response that there was simply no alternative, especially if they needed to ensure access to the data from other hospitals that use the same vendor even when the physicians generally dislike the EHR vendor.

There is nothing worse than feeling stuck buying and implementing a system to keep your operations going and maintaining the status quo, all while knowing that the transactional nature and barriers of the healthcare system will continue to disappoint clinicians and patients.

As major vendors like Epic and Oracle deploy more AI features, smaller competitors (in a bid to survive) will be forced to build new capabilities to help retain physicians within these dominant platforms.

Without deliberate effort to involve clinicians and patients in guiding AI development to meet *their* priorities or even principles of human-centeredness, the current market leaders will likely strengthen their control, leaving little room for new entrants.

Consequently, decisions about AI will focus on streamlining administrative processes for transactional healthcare, as revenue will continue to flow to those who enable (and remove friction) in existing system operations.

We seem to be on the high-speed road of continuing to deepen long-term divisions in healthcare, unless we take this opportunity to guide AI development toward more of a research-orientation with a focus on the quality of clinical data. Otherwise, we may not get a chance for several generations.

I hope this time will be different.

"The process of industrial mutation that incessantly revolutionizes the economic structure from within, destroying the old one, and creating a new one. Creative Destruction is the essential fact about capitalism."[119]

~ Joseph Schumpeter, economist

CONCLUSION

In writing this book, my aim was to connect my own journey to the broader story of health IT—how it has transformed modern medicine in the U.S., and how we now stand together at a pivotal moment to shape healthcare AI as it, in turn, begins to transform health IT itself.

This story has always been about context: the path we have traveled and the future we can have in thoughtfully developing healthcare AI.

Eighteen months ago, when I guided Veradigm's entry into generative AI, it was a strategic step aimed at addressing a long-standing gap between clinical care and clinical research. Though coming from an unlikely place, as an incumbent EHR serving independent clinics, we faced a timely, foundational moment with the opportunity to connect two disparate health IT ecosystems and guide the path toward improving U.S. healthcare. But it would have to happen quickly, decisively, and steadfastly.

Since then, the healthcare AI landscape has simply accelerated at warp speed, not only spurring the development of new companies but also forcing existing healthcare entities to consider how best to apply AI tools to meet market expectations.

This pace has raised all kinds of questions, which take more than a moment to consider: where is it prudent for an AI application or an AI agent? What models require oversight? What process should keep a human in the loop? What should be sped up and what should be slowed down? Where has AI implementation already met or created unexpected problems?

The new emerging companies are trying to define novel ways to perform the tasks of healthcare IT and data management. Some have sped up data capture in real time; others have expanded data sources and radically improved the usability of data.

Health systems and physicians are directly experiencing and using AI tools embedded in their digital clinical workflow as EHR vendors form and deepen their relationships with Big Tech and AI companies. In fact, these vendors are now deploying their engineers to directly build in functionalities reliant on a host of LLM models.

Experiments abound with AI tools including ambient scribe, AI assistants, prior authorization battle agents, and even the bold step of using agentic AI to make care suggestions. Small and large studies continue to get published with head-to-head matchups of AI capabilities against human capabilities, particularly around diagnosis and outcomes management.

But where is the long-term path and what is the ultimate goal?

Everybody's Moving

Over this past year, I have spoken to many physicians, entrepreneurs, new and small healthcare AI companies, a wide range of investors, and listened to many large company presentations. There is both profound and vague uncertainty and excitement about what AI can do for healthcare.

I have met with companies trying to empower patients by making information easier to find and review; but these new companies are up against new regulations that are both slow-moving and expensive. As expected, new regulations favor existing companies' immense capital base and market position. We are seeing early discussions about healthcare AI-accreditation.

There is also optimism among the new healthcare AI entrepreneurs. Some see opportunity in enriching data; others see care gaps that could get closed by empowering patient decision-making. While many may lack the ability to scale their products inside traditional healthcare entities, their provisioning of tools to help patients and other entities tap into or improve their own data may ultimately prove to be disruptive.

There are also the fiercely independent clinics, which despite market forces of consolidation, have managed to hold on, survive, and even expand. These clinics are not operating in the hospital EHR incumbency, but within a smaller marketplace of existing and new EHR vendors. And by managing their own tech stack, these clinics may create an ideal setting where a mix-and-match approach to AI capabilities becomes the best way to both adopt new tools and experiment, allowing innovation to flourish in a marketplace-style environment.

While some of the new healthcare AI entrepreneurs will ultimately sell their capabilities by partnering with the large incumbent EHR companies, they are also learning how their capabilities mesh with or exacerbate workflow challenges.

Finally, the new healthcare AI entrepreneurs are creating networks facilitated by AI to address the information asymmetry for patients about trials and for sponsors around quality data to find eligible patients.

The Analytics Paradox

With the race to train LLMs on data within current systems, there may be an interesting demand developing for analytical and specialized data analytics companies to support both data origination and aggregation companies.

Many of these analytical companies are midsize, ten-plus years old, and have tried to capitalize on the excitement of real-world evidence but have never fully been able to capture the dominant market position for providing analysis for research. The costs of accessing, interpreting, and abstracting data were simply too high, but the analytics they provided created a reasonable workaround. The work was complex and was often impeded by the poor-quality data available. These companies' investors have grown impatient, liquidity is more locked in 2025 (if it is not AI-oriented), and mergers and acquisitions seem to be the only way to survive.

What is interesting is that these companies who have been providing analytical tools, software, and consulting services have actually been the *de facto* bridge between data from clinical care to clinical research but have operated more piecemeal and in a one-way direction to support research work.

Over the last decade of providing these specialized services, these companies have developed valid methodologies to use datasets from disparate health delivery systems within a variety of privacy-related environments to support life sciences research and value-based care.

While many recognize new opportunities to help improve and enrich the data quality for their customers, these companies would need to make a technology investment in AI well beyond their financial means. These firms' current operating models tend to be more manual, highly dependent on expertise, and involve paying for data access while sometimes using their staff to do manual abstraction in order to conduct analysis for their customers. As such, it doesn't feel like any of these small or midsize companies are in a position to close the system-wide gap and take advantage of creating a two-way road.

Unfortunately, this care–research gap has never been *a priority* for the larger healthcare IT and EHR players who could be investing in improving the clinical data itself. Their rush to apply AI and LLMs without a deep understanding of real-world evidence or rigorous outcomes research is the latest example of producing superficial solutions that could ultimately worsen the problem, especially because the application of AI will likely be used to either improve operations or fuel the arms race of better revenue cycle management between providers/health systems and payers.

This means the market may remain permanently fragmented and transaction-driven, with AI and LLMs grafted onto legacy infrastructure and entrenched system dynamics absorbed by the status quo rather than disrupting it.

It would be a profound missed opportunity for us all if, in order to merely survive in a market shaped by the largest players, we resign ourselves to once again focus solely on providers, payers, and the efficiency of transactions rather than seizing the chance to truly bridge care and research in service of advancing human health.

The market may remain permanently fragmented and transaction-driven, with AI and LLMs grafted onto legacy infrastructure and entrenched system dynamics absorbed by the status quo rather than disrupting it.

Will we once again overlook the opportunity to focus on the narrative data layer, where the true nuance and variability of disease and human experience reside, thereby limiting our collective research progress and our capacity to drive better outcomes for patients?

Domain Experts and Vibe Coding

What gives me hope is not just how far and fast generative AI tools have progressed, but who can develop them.

A few months ago, in the heat of summer, I was vibe-coding, where you instruct generative AI to code for you and subsequently turn an idea into a working prototype. I was using Lovable, a front-end AI tool, to build a quick prototype interface for a new kind of EHR, one that includes the elements of what a physician would want to see if she were the patient.

I prompted the AI about what specific information to show upfront: which information to graph and visualize and how to create different views and change parameters. I had the benefit of already knowing what I wanted to see as a former physician and health IT veteran, but it still took me roughly one hour.

In the process, I remembered a conversation I had had a year ago when I was asked why it was so important for Veradigm to acquire AI capabilities through mergers and acquisition. My answer then was that in the history of healthcare IT, most companies providing healthcare services never had the will, opportunity, financial strength, or technical prowess to even be able to purchase new technology capabilities to rapidly scale their domain knowledge and unlock the value of their data.

And yet, here I was, one year later, creating a rapid prototype by myself for a potential new EHR interface. While it didn't include data and was only a mockup, it also signified the rapidly narrowing chasm where coding capabilities are becoming available to non-technical folks to design and create their own applications. This should give everyone pause.

How far away are we from the day when a new generation of EHRs or PHRs can emerge and are created directly by domain experts or even a motivated patient rather than a vendor or a team of engineers? That day may not be that far away.

Given the history of the low status physicians have held in the health IT driven ecosystem, it would not be too big a leap to imagine a group of physicians and medical professionals "rage-building" a product truly designed around their needs, and I am willing to bet that it would support clinical research far better than the current legacy commercial products, even those embedded with AI tools. Perhaps reclaiming this newfound agency will also allow physicians to return to the cornerstone of the physician-patient relationship.

Innovation can come from anywhere as more people learn to use AI to create AI. With the right tools and expertise in place, this is not just possible, but highly probable. In fact, I am most excited to see what motivated patients with their physicians might do to finally gain some real voice in their healthcare journey. Today, we have an accessible technical capability for *anyone* interested to create and code an application by themselves, without having to hire a team of engineers.

The arrival of democratic AI tools in healthcare holds enormous promise; patients and physicians may finally have a real seat at the table, helping to shape health IT based on lived experience and practical needs. With these available tools and models, those willing to learn can design, build, and prototype solutions uniquely suited to their fields, making experts into their own technical teams and ushering in a new era of innovation.

Innovation can come from anywhere as more people learn to use AI to create AI.

But there is also genuine uneasiness and concern. As companies and AI advocates and evangelists push for rapid adoption and use, there is a risk there will not be sufficient discussion about the essential roles of humanity, personal and professional judgment, and user preference. As large-scale AI initiatives and advanced models unfold, we must ensure that human insight and the will of those most affected remain at the forefront, because the story of healthcare's future is ours to write together.

So while today's marketplace will still prioritize the gains made from eking out more efficiencies or removing friction in healthcare transactions and operations, this does NOT have to be a zero-sum game.

We have the ability to develop multiple systems focused on data to drive greater knowledge and insights. Even with the possibility of disruption, the issues of data governance and quality will still be important.

———

For the foreseeable future, the dominant healthcare AI use-cases will center on reduction of administrative tasks to streamline how the money flows and how health systems and professionals are paid for care.

The tug-of-war between what a physician deems medically necessary and what an insurer is willing to pay will persist and get more intense with AI agents.

The secondary use of clinical data for real-world evidence will require more care and attention to quality of the data, particularly with the development of AI-enabled abstraction methods, new inputs, and synthetic values. It is also a moment when AI tools may allow us to incorporate additional sources of clinical data including radiological, microscopic images.

There will hopefully be a growing demand among patients and physicians to reclaim some agency in determining what they need and want, and that they too can directly benefit from developing and wielding AI tools.

The U.S. healthcare system remains fragmented, governed by complex regulations and reactive to competing interests. This will not change easily.

Once again, we have another presidential focus on interoperability and an *optional* push for data sharing among all the vendors to create a patient-centric healthcare system.

But this time *might* be different.

Although patients have always theoretically had the right to access their data, the reality is it is a gargantuan task for most of them to assemble.

My hope is that as more people grow aware of the asymmetry of power around one's own personal health data, both form and function, as well as the lost opportunity around research, there will be new demand, new companies, and bold efforts trying to change that dynamic.

My hope is that as more people grow aware of the asymmetry of power around one's own personal health data, both form and function, as well as the lost opportunity around research, there will be new demand, new companies, and bold efforts trying to change that dynamic.

With everything happening everywhere and all at once, collectively, we are compelled to take the leap. The tools, transformative technologies, and continuous improvements in AI models are more accessible than ever—to professionals and the public alike. The current spirit of the times favors disruption, presenting a rare and powerful opportunity to reshape existing systems, for the better.

As Thucydides* said, "The bravest are surely those who have the clearest vision of what is before them, glory and danger alike, and yet notwithstanding, go out to meet it."

It is now time to close the gap by building anew.

---

* Thycydides was an Athenian historian and general (c460-c400 BC). While known for his History of the Peloponnesian War, he has also been called the father of "scientific history" because of his application of strict standards of impartiality, evidence-gathering, and analysis of cause-and effect without reference to divine intervention or the intervention of the gods.

ACKNOWLEDGEMENTS

There are countless people I need to thank for making this book possible, but a special note of gratitude to the following:

J.D. Kleinke, Dr. Lisa Sanders, Peter Frishauf, Emily Rubinstein, Dr. Henry Hsia, and Viola Hsia for their guidance, advice, and support with the writing of this book.

An enormous debt of gratitude to Vita Cassese, Ken Getz, Dr. April Wazeka, Sejal Shah Gulati, Stephanie Davis, Jocelyn Anker, Jon Swope, Talia Hsia, Margaret Crotty, Rory Riggs as my early readers whose expert feedback, critical insights, and thoughtful review gave the book its center of gravity.

And my deepest thanks to these distinguished experts who reviewed my book: Dr. Pauline Chen, Dr. Nancy Brown, Dr. Ayman El-Mohandes, Stephane Bancel, Peter Pitts, Bunny Ellerin, Jodie Gillon, Missy Krasner, Shashi Shankar, Dr. Xinkun Nie, Deborah Perry Piscione, and. Dr. Carri Chan. I am truly humbled by your support and kind words.

I also want to express my gratitude to my team at Rigani Press and Jennifer S. Wilkov at Your Book Is Your Hook, LLC. I couldn't have developed this book without your expertise and care.

Most of all, I am eternally grateful to the many experts, colleagues, entrepreneurs, leaders, friends, and family who have had so many thought-provoking and lengthy conversations with me, both during the writing of this book and over the last three decades, about why our healthcare system didn't work, our enduring hopes for health information technology, exciting ideas, new startups, and an overwhelming desire for patients and physicians to recapture their own agency.

To those who exchanged ideas, shared their wisdom, and worked alongside me over the years: your insights and collaboration across countless conversations, projects, and adventures profoundly shaped my perspective on healthcare IT and enriched every step of this journey. Thank you for your brilliance and generosity.

Travis Donia, Brenda Gleason, Dr. Amber Batata, David Hepler, Tracy Blumenfeld, Wes McCain, Traci Entel, Mitchell Smith

Dr. Briggs Morrison, Dr. Jack McMillan, Dr. Rito Bergemann, Dr. Newell McElwee, Dr. Kimberly McGuigan, Dr. Mark Horn, Gustav Ando, Joseph DiCesare, Neal Masia

Dr. Paul Greenberg, Anita Burrell, Ari Gnanasakthy, Jeff Zheng, Jeff Hille, Moreno Perguini, Anouchka Vidal, Bill Morrison, Mary Chan, and Jason Tse.

Rachel Jao, Ashley Jaksa, Boaz Adler, Mingfeng Shen, Sari Tower, Humeyra Etik, Dr. Harshika Satyarthi, Tom Dever, Joan Gaffney, Rachel Sliman, Lorraine Versoza, Ruth Chang, Judith Rubinstein, Dan Liden, Daniel Sanchez, Shayna Rosenblum, Briana Lurie, Anson Pontynen, Johnna Mason, Yvonne Lovaglio Bauer, Anand Gan, Landon Westbrook, John Weaver, Gil Breiman, and the entire original team and all investors at Context Matters.

Joshua Schultz, Kevin Hutchinson, Stuart Charney, Siobhán Ní Bhuachalla, Sue Braithwaite Torgersen, Paulash Mohsen, Tatyana Daniels, Dr. Elaine Daniels, Dr. Steve Labkoff, Doug Giordano.

Sundeep Bhan, Asaf Evenheim, Andy Willis, Dr. Mark Braunstein, John Kamp, Mark Bard, Joe Farris, Devi Ramanan, Lineene Krasnow, Mukhtar Ahmed, Rick Piazza, Joe Rugilio, Justin Thomson, Steve Hirschfeld, Alan Mateo, Ari Feldman, Tarek Sherif.

Dr. Sebastian Schneeweiss, Dr. Jeremy Rassen, Kristin Coletto, Eliot Bradshaw, JL Novosad, Susan Rodriguez, Gena Cook, Michael Langer, Lorraine Marchand, Frank Corvino, Jeannie Forrest, Will Manidis, Gaurav Kaushik, Aleck McCathie, the late Douwe Rademaker, and the late Glen deVries.

Finally, a huge hug from the bottom of my heart to those who shared their stories and gave me inspiration throughout my journey:

Dr. Farhad Riahi, Dr. Lillian Oshva, Dr. Arlene Rogachefsky, Dr. Caitlin Fiss, Ramona Shih, my parents – Drs. C.H. and Patience C. Ho, and the late Dr. Wolffe Nadoolman.

My sincerest apologies to anyone I have left off this list. I have enduring gratitude and respect to all my colleagues, friends, mentors, and advisors whom I have had the privilege of knowing and collaborating with over all these years. This book is a reflection of all the conversations, endeavors, and adventures we have had together.

APPENDIX I

GLOSSARY OF ACRONYMS AND ABBREVIATIONS

AHRQ – Agency for Healthcare Research and Quality
A U.S. government agency under HHS that supports research to help people make more informed decisions and improve the quality of healthcare services.

AOL – America Online
An American web portal and online service provider. It was one of the early pioneers of the internet in the 1990s. It is currently owned by Apollo Global Management, which also owns Yahoo, and continues to offer email services.

API – Application Programming Interface
A set of rules and tools that allows different software applications to communicate with each other. APIs enable the integration and exchange of data between systems.

CCR – Continuity Care Record
A health record standard designed to create a summary of a patient's core health information. It helps improve communication during patient handoffs.

CDA – Clinical Document Architecture
An HL7 standard that specifies the structure and semantics of clinical documents for exchange between healthcare providers and patients.

CDISC – Clinical Data Interchange Standards Consortium
A global, non-profit organization that develops and promotes data standards for acquiring, exchanging, submitting, and archiving data in clinical trials.

CIO – Chief Information Officers
Executive-level managers responsible for overseeing the information technology (IT) strategy and implementation within an organization.

CISCRP – Center for Information and Study on Clinical Research Participation
A non-profit organization focused on educating and informing the public, patients, and healthcare professionals about clinical research participation. Founded by Ken Getz of Tufts University.

CME – Continuing Medical Education
Educational activities that help medical professionals maintain, develop, or increase their knowledge, skills, and professional performance.

CMS – Center for Medicare and Medicaid Services
A federal agency within HHS that administers the Medicare program and works with state governments to administer Medicaid, CHIP, and health insurance portability standards.

CRO – Contract Research Organizations
Companies that provide support to the pharmaceutical, biotechnology, and medical device industries in the form of research services outsourced on a contract basis. CROs are usually employed for conducting clinical trials.

DERP – Drug Effectiveness Review Project
A project from Oregon Health Sciences University that conducts systematic reviews of the comparative effectiveness and safety of drugs in various classes. It provides evidence-based information to help policymakers and healthcare providers.

EBM – Evidence Based Medicine
In medical practice, this term refers to using the most current and best evidence to support decisions around care (mainly treatment) of individual patients. Defined by David Sackett as: "The conscientious, explicit, and judicious use of current best evidence in making decisions about the care of individual patients."

EDC – Electronic Data Capture
A computerized system designed for the collection of clinical data in electronic format for use mainly in human clinical trials. The largest companies who offer EDC are Oracle Clinical (Oracle) and Medidata (Dassault Systems).

eHI – eHealth Initiative
A non-profit organization founded in 2001 and closed in 2023. It was dedicated to convening stakeholders around improving healthcare through the use of information technology and data.

EHR – Electronic Health Record
A digital version of a patient's paper chart. EHRs are real-time, patient-centered records that make information available instantly and securely to authorized users.

EMR – Electronic Medical Record
A digital version of a patient's chart from one practice. While EHRs focus on total health, EMRs are often specific to a single provider or clinic.

EPC – Evidence Based Practice Centers
Centers designated by AHRQ to conduct systematic reviews of healthcare topics. These reviews help inform clinical guidelines and coverage decisions.

FDA – Federal Drug Administration
A federal agency of HHS responsible for protecting public health by ensuring the safety, efficacy, and security of human and veterinary drugs, biological products, and medical devices. FDA is also responsible for manufacturing facilities and food safety.

FHIR – Fast Healthcare Interoperability Resources
A standard describing data formats and elements (known as "resources") and an API for exchanging EHRs. It aims to simplify interoperability.

FTE – Full-Time Equivalent
A unit that indicates the workload of an employed person in a way that makes workloads comparable across various contexts.

G-BA – Federal Joint Committee (Gemeinsamer Bundesausschuss)
The highest decision-making body of the joint self-government of physicians, dentists, hospitals, and health insurance funds in Germany.

Gen X – Generation X
Refers to the demographic cohort born between 1965 and 1980, following Baby Boomers and preceding Millennials.

Gen Z – Generation Z
Refers to the demographic cohort born between 1997 and 2012. They are often called "digital natives" due to growing up in the digital age.

HHS – Health and Human Services
The U.S. government's principal agency for protecting the health of all Americans and providing essential human services.

HIE – Health Information Exchange
The mobilization of healthcare information electronically across organizations within a region, community, or hospital system. HIE allows for the secure sharing of patient data.

HIMSS – Healthcare Information Management Systems Society
A not-for-profit global, advisor, thought leader, and member-based society committed to reforming the global health ecosystem through the power of information and technology. It was founded in 1961 as the Hospital Management Systems Society. Headquartered in Chicago, IL.

HL7 – Health Level 7 International
A non-profit organization that develops standards for the exchange, integration, sharing, and retrieval of electronic health information.

HTA – Health Technology Assessment
The systematic evaluation of the properties and impacts (clinically and economically) of health technology. Health technology is defined as interventions, therapies, diagnostics, and systems. Used primarily outside the U.S. and through government sanctioned HTA agencies to inform decision-making for healthcare resource allocation.

HTE – Heterogeneity of Treatment Effect
The variation in how individuals respond to a specific treatment or intervention. Defined initially as a statistical variation phenomenon in 1999, HTE emerged from the observation that treatment responses vary among individuals and that the average treatment effect observed in a clinical trial may not be representative of all individuals within a population. Understanding HTE helps tailor treatments to patients.

ICER – Institute for Clinical and Economic Review

An independent non-profit organization that evaluates the clinical and economic value of prescription drugs, medical tests, and other healthcare interventions. Founded by Steven D. Pearson in 2006 as a research program at Harvard Medical School and within Massachusetts General Hospital. Today, it is funded through grants and considers itself "the nation's drug pricing watchdog."

ICMJE – International Committee of Medical Journal Editors

A group of general medical journal editors who establish guidelines on the ethical and technical aspects of medical publishing.

IOM – Institute of Medicine

Now known as the National Academy of Medicine (NAM), it is an independent organization that provides unbiased and authoritative advice to decision-makers and the public.

ISPOR – International Society for Pharmacoeconomics and Outcomes Research

A professional scientific society that focuses on promoting the science of pharmacoeconomics (health economics) and outcomes research.

LAN – Local Area Networks

A computer network that interconnects computers within a limited area such as a residence, school, laboratory or office building.

LLM – Large Language Model

An advanced type of artificial intelligence (AI) algorithm that uses deep learning techniques and massive datasets to understand, summarize, generate, and predict new content. Trained on enormous datasets, including text, images, and audio, to learn the statistical relationship between words, phrases, concepts, and overall structure of language. The term "large" refers to billions of parameters, a shifting size definition as models become more sophisticated. In 2025, well-known LLMs include ChatGPT, Claude, Microsoft Copilot, Gemini, Meta AI, and xAI.

MVP – Minimum Viable Product

A version of a new product that allows a team to collect the maximum amount of validated learning about customers with the least effort. A common development approach to testing a new product.

NACDS – National Association of Chain Drug Stores
Trade association that represents traditional drug stores and supermarkets and mass merchants with pharmacies. It advocates for the chain pharmacy industry.

NCPA – National Community Pharmacy Association
Trade association that represents the professional and proprietary interests of independent community pharmacists in the United States.

ONCHIT – Office of the National Coordinator of Health Information Technology
An entity within HHS that leads national health IT efforts and is charged with implementing the HITECH Act and promoting health information technology. Established by Executive Order from President George W. Bush on April 27, 2004.

OHSU – Oregon Health and Science University
A public research university and academic health center in Portland, Oregon, focused on health sciences education, research and patient care.

P4P – Pay for Performance
A healthcare payment model where providers receive financial incentives for meeting certain performance measures for quality and efficiency.

PBM – Pharmacy Benefit Managers
Third-party administrators of prescription drug programs for commercial health plans, self-insured employers, Medicare Part D plans, and government employee plans. PBMs negotiate with pharmaceutical companies (manufacturers) to secure discounts and rebates, develop formularies (lists of covered drugs) and contract with pharmacies. PBMs manage the overall benefits and clearinghouses handling claims processing and communication between pharmacies and PBMs, providing information about formulary coverage, copays, and other benefit details.

PHI – Protected Health Information
Any health information that can be used to identify an individual and relates to their health status, provision of healthcare, or payment

for healthcare that is created or collected by a covered entity under HIPAA. Covered entities include hospitals, clinics, physicians, and health insurance companies, and any organization or person that transmits health information electronically in connection with HIPAA-covered transactions. PHI includes information like names, dates of birth, medical records, mental health utilization, and insurance details.

PHR – Personal Health Record
An electronic application through which patients can maintain and manage their health information in a private, secure, and confidential environment.

POA – Power of Attorney
A legal document that grants one person (the agent) the authority to act on behalf of another person (the principal) in specific or all legal or financial matters.

QALY – Quality-Adjusted Life Year
A measure of disease burden, including both the quality and the quantity of life lived. It is used in economic evaluations to assess the value for money of medical interventions.

QHIN – Qualified Health Information Networks
Entities designated under TEFCA that agree to specific terms and conditions to enable secure, nationwide health information exchange.

RAG – Retrieval-Augmented Generation
An AI framework for improving the quality of large language model (LLM) responses by grounding the model on external sources of knowledge.

RBRVS- Resource-Based Relative Value Scale
A relative ranking scale combining time, intensity, and cost of care into a single calculation to determine payment for physician services. Expected to correlate directly with all the resource costs for providing those services.

RDE – Remote Data Entry
The process of entering data into a system from a location outside of where the main system or server is located. Often used in clinical trials.

RVU- Relative Value Unit
A standardized metric used in healthcare to measure the value of a medical service or procedure; a component of RBRVS.

RWD – Real World Data
Data relating to patient health status and/or the delivery of healthcare routinely collected from a variety of sources. Unlike data collected in a clinical trial, real world data is collected in the course of care.

RWE – Real World Evidence
Clinical evidence about the usage and potential benefits or risks of a medical product derived from analysis of RWD.

SDOH – Social Determinants of Health
The conditions in the environments where people are born, live, learn, work, play, worship, and age that affect a wide range of health, functioning, and quality-of-life outcomes.

SLM – Small Language Models
More compact AI language models compared to LLMs, requiring fewer computational resources. They are designed for more specific tasks or deployment on smaller devices.

TEFCA – Trusted Exchange Framework and Common Agreement
A set of principles, terms, and conditions developed by ONC to enable nationwide exchange of electronic health information across different networks. Created in January 2018, final draft in April 2019. The Common Agreement, which is the core document of TEFCA, was published on January 18, 2022.

VBC – Value-Based Care
A healthcare delivery model in which providers, including hospitals and physicians, are paid based on patient health outcomes rather than the quantity of services delivered.

APPENDIX II

TIMELINE

Pre-internet

1973: The U.S. Congress passed the Health Maintenance Organization (HMO) Act. HMOs gained significant prevalence in the late 1980s and early 1990s as employers turned to them to cut healthcare costs.

1990-1995: Enrollment in public and private HMOs increased from 36.5 million to 58.2 million. By 1995, most Americans with employer-provided health insurance were part of a managed care plan.

1993: The Clinton Health Plan, developed by the Task Force for Health Care Reform under President Bill Clinton and First Lady Hillary Clinton, was introduced. Its main objective was to establish universal health coverage. The plan proposed a health care security card through enrollment in qualified health plans, mandates for insurers, regional health alliances, and subsidies for low-income individuals. It also mentioned electronic health record keeping for enrollment management. The plan faced controversy for its perceived secrecy, opposition from conservatives, libertarians, and the insurance industry, concerns about affordability from employers, and a lack of physician input.

1993: The Association of Physicians and Surgeons (AAPS) and other groups filed a lawsuit against Hillary Clinton and HHS Secretary Donna Shalala regarding closed-door meetings and seeking access to task force member lists.

1994: Despite efforts at compromise bills, no healthcare legislation passed. The midterm elections resulted in the GOP gaining control of both the House and Senate, effectively ending the Clinton healthcare overhaul efforts. House Speaker Newt Gingrich would later advocate for electronic health records and e-prescribing in 2004 after leaving

Congress. Healthcare insurance reform would return under President Barack Obama's Affordable Care Act in 2009-2010.

1995: Known as 'The Internet Moment", this year marked the beginning of the internet's widespread impact on business and society. Netscape was the leading web browser.

1st Era: Healthcare Content and Patient Privacy

1995: Medscape launched, offering free access to trusted medical information for both consumers and clinicians.

1996: The Health Insurance Portability and Accountability Act (HIPAA) was signed by President Bill Clinton. This law would govern protected patient information (PHI) and continue to be expanded and amended over the next thirty years.

1996: The Communications Decency Act, including Section 230, was passed. Section 230 protected social media sites by allowing them to host third-party content without being treated as the publisher.

1997: FDA issued final 21 CFR Part 11 regulations that allowed acceptance of electronic records, electronic signatures, and handwritten signatures executed to electronic records as equivalent to paper records and handwritten signatures executed on paper. These regulations, which apply to all FDA program areas, were intended to permit the widest possible use of electronic technology, compatible with FDA's responsibility to protect the public health.

1999: Section 510 of Labor-HHS Appropriations Bill forbids any federal funding for the development of a unique health identifier or a National Patient Identifier. It has been renewed annual since initial passage

1999-2001: The dot.com era experienced its boom-and-bust cycle. A prominent example from that era is DrKoop.com, launched in 1997 by former U.S. Surgeon General, Dr. C. Everett Koop, as a health information website. The company went public in 1999 with a valuation of over $1 billion and collapsed within a couple of years with both an unsustainable business model and the dot.com bust.

2nd Era: Insurance Reform, Infrastructure, and Interoperability

2003: Health Savings Accounts (HSAs) were introduced as part of the Medicare Prescription Drug Improvement and Modernization Act of 2003 signed by President George W. Bush.

2004: The Office of the National Coordinator for HIT (ONCHIT) was established by presidential executive order under President Bush. Its mission was to coordinate the health IT ecosystem, emphasizing standards for data sharing and interoperability between systems.

2005: Vioxx was withdrawn from the market following numerous lawsuits concerning heart disease and stroke risks. This event highlighted that adverse effects could appear after the conclusion of clinical trials, leading to the FDA Amendments Act (FDAAA) in 2007, which would mandate the listing of all pharmaceutical trials on clinicaltrials.gov.

2008: The U.S. faced a significant housing market collapse which triggered a global financial crisis

2009: The Health Information Technology for Economic and Clinical Health (HITECH) Act was signed by President Barack Obama as part of the American Recovery and Reinvestment Act (ARRA). HITECH aimed to transform healthcare relationships through the implementation and use of HIT. It bolstered HIPAA's privacy and security rules, increased enforcement, provided substantially large adoption incentives ("meaningful use"), and penalties to physicians and hospitals to drive EHR adoption and health information exchanges (HIEs).

2010: The Affordable Care Act (ACA), or "ObamaCare" was passed, primarily to expand health insurance coverage and provide a marketplace for it. It also reinforced EHR adoption incentives, meaningful use, and promoted care coordination, quality metrics, outcomes-based payment reform, and interoperability.

2012: The FDA Safety and Innovation Act (FDASIA) was passed. It introduced patient-focused drug development, created a "breakthrough" designation to speed up drug approvals, and encouraged FDA collaboration with life sciences companies. FDASIA also directed the FDA to collaborate with ONCHIT to create a regulatory framework for Health IT.

3rd Era: Expansion of Data and Data Sharing

2015: ONCHIT released the Federal Health IT Strategic Plan (2015-2020). This plan aimed to leverage Health IT to improve care coordination, information sharing, and overall health outcomes. It specifically called out and addressed the issue of "information blocking" by certain EHR vendors and health systems.

2016: The 21st Century Cures Act passes. This law had significant implications for Health IT and drug development, notably introducing the use of real-world data and evidence (RWD/RWE) into FDA considerations. For Health IT, it focused on improving the flow and exchange of health information. ONCHIT was made responsible for implementing these provisions, including advancing interoperability, preventing information blocking, enhancing usability and security, and ensuring patients could access their electronic data.

4th Era: AI Models and the Rise of Multimodal Data, Health Surveillance, and Privacy Risk

2017: The Transformer Model Architecture, a key development in AI, was introduced by Google as a neural network architecture which supercharged natural language processing (NLP).

2020-2023: The world grappled with the SARS-CoV-2 (COVID-19) Pandemic. Globally, over seven million people died from COVID during the pandemic, including over one million in the U.S. mRNA vaccines were developed in record time in 2020. mRNA (messenger RNA) technology was used to instruct cells to produce the SARS-CoV-2 spike protein to prompt an immune response without using the live virus. Once the viral genome was sequenced, this technology enabled rapid design and large-scale production.

2020: Operation Warp Speed was launched by presidential executive order under President Donald Trump to accelerate COVID-19 vaccine development and distribution.

2022: The U.S. Supreme Court overturned Roe v. Wade on June 24 and returned the authority to regulate abortion to individual states. Close to half of the states moved to ban or severely restrict abortion. And states with protective laws, such as California, Maryland, and New York expanded access and became destinations for those seeking abortion care. Because access was now determined at the state level, new concerns emerged about whether the data contained in EHRs and digital health applications could be accessed by law enforcement or used as evidence in states where abortion is illegal. Safeguarding PHI and patient-physician confidentiality became a concern, exposing gaps in HIPAA and the unexpected conflict with state laws. Digital tracking from the proliferation of health and reproductive applications became a new source of sensitive data often shared with third parties. The increase in telemedicine, especially during the CoVID pandemic, meant new challenges for safeguarding patient data and complying with varying state laws.

2022: ChatGPT was launched in November, bringing generative AI into mainstream awareness.

2024: The focus of AI use cases in healthcare shifted toward improving healthcare delivery and revenue cycle management.

2024: There was an increase in AI safety bills at the state level around the issue of accountability. California's Senate Bill 1047, which aimed to establish safety measures and accountability for tech companies releasing AI models, was vetoed on September 29, 2024, as it was criticized for being vague and a hindrance to innovation. The regulation of AI, particularly at the state level, continues to be a prominent issue.

2025: Rise of agentic AI (autonomous systems capable of independently initiating actions, planning, and complex tasks) and integration of autonomous digital agents. AI models begin incorporating multi-modal data and seamlessly integrate across multiple data types including images, audio, and video, changing how healthcare diagnostics processed information. Quantum computing has started to intersect AI with quantum-powered algorithms for applications in material sciences, drug discovery, and supply chain optimization.

2025: On September 29, 2025, California Governor Gavin Newsom signed into law Senate Bill 53, The Transparency in Frontier Artificial Intelligence Act (TFAIA). It is the first state law to specifically regulate AI developers. The law requires large AI model developers to release transparency reports on a model's intended uses and restrictions. It also mandates that large developers summarize a model's catastrophic risks and to report any "critical safety incidents." Whistleblower protections are enacted for employees working on these frontier models.

APPENDIX III

MAJOR FEDERAL LEGISLATION AFFECTING HEALTH IT (1996-2016)

1996: HIPAA – Health Insurance Portability and Accountability Act

The Health Insurance Portability and Accountability Act (HIPAA) was signed into law on August 21, 1996, and was designed to protect the privacy and security of individuals' medical information and set national standards for safeguarding "protected health information" (PHI), which includes any health data that can identify an individual and is maintained or exchanged in any form.

Created to protect health insurance for workers and their families when changing or losing jobs, HIPAA contained provisions to improve the portability of health insurance coverage and was the first law attempting to prohibit discrimination based on pre-existing conditions and standardization of electronic health transactions.

Best known for its Privacy Rule, which both establishes a federal baseline of privacy protections for PHI and restricts how healthcare providers, insurers, and their business associates can use and disclose this information without patient authorization. The Privacy Rule grants patients' rights over their health data, such as the ability to access their records and request corrections. Another component, known as The Security Rule, sets standards for the protection of electronic PHI, requiring administrative, physical, and technical safeguards to ensure confidentiality, integrity, and availability.

HIPAA would later be amended in 2009 via HITECH to include The Breach Notification Rule which would mandate that all covered entities notify affected individuals of any unauthorized release of their PHI. Breaches were subject to both civil and criminal penalties.

1997: Balanced Budget Act of 1997 and CHIP

The Children's Health Insurance Program (also known as SCHIP) was signed into law on August 5, 1997, and was created in response to the high number of uninsured children in the United States, particularly those from working families with incomes too high to qualify for Medicaid but too low to afford private insurance. CHIP provides federal matching funds to states to offer health insurance coverage for children under age nineteen in families with incomes generally up to 200 percent of the federal poverty level, though states have flexibility to set higher thresholds.

States can use CHIP funds to expand their Medicaid programs, create separate child health programs, or use a combination of both. The program offers an "enhanced" federal matching rate, meaning the federal government pays a larger share of costs compared to Medicaid, incentivizing states to participate. States are required to submit plans to HHS outlining use of funds, and states contracting with Medicaid managed care organizations were required to develop and implement quality assessment and monitoring procedures. Subsequent legislation such as the reauthorization of CHIP (CHIPRA) will build on this foundation by introducing HIT demonstration grants for the development of electronic health record formats for children in CHIP and Medicaid.

CHIP also includes important protections and requirements, such as prohibiting discrimination based on diagnosis, allowing for twelve months of continuous eligibility, and requiring outreach to enroll eligible children.

2003: MMA – Medicare Prescription Drug, Improvement, and Modernization Act

The Medicare Prescription Drug, Improvement, and Modernization Act (MMA) was signed into law on December 8, 2003, with the aim of reforming the Medicare program to cover more prescription drugs, expand the role of private health plans in Medicare, and encourage health information technology as a means to modernize prescribing and improve patient safety. The Act created Medicare Part D, a prescription drug benefit for Medicare beneficiaries. Part D was not to be implemented until 2006 but allowed beneficiaries to enroll in private drug plans subsidized by Medicare versus paying out-of-pocket and expanded their access to prescription drugs.

MMA also expanded the role of private health plans in Medicare through the creation of Medicare Advantage (Part C). This program allowed beneficiaries to receive their Medicare benefits through private insurers, with additional benefits and expected lower out-of-pocket costs compared to traditional Medicare. The MMA was designed to foster competition among private plans to improve quality and efficiency and offer more choices to beneficiaries.

The law also created provisions to modernize Medicare's administration and promote the use of health information technology (HIT) to improve patient safety and enhance the efficiency of the prescription process. It encouraged the adoption of electronic prescribing (e-prescribing) and electronic health records (EHRs) by introducing pilot projects and incentives for hospitals to adopt these technologies. Higher reimbursement rates went to hospitals which adopted electronic systems and set standards around ePrescribing. The timeline for adoption was meant to coincide with the launch of Part D prescription drug benefit.

MMA also encouraged the development of internet-based portals allowing Medicare beneficiaries to access their claims information securely.

2009: CHIPRA – Children's Health Insurance Program Reauthorization Act of 2009

The Children's Health Insurance Program Reauthorization Act (CHIPRA) was signed into law on February 4, 2009, and designed to expand and improve the 1997 created Children's Health Insurance Program (CHIP). While the main goal was to extend CHIP funding four years through September 30, 2013, and increase federal support to cover more uninsured children, the law also called for developing and adopting new child healthcare quality measures and provided demonstration grants for quality improvement and health information technology. Administratively, CHIPRA also simplified enrollment and renewal processes and expanded eligibility in many states. To encourage efficiency, states that streamlined enrollment and increased children's Medicaid enrollment above baseline levels were awarded performance bonuses. To expand eligibility, CHIPRA provided options for covering legal immigrant children and pregnant women without a five-year waiting period.

CHIPRA also required the development of a model EHR format for children enrolled in CHIP and Medicaid.

2009: HITECH Act – Health Information Technology for Economic and Clinical Health Act

The Health Information Technology for Economic and Clinical Health (HITECH) Act, was signed into law on February 17, 2009, as part of the American Recovery and Reinvestment Act and aimed to accelerate the adoption and meaningful use of electronic health records (EHRs) across the entire healthcare system, strengthen the privacy and security provisions of HIPAA, and promote the development of Health Information Exchanges (HIEs).

HITECH accelerated the adoption and meaningful use of EHRs by providing billions of dollars in incentives to hospitals and health care providers for implementing certified EHR systems and meeting specific usage criteria. To qualify for incentive payments, providers had to demonstrate that they were using EHRs in ways that enhanced quality, safety, efficiency, and patient engagement, such as e-prescribing, sharing data securely, and reporting clinical quality measures.

HITECH strengthened the privacy and security provisions of HIPAA by adding The Breach Notification Rule, which requires notification to affected individuals and authorities in the event of unauthorized disclosures of PHI. Breaches of PHI would now result in both civil and criminal penalties, with a tiered system based on level of culpability ranging from unintentional violation to willful neglect. Fines are exacted on a per violation basis with penalties associated with lack of timely cure or repeated violations.

HITECH also supported the development of Health Information Exchanges (HIEs) in order to engage patients in their care, increase coordination among care providers, and facilitate the secure exchange of health information.

2010: ACA – Affordable Care Act

The Affordable Care Act (ACA), also known as "Obamacare" was signed into law March 23, 2010, and aimed to expand access to health insurance, improve the quality of care, and control health care costs. The act was created in response to millions of uninsured Americans and high costs and insurance market practices that excluded people with pre-existing conditions or charged them unaffordable premiums.

The main goals were to increase insurance coverage primarily through the creation of state-based health insurance marketplaces (exchanges), expansion of Medicaid eligibility to adults with incomes up to 138 percent of the federal poverty level (optional for states), and the provision of income-based subsidies and tax credits to help individuals and families afford private insurance. The law also introduced an individual mandate, requiring most Americans to have health insurance or face a penalty (penalty phased out to zero starting in 2019), and an employer mandate requiring larger employers to offer health coverage to their employees.

Insurers were prohibited from denying coverage or charging higher premiums due to pre-existing conditions. They were also prohibited from imposing annual or lifetime limits on essential health benefits. All plans are required to cover a standardized set of benefits including preventive care, maternity and newborn care, mental health services, and prescription drugs.

To control costs, the ACA established minimum medical loss ratio standards, requiring insurers to spend a set percentage of premiums on health care services rather than administrative costs or profits with rebates to consumers if these standards are not met. Reforms to Medicare included closing the Part D "donut hole", reducing overpayments to Medicare Advantage plans, and creating incentives for value-based care models.

The ACA also accelerated the adoption and integration of electronic health records (EHRs) by building upon the foundation set by the HITECH Act of 2009, which established incentives and standards for EHR use. It expanded these provisions by promoting the widespread use of digital health records with an emphasis on interoperability. The law strengthened incentive programs such as "Meaningful Use", which tied Medicare and Medicaid reimbursements to the effective adoption and utilization of certified EHR systems. Providers who demonstrated meaningful use, such as electronic prescribing, improved patient engagement, and data-driven clinical decision-making, were eligible for financial incentives, encouraging rapid EHR adoption across hospitals and clinics.

2012: Food and Drug Administration Safety and Innovation Act (FDASIA)

The Food and Drug Administration Safety and Innovation Act (FDASIA) was signed into law on July 9, 2012, and significantly expanded the FDA's authority and resources to safeguard and advance public health.

Specifically, it reauthorized and expanded user fee programs to include innovator drugs, generic drugs, and biosimilars to supplement previous programs for prescription drugs and medical devices. The Act created a "breakthrough therapy" designation to expedite the development and review pathway for any therapy that could show substantial improvement over existing therapies for serious or life-threatening conditions. In addition, innovation incentives were expanded to extend priority review for rare pediatric diseases. The Act also expanded the FDA's authority over the drug supply chain, allowing the agency to focus on shortages, security, and counterfeit drugs.

Section 618 directed the Secretary of HHS, acting through the FDA and in consultation with ONC and Chairman of the Federal Communications Commission to develop a report with a strategy and recommendations about an appropriate risk-based regulatory framework for health IT including medical mobile applications and which would directly address patient safety and avoid regulatory duplication.

2015: Medicare Access and CHIP Reauthorization Act (MACRA)

The Medicare Access and CHIP Reauthorization Act (MACRA) signed into law on April 16, 2015, aimed to promote value-based care payment programs and extend funding of the Children's Health Insurance Program. The Act repealed the Sustainable Growth Rate (SGR) formula, used to calculate annual cuts to physician payments. In its place, it created the Quality Payment Program (QPP), offering clinicians two main tracks for Medicare reimbursement: the Merit-based Incentive Payment System (MIPS) and Advanced Alternative Payment Models (APMs).

MIPS consolidates existing quality reporting programs with rewards or penalties to clinicians based on performance in quality, cost, use of health IT, and clinical practice improvement. Advanced APMs offer greater rewards for clinicians who participate in risk-based, coordinated care models and meet specific quality and cost benchmarks. The goal of the legislation was to shift to value-based care, focused on improving outcomes as a way to reduce costs.

MACRA also extended funding for the Children's Health Insurance Program (CHIP), but CHIP would lapse for 114 days in 2017 and then in early 2018, Congress would extend funding through fiscal year 2023. Then a month later through the Bipartisan Budget Act, they would extend CHIP an additional four years through the end of 2027.

2016: The 21st Century Cures Act

The 21st Century Cures Act, signed into law on December 13, 2016, aimed at accelerating medical innovation, improving patient care, and modernizing the U.S. healthcare system.

> ➤ Streamlined the approval processes for drugs, biologics, and medical devices by modernizing clinical trial designs to allow the use of real-world evidence and expediting the review of certain innovative therapies and devices

> ➤ Allocated $4.8 billion over ten years of new funding to the National Institutes of Health (NIH) to support major

initiatives such as the Cancer Moonshot, the Precision Medicine Initiative, the BRAIN Initiative, and regenerative medicine research

➤ Provided substantial resources for combating the opioid epidemic and improving mental health services, including reforms to mental health care delivery and funding for related research

➤ Included provisions to enhance interoperability of electronic health records (EHRs), prevent information blocking, and ensure patients have secure, easy access to their health data.

➤ Amended the Federal Food, Drug, and Cosmetic Act (FDCA) and the Public Health Service Act (PHSA) to accelerate the discovery and delivery of new medical technologies through expedited programs for regenerative medicine and breakthrough devices

➤ Reauthorized priority review voucher programs for rare pediatric diseases

➤ Reduced administrative burdens and pushes to expand participation in clinical research by encouraging data sharing and promoting the inclusion of diverse populations in clinical studies

➤ Limits FDA regulation of low-risk mobile health apps that promote healthy lifestyles but are not directly involved in disease diagnosis or treatment

Defined the Role of Real-World Evidence (RWE)

➤ Distinguished between real-world data (RWD) and real-world evidence (RWE).

➤ Mandated and Required the FDA to

➤ Evaluate use of RWE to support the approval of new indications for already approved drugs

➤ Fulfill post-approval study requirements and monitoring safety and effectiveness in post-market surveillance, especially for populations underrepresented in clinical trials

➤ Create a comprehensive framework for evaluating RWE, including standards for data collection, methodologies for analysis, and identification of priority areas and data gaps

➤ Issue draft and final guidance documents to clarify how RWE can be used in regulatory submissions (how RWE can supplement RCTs by providing insights from broader, more diverse patient populations and real-world clinical settings)

Defined and Mandated Adoption of Interoperability Requirements

➤ Defined interoperability as the ability to securely exchange EHI between different health IT systems without special effort from users. It mandates that EHRs and other HIT systems must allow seamless, secure access and exchange of health data across platforms and organizations

➤ Prohibited of Information Blocking: Defines "information blocking" as any practice likely to interfere with, prevent, or materially discourage access, exchange, or use of EHI. Definition applied to healthcare providers, health IT developers, health information networks, and health information exchanges. Violations have significant financial penalties.

➤ Required patients be able to electronically access all their EHI, structured and unstructured, at no cost. This includes clinical notes, test results, and medications released in near real-time via patient portals

➤ Required adoption of standardized application programming interfaces (APIs), making it easier for patients and providers to access and share health information using apps and other digital tools.

> ➤ Updated certification requirements for health IT products to ensure compliance with interoperability and information blocking rules

The Office of the National Coordinator for Health Information Technology (ONCHIT) issued a final rule in 2020 to implement interoperability provisions. The rule outlined technical requirements, compliance timelines, and exceptions to information blocking, and expanded the scope of data that must be made available from a limited set (USCDI) to all EHI.

APPENDIX IV

MEDICAL RECORD
OWNERSHIP BY STATE

State	Medical Record Ownership Laws
Alabama, Arizona, Arkansas, Colorado, Connecticut, Delaware, District of Columbia, Hawaii, Idaho, Illinois, Iowa, Kentucky, Maine, Massachusetts, Michigan, Minnesota, Montana, Nebraska, Nevada, New Jersey, New Mexico, New York, North Dakota, Ohio, Oklahoma, South Dakota, Vermont, Washington, West Virginia, Wisconsin	No law identified conferring specific ownership or property right to medical record
Alaska, California, Florida, Georgia, Indiana, Kansas, Louisiana, Maryland, Mississippi, Missouri, New Mexico, North Carolina, Oregon, Pennsylvania, Rhode Island, South Carolina, Tennessee, Texas, Utah, Virginia, Wyoming	Hospital and/or physician owns medical record
New Hampshire	Patient owns information in medical record

Source: Health Information & Law Project (last updated 2015). Milken Institute School of Public Health, George Washington University, funded by a grant from Robert Wood Johnson Foundation

APPENDIX V

FINANCING HEALTHCARE: PAYMENT MODELS, COST MANAGEMENT, REVENUE STREAMS

Public (Government) Payers Payment Models

Type	Payment Model	Key Payment Mechanisms/ Terms	Who Pays Whom	Notable Features/ Controversies
Medicare (Traditional FFS)	Fee-for-Service (FFS)	Physician Fee Schedule (PFS), Diagnosis-Related Groups (DRGs) for hospitals	CMS to Providers	Direct payment for each service; 80/20 split with beneficiary coinsurance
Medicare Advantage	Capitated (Risk-Adjusted)	Hierarchical Condition Categories (HCCs), Risk Adjustment Factor (RAF)	CMS to MA Plans; MA Plans to Providers	Private administration of public funds; "coding intensity" concerns; prior authorization often required
Medicaid (FFS)	Fee-for-Service (FFS)	Federal Medical Assistance Percentage (FMAP), Upper Payment Limit (UPL), Disproportionate Share Hospital (DSH) payments	States (with federal match) to Providers	Lower physician rates than Medicare; supplemental payments for certain providers
Medicaid (Managed Care)	Capitated	State-Directed Payments	States (with federal match) to MCOs; MCOs to Providers	Covers ~75% of Medicaid population; states can direct MCO payments; transparency concerns for MCO rates
VA Healthcare	Direct Care / Community Care	VA Fee Schedule (VAFS), Medicare rates for community care	VA to Internal Providers; VA to Community Providers	Direct care within VA facilities; community care requires VA authorization; patient copays paid to VA

Currently, there is a significant transition from traditional fee-for-service models to value-based care, most notably in Medicare Advantage's use of risk-adjusted capitated payments and Medicaid's state-directed payment initiatives.[120] The goal in this shift is to incentivize physicians/providers and payers to focus on patient outcomes and cost-effectiveness rather than simply the volume of services provided. This transition has introduced new complexities and potential for financial manipulation, as seen with coding intensity in Medicare Advantage.

Private Payers Cost Management Strategies

Private payers in the U.S. healthcare system are primarily private insurance companies and employer-sponsored health plans that provide coverage for medical expenses.

A range of plan types are offered including:

> Health Maintenance Organizations (HMOs)

> Preferred Provider Organizations (PPOs)

> Point of Service (POS) plans

> Fee-for-Service (FFS)

> High-Deductible Health Plans (HDHPs

Each has different rules about which physicians and hospitals a patient can use, how much a patient pays out-of-pocket, and whether referrals are needed to see a specialist.

Most Americans receive private insurance through their employer, which allows for risk pooling and generally lower costs compared to individually purchased plans. Private payers negotiate rates with healthcare providers, process claims, and reimburse providers for services rendered.

To control costs, they use various strategies:

> tiered provider pricing

> increased cost-sharing

> utilization controls

The most prominent mechanisms to achieve utilization control are prior authorization (PA) and claim denials.

Prior authorization means evaluating the medical necessity, safety, and cost-effectiveness of proposed services or drugs before approving coverage.[121] This process is to allow payers to direct patients towards less expensive treatment options if deemed sufficient and to ensure adherence to their formulary and policy rules.

Claim denial is another critical tool, but one that creates a great deal of stress for patients and physicians. Payers deny claims for a multitude of reasons, including administrative errors (e.g., incomplete or incorrect information), lack of medical necessity, services not covered by the policy, or issues with coding. These denials effectively reduce the financial outlay for the payer and shift the burden of payment, or the administrative effort to rectify the claim, onto the provider or patient. But the ability to deny claims creates systemic friction where payers can influence physician reimbursement and patient's access to care. The effects can be financial toxicity and administrative waste trying to manage.

PBM Revenue Streams

Revenue Stream	Mechanism	Associated Controversy/Impact
Rebates from Manufacturers	PBMs negotiate discounts from drug manufacturers for formulary placement	Lack of transparency; PBMs retain portion of rebates; incentivizes higher list prices; favors high-rebate drugs over cheaper alternatives
"Spread Pricing"	PBMs charge payers more for a drug than they reimburse pharmacies, keeping the difference	Inflated drug costs for payers; reduces reimbursement for independent pharmacies; opaque to payers and patients
Directing Business to Affiliated Pharmacies	PBMs own or are affiliated with pharmacies (e.g., mail-order, specialty) and direct patients to them	Creates conflicts of interest; disadvantages independent pharmacies, potentially leading to "pharmacy deserts"; can increase patient costs
Administrative Fees from Payers	Fees charged to health plans for managing prescription drug benefits	Can be opaque and complex, making it difficult for clients to understand true costs; contributes to overall administrative waste

APPENDIX VI
STANDARDS FOR INTEROPERABILITY

In 2011, Fast Healthcare Interoperability Resources (FHIR) was conceived as Resources for Healthcare (RFH) and formally proposed to Health Level 7 (HL7). Led by Grahame Grieve who is credited as the inventor of FHIR, the concept was presented in May 2012 and has since become the most widely adopted, API-focused standard for representing and exchanging health information.[122]

The goal of FHIR was to foster a more connected health ecosystem and strengthen health *data* interoperability. Utilizing modular components (termed "Resources") for data exchange, this would allow for flexible and efficient sharing of clinical and administrative data.[123]

Standard Name	Purpose/Application/ Maintained
HIPAA (Health Insurance Portability and Accountability Act)	1996 law which defined privacy and security of Protected Health Information (PHI) and electronic transaction standards; can be referred to as a standard
FHIR (Fast Healthcare Interoperability Resources)	Electronic exchange of clinical and administrative health information via APIs; modern interoperability
HL7 (Health Level 7)	Messaging standard for electronic health information exchange (foundational for FHIR)
SNOMED CT (Systematized Nomenclature of Medicine—Clinical Terms)	Comprehensive clinical terminology for consistent representation of clinical content in EHRs (e.g., diagnoses, symptoms, procedures); often provides the "answer" to a clinical observation or test

LOINC (Logical Observation Identifiers Names and Codes)	Universal code system for identifying health measurements, observations, and documents (e.g., lab test questions); represents the "question" for a test or measurement
RxNorm	Normalized names for clinical drugs; links drug vocabularies for facilitating communications between different pharmacy management and drug interaction software systems
DICOM (Digital Imaging and Communications in Medicine)	Standard for storing, transmitting, and viewing medical imaging data
CPT (Current Procedural Terminology)	Procedure codes for billing outpatient and office medical services, maintained by the American Medical Association (AMA)
ICD-10 (International Classification of Diseases, 10th Revision)	Medical classification list by the World Health Organization (WHO) containing codes for diseases, signs, symptoms, and abnormal findings, primarily used for diagnosis coding
HCPCS (Healthcare Common Procedure Coding System)	Healthcare Common Procedure Coding System; procedure codes based on CPT, leveraged for Medicare reimbursement
NDC (National Drug Code)	National Drug Code; unique identifier for commercially distributed drugs in the US; list of all drugs manufactured, prepared, propagated, compounded, or processed for commercial distribution, maintained by the FDA

Despite the existence and continuous development of these robust data standards (e.g., FHIR, SNOMED CT, LOINC) and regulatory frameworks (HIPAA and all subsequent regulatory and policy legislation), significant challenges persist in achieving true interoperability due to the widespread data fragmentation.

The healthcare system is fragmented by not only disparate systems but also because of inconsistent coding practices and poorly formatted data. This not only makes it difficult to use the data and create easy seamless exchange, it also becomes more difficult to abstract relevant information to determine cause and correlation for research purposes. In essence, data is still in silos, and many manual processes and custom software are implemented and built to bridge the gaps. All this contributes to the increased costs and inefficiencies across the system.

From an interoperability perspective, the technical capacity and specifications exist, but the practical and consistent implementation across a fragmented healthcare system and diverse competitive landscape remains the greatest barrier. The barrier is not technical. It is ensuring consistency in data, which requires more cooperation than currently exists. It is this lack of consistency in data, often referred to as the "last mile" problem in data connectivity, that remains the bane of most informaticians, CIOs, and data managers.

ABOUT THE AUTHOR

A physician-turned-entrepreneur and visionary executive, S. Yin Ho, MD, MBA has led transformative Health IT and clinical research companies for over twenty-five years, including serving as interim CEO at Veradigm where she spearheaded the acquisition of Science IO to bring in-house generative AI to EHR and founding Context Matters, the pioneering health economics data analytics platform now part of Clarivate Analytics. Previously, she led eHealth at Pfizer, guided Medidata's strategy through IPO, and held senior leadership roles at Aetion. Trained as an emergency physician at Yale and holding an MBA from Harvard, Dr. Ho co-founded the influential New York City Health Business Leaders group, now AlleyCorp's Digital Health New York. She currently advises many AI healthcare startups and is on the Board of Directors at Segmed (an AI radiology platform) while advocating for responsible AI development in healthcare.

Dr. Ho calls New York City her home with her husband and two grown daughters. She is an avid swimmer, home cook, wine lover, and community organizer.

Stay Connected:

🌐 syinho.com

in linkedin.com/in/yin-ho

ENDNOTES

Introduction

1 Centers for Medicare & Medicaid Services. (2025, June 3). White House, tech leaders commit to create patient-centric healthcare ecosystem. https://www.cms.gov/newsroom/press-releases/white-house-tech-leaders-commit-create-patient-centric-healthcare-ecosystem

2 Lundberg, G. D. (2005). Medscape – The first 5 years. Medscape General Medicine. https://www.ncbi.nlm.nih.gov/pmc/articles/PMC1681598/

3 American College of Physicians, remarks 2004

4 Society for Participatory Medicine. (n.d.). About us. https://participatorymedicine.org/about/

Chapter 1

5 Liu, C.-H., Magesh, S., & Ioannidis, J. P. A. (2024). Assessing the landscape of generative AI in biomedical research. medRxiv. https://www.ncbi.nlm.nih.gov/pmc/articles/PMC11215012/

6 Broad Institute. (n.d.). Peer review: A historical perspective. MIT Communication Lab. https://mitcommlab.mit.edu/broad/commkit/peer-review-a-historical-perspective/

7 Lundberg, G.D. (2005). Medscape- The first 5 Years. Medscape General Medicine. https://www.ncbi.nlm.nih.gov/pmc/articles/PMC1681598/

8 Lundberg, G. D. (2020, November 5). Why Medscape worked: A look back. Medscape. https://www.medscape.com/

9 *The New York Times*. (2001, December 27). Technology briefing: Internet; WebMD buys Medscape portal. *The New York Times*. https://www.nytimes.com/

10 Sibbald, B. (2004, October 19). Rofecoxib (Vioxx) voluntarily withdrawn from market. CMAJ, 171(9), 1027–1028. https://doi.org/10.1503/cmaj.1041553

11 Graham, D. J., et al. (2005). Risk of acute myocardial infarction and sudden cardiac death in patients treated with cyclo-oxygenase 2 selective and non-selective non-steroidal anti-inflammatory drugs: Nested case-control study. *The Lancet*, 365(9458), 475–481. https://doi.org/10.1016/S0140-6736(05)17868-9[1]

12 International Committee of Medical Journal Editors. (2007, June). Clinical trial registration: Looking back and moving forward. ICMJE. https://www.icmje.org/recommendations/

Chapter 2

13 Stead, W. W., & Lorenzi, N. M. (1999). Health informatics: Linking investment to value. Journal of the American Medical Informatics Association, 6(5), 341–348. https://doi.org/10.1136/jamia.1999.0060341

14 Johnson, M. (2025, January 23). A grim prognosis, a gamble and one patient's fight to defy cancer. The Washington Post. https://www.washingtonpost.com/

Chapter 3

15 NYC Health Business Leaders. (n.d.). EMR & PHR progress report (October 14). NYC Health Business Leaders.

16 CNN Money. (2007, January 23). AOL co-founder Case debuts Web health service offering. CNN. https://money.cnn.com/

17 Lohr, S. (2007, October 4). Microsoft rolls out personal health records. *The New York Times*. https://www.nytimes.com/

18 Singer, E. (2008, May 19). Google Health launches. MIT Technology Review. https://www.technologyreview.com/

19 MobiHealthNews. (2018, December 20). Apple's busy 2018 in healthcare, from Health Records to Watch ECG. MobiHealthNews. https://www.mobihealthnews.com/

20 UC San Diego Research IT. (n.d.). Data curation: Definition. https://research-it.ucsd.edu/data-curation/definition.html

Chapter 4

21 National Committee on Vital and Health Statistics. (2009, September). Health data stewardship: What, why, who, how — An NCVHS primer. U.S. Department of Health and Human Services.

Chapter 5

22 National Cybersecurity Center of Excellence. (2020, December). Securing Picture Archiving and Communication System (PACS): A NIST cybersecurity practice guide (NIST Special Publication 1800-26A). National Institute of Standards and Technology.

23 Sternstein, A. (2005, September 16). Gingrich: 'Paper kills,' electronic medical records save lives. HIMSS. https://www.himss.org/

24 Shen, Y., Yu, J., Zhou, J., & Hu, G. (2025). *Twenty-five years of evolution and hurdles in electronic health records and interoperability in medical research: Comprehensive review. Journal of Medical Internet Research*, 27, e59024. https://doi.org/10.2196/59024

25 Brown, S. H., Lincoln, M. J., Groen, P. J., & Kolodner, R. M. (2003). *VistA — U.S. Department of Veterans Affairs national-scale HIS. International Journal of Medical Informatics*, 69(2–3), 135–156. https://doi.org/10.1016/S1386-5056(02)00131-4

26 Institute of Medicine (US) Committee on Improving the Patient Record. (1991). The computer-based patient record: An essential technology for health care (R. S. Dick & E. B. Steen, Eds.). National Academies Press.

27 Mullaney, T. (2001, October 9). *Pfizer, IBM, Microsoft launch health-care software venture. The Wall Street Journal.* https://www.wsj.com/articles/SB1002726212272568120

28 The Pharma Letter. (2001, October 10). Pfizer, IBM and Microsoft launch Amicore. The Pharma Letter. https://www.thepharmaletter.com/

29 Garrett, P., & Seidman, J. (2011, January 4). *EMR vs EHR – What is the difference?* Health IT Buzz. https://www.healthit.gov/buzz-blog/electronic-health-and-medical-records/emr-vs-ehr-difference

Chapter 6

30 Health Affairs. (n.d.). Meaningful use of electronic health records.https://www.healthaffairs.org/content/briefs/meaningful-use-electronic-health-records

31 RTTNews. (2009, June 9). GE to provide 'Stimulus Simplicity' electronic medical records program to physicians – Update. RTTNews. https://www.rttnews.com/

32 Institute of Medicine (US) Committee on Health Research and the Privacy of Health Information. (2009). Beyond the HIPAA Privacy Rule: Enhancing privacy, improving health through research (S. J. Nass, L. A. Levit, & L. O. Gostin, Eds.). National Academies Press.

Chapter 7

33 Manos, D. (2009, May 8). Blumenthal names new HIT panel members, first meetings next week. *Healthcare IT News.* https://www.healthcareit-news.com/

34 Mandl, K. D., & Kohane, I. S. (2020, January 27). Epic's call to block a proposed data rule is wrong for many reasons. STAT. https://www.statnews.com/

35 Farr, C. (2017, August 7). Joe Biden took on Epic Systems CEO Judy Faulkner over patient data — here's what happened. CNBC. https://www.cnbc.com/

36 Cerner Corporation. (2011). 2011 annual report. https://www.cerner.com/about/investors/annual-reports

37 Saporito, B. (2005, June 20). The E-health revolution. Time.

38 Miliard, M. (2010, June 9). Allscripts, Eclipsys to merge in $1.3 billion deal. Health IT News. https://www.healthcareitnews.com/

39 Carlson, J. (2012, December 9). Allscripts CEO Tullman steps down. Modern Healthcare. https://www.modernhealthcare.com/

40 Acquired FM. (2025, April 20). Episode 4 Epic Systems (MyChart) [Audio podcast episode]. In Acquired FM. https://www.acquired.fm/

Chapter 8

41 Stigler, G. J. (1971). The theory of economic regulation. The Bell Journal of Economics and Management Science, 2(1), 3–21. https://doi.org/10.2307/3003160

42 Milliard, M. (2020, January 29). Epic continues campaign for changes to forthcoming ONC info blocking rules. *Healthcare IT News*. https://www.healthcareitnews.com/

43 Fox, A. (2025, May 27). Epic Nexus connects 625 hospitals to TEFCA. *Healthcare IT News*. https://www.healthcareitnews.com/

44 MedPage Today. (n.d.). Practice management: Information technology. https://www.medpagetoday.com/practicemanagement/informationtechnology/102812

45 Health Affairs. (n.d.). Universal patient identification and why the U.S. needs it. https://www.healthaffairs.org/content/forefront/universal-patient-identification-and-why-us-needs

46 Health Data Management. (n.d.). More than 100 organizations urge Congress to pave way for a national patient ID. https://www.healthdatamanagement.com/articles/more-than-100-organizations-urge-congress-to-pave-way-for-a-national-patient-id?id=130210

47 Pifer, R. (2024, May 15). VA watchdog finds software flaw in Oracle Cerner EHR led to patient harm. *Fierce Healthcare*. https://www.fiercehealthcare.com/

Chapter 9

48 Pharmacy Times. (2002, October). E-prescribing—Making the first connections. Pharmacy Times.

49 Surescripts. (2008, April 29). CVS/Caremark, Express Scripts and Medco Health Solutions join U.S. chain and independent pharmacies to accelerate transition from paper-based to paperless prescribing [Press release]. https://surescripts.com/

50 Surescripts. (2024, August 13). Surescripts announces strategic partnership with TPG to enhance patient care and meet evolving healthcare needs nationwide [Press release]. https://surescripts.com/

51 American Hospital Association. (2025, January). Change Healthcare cyberattack underscores urgent need to strengthen cyber preparedness for individual health care organizations and as a field. https://www.aha.org/change-healthcare-cyberattack-underscores-urgent-need-strengthen-cyber-preparedness-individual-health-care-organizations-and

52 U.S. House Committee on Energy & Commerce. (2024, May 3). What we learned: Change Healthcare cyber attack. https://energycommerce.house.gov/posts/what-we-learned-change-healthcare-cyber-attack

53 BankInfoSecurity. (n.d.). Change Healthcare attack cost estimate reaches nearly $2.9B. https://www.bankinfosecurity.com/change-healthcare-attack-cost-estimate-reaches-nearly-29b-a-

Chapter 10

54 Boben, P. J. (1996). Medicaid reform in the 1990s. Health Care Financing Review, 18(1), 1–4.

55 Toner, R. (1994, August 23). Health care debate; Once in forefront, H.M.O.'s lose their luster in health debate. *The New York Times*. https://www.nytimes.com/

56 Goodson, J. D., Bierman, A. S., Fein, O., Rask, K., Rich, E. C., & Selker, H. P. (2001). The future of capitation: The physician role in managing change in practice. Journal of General Internal Medicine, 16(4), 250–256. https://doi.org/10.1046/j.1525-1497.2001.016004250.x

57 Hsiao, W. C., Braun, P., Yntema, D., & Becker, E. R. (1988, September 29). Estimating physicians' work for a resource-based relative-value scale. *New England Journal of Medicine*, 319(13), 835–841. https://www.nejm.org/doi/full/10.1056/nejm198809293191305

58 Center to Advance Palliative Care. (n.d.). Everything you always wanted to know about RVUs but were afraid to ask. https://www.capc. org/blog/everything-you-always-wanted-to-know-about-rvus-but-were-afraid-to-ask/

59 Legacy.com. (n.d.). Wolffe Nadoolman obituary. https://www.legacy.com/us/obituaries/nytimes/name/wolffe-nadoolman-obituary?id=20123113

60 Nadoolman, W. (2009, March 23). Slow medicine. The Empathic Pediatrician.

Chapter 11

61 Rosen, J. (2022, September 28). Lauren Gardner wins Lasker Award for COVID-19 dashboard. The Hub. https://hub.jhu.edu/

Chapter 12

62 Guyatt, G. H., Cairns, J., et al. (1992). Evidence-based medicine: A new approach to teaching the practice of medicine. JAMA, 268(17), 2420–2425. https://doi.org/10.1001/jama.1992.03490170092032

63 Lewis, M. (2004). Moneyball: The art of winning an unfair game. W. W. Norton & Company.

64 Sackett, D. L., Rosenberg, W. M., Gray, J. A., Haynes, R. B., & Richardson, W. S. (1996). Evidence based medicine: What it is and what it isn't. BMJ, 312(7023), 71–72. https://doi.org/10.1136/bmj.312.7023.71

65 Linskey, M. E., & Kalkanis, S. N. (2009). Evidence-linked, clinical practice guidelines—getting serious; getting professional. Journal of Neurosurgery, 111(6), 1101–1103. https://doi.org/10.3171/2009.9.JNS091156

66 The Dartmouth Institute for Health Policy & Clinical Practice. (n.d.). The Dartmouth Atlas of Health Care. https://www.dartmouthatlas.org/

67 Wennberg, J. E., Fisher, E. S., & Skinner, J. S. (2002). Geography and the debate over Medicare reform. Health Affairs, Suppl Web Exclusives, W96–W114. https://doi.org/10.1377/hlthaff.w2.96

68 McElwee, N., Ho, S. Y., McGuigan, K., & Horn, M. (2006). Evidence-based coverage decisions? Primum non nocere. Health Affairs, 25(3), w279–w289. https://doi.org/10.1377/hlthaff.25.w279

69 Oregon Health & Science University. DERP reports. Evidence-based Practice Center.

Chapter 13

70 Health Affairs. (n.d.). Comparative effectiveness research. https://www.healthaffairs.org/content/briefs/comparative-effectiveness-research

71 Barenie, R. E., Avorn, J., Tessema, F. A., & Kesselheim, A. S. (2021). Public funding for transformative drugs: The case of sofosbuvir. Drug Discovery Today, 26(1), 273–281. https://doi.org/10.1016/j.drudis.2020.10.001

72 Decision Resources Group. (2017, August 16). Decision Resources Group acquires Context Matters to expand global market access intelligence offerings [Press release]. PR Newswire. https://www.prnewswire.com/

73 Elvers, E. (2019, February 2). Explaining ICER: America's answer to NICE. Source Health Economics. https://source-he.com/explaining-icer-americas-answer-to-nice/

Chapter 14

74 U.S. Food and Drug Administration. (2024, March 18). Real-world evidence. https://www.fda.gov/science-research/science-and-research-special-topics/real-world-evidence

Chapter 15

75 Bain, L. J. (2005). Crossroads in clinical trials. NeuroRx, 2(4)

76 Getz, K., Casey, C., Chambers, J., de Bruin, A., McNair, J., & the CISCRP Team. (2022, April 22). Remembering that TIME magazine issue; celebrating progress in patient engagement. Applied Clinical Trials. https://www.appliedclinicaltrialsonline.com/

77 Henry, T. A. (2021, May 27). "Trial-in-a-box" to help more practices take part in clinical trials. American Medical Association. https://www.ama-assn.org/

78 Wang, L., & Motti, E. F. (n.d.). The increasing shift of clinical trials to CROs. Pharma Outsourcing. https://www.pharmoutsourcing.com/Featured-Articles/174597-The-Increasing-Shift-of-Clinical-Trials-to-CROs/

79 Unger, J. M., Gralow, J. R., et al. (2024). National estimates of the participation of patients with cancer in clinical research studies based on Commission on Cancer accreditation data. Journal of Clinical Oncology, 42(15), 1735–1745. https://doi.org/10.1200/JCO.23.00786

80 BioSpace. (2023, September 12). Tufts' Ken Getz: Onerous clinical trial protocols contribute to high failure rates. *BioSpace*. https://www.biospace.com/outdated-clinical-trial-approaches-leading-to-high-failure-rate

Chapter 16

81 Johnson, T., Joyner, M., DePourcq, F., Drezner, M., Hutchinson, R., Newton, K., Uscinski, K. T., & Toussant, K. (2010). Using research metrics to improve timelines: Proceedings from the 2nd Annual CTSA Clinical Research Management Workshop. *Clinical and Translational Science*, 3(6), 305–308. https://doi.org/10.1111/j.1752-8062.2010.00246.x

82 Warnock, N., & Lester, M. (2010, April). Financial steps for sites. *Applied Clinical Trials*. https://www.appliedclinicaltrialsonline.com/view/financial-steps-sites

Chapter 17

83 Kleinke, J. D. (2005, September). Dot-Gov: Market failure and the creation of a national health information technology system. Health Affairs, 24(5), 1246–1262. https://doi.org/10.1377/hlthaff.24.5.1246

84 Institute of Medicine (US) Committee on Quality of Health Care in America. (2000). To err is human: Building a safer health system (L. T. Kohn, J. M. Corrigan, & M. S. Donaldson, Eds.). National Academies Press. https://doi.org/10.17226/9728

85 Centers for Medicare & Medicaid Services. (n.d.). Get your Medicare claims with connected apps. Medicare.gov. https://www.medicare.gov/manage-your-health/get-medicare-claims-with-connected-apps

86 Parikh, R. S., Kreinces, J. B., & Pohlman, K. L. (2021). Importance of pharmacy partnerships in effective COVID-19 vaccine distribution. Journal of the American Pharmacists Association, 61(5), e1–e4. https://doi.org/10.1016/j.japh.2021.06.002

87 Fierce Healthcare. (n.d.). Walgreens eyes 'tremendous growth' in clinical trials as part of transformation strategy.

https://www.fiercehealthcare.com/retail/walgreens-eyes-tremendous-growth-clinical-trials-part-transformation-strategy

88 CVS Health. (n.d.). CVS Health introduces Clinical Trial Services. https://www.cvshealth.com/news/clinical-trial-services/cvs-health-introduces-clinical-trial-services.html/1000

89 Alsumidaie, M. (n.d.). Why did CVS shutter its clinical trials unit? Applied Clinical Trials. https://www.appliedclinicaltrialsonline.com/view/why-did-cvs-shutter-its-clinical-trials-unit-

90 Beaney, A. (2024). Walgreens sets sights on clinical trial network growth in recruitment. Clinical Trials Arena. https://www.clinicaltrialsarena.com/interviews/walgreens-sets-sights-major-clinical-trial-network-growth/

Chapter 18

91 Shaywitz, D. (2018, February 18). The deeply human core of Roche's $2.1 billion tech acquisition – and why it made it. *Forbes*. https://www.Forbes.com/

Chapter 19

92 Kutner, A. (2023, June 30). Lawyers sanctioned for using ChatGPT to write legal brief with 6 fake cases. Legal Dive. https://www.legaldive.com/

Chapter 20

93 EY. (2024, December 18). Venture capital investment in generative AI almost doubles globally in 2024 as momentum accelerates in transformative sector. EY. https://www.ey.com

94 Gartner. (2025, March 31). Gartner forecasts worldwide GenAI spending to reach $64.4 billion in 2025. *Gartner*. https://www.gartner.com

95 Crownhart, C. (2024, September 26). Why Microsoft made a deal to help restart Three Mile Island. *MIT Technology Review*. https://www.technologyreview.com/2024/09/26/1104516/three-mile-island-microsoft/

96 Powell, A. (2025, February 10). It's inoperable cancer. Should AI make call about what happens next? *The Harvard Gazette*. https://news.harvard.edu/gazette

97 Appel, G., Neelbauer, J., & Schweidel, D. A. (2023, April 7). Generative AI has an intellectual property problem. *Harvard Business Review*. https://hbr.org

98 O'Neil, C. (2016). *Weapons of Math Destruction*. Broadway Books.

99 Straw, I., & Callison-Burch, C. (2020, December 17). Artificial intelligence in mental health and the biases of language based models. *PLoS One*, 15(12), e0240376. https://doi.org/10.1371/journal.pone.0240376

Chapter 21

100 Manos, D. (2014, February 7). Malcolm Gladwell tells 3 tales of interoperability. *Healthcare IT News*. https://www.healthcareitnews.com

101 Veradigm. (2024, March 4). Veradigm completes acquisition of ScienceIO. *Veradigm*. https://www.veradigm.com

102 Landi, H. (2024, February 27). ViVE 2024: Veradigm buys ScienceIO in $140M deal to build out healthcare AI solutions. *Fierce Healthcare*. https://www.fiercehealthcare.com

103 Jennings, K. (2024, April 18). How a decades-old medical records company made a huge AI bet to save itself. *Forbes*. https://www.*Forbes*.com

Chapter 22

104 Duggan, M. J., Gervase, J., Schoenbaum, A., Hanson, C., Howell, E., Sheinberg, E., & Johnson, K. B. (2025). Clinician experiences with ambient scribe technology to assist with documentation burden and efficiency. JAMA Network Open, 8(2), e2460637. https://doi.org/10.1001/jamanetworkopen.2024.60637

105 RSNA. (2019, January 23). AI for chest X-rays could improve patient care in underserved communities. RSNA News. https://www.rsna.org/news/2019/january/ai-for-chest-x-rays

106 Kent, J. (2024, October 30). Yale New Haven radiologists boost CT scan reviews with AI. *Healthcare IT News*. https://www.healthcareitnews.com/news/yale-new-haven-radiologists-boost-ct-scan-reviews-ai

Chapter 23

107 American Hospital Association. (2024, August 6). Analysis: Medicare Advantage prior authorization requests increase 9 million in 3 years. AHA News. https://www.aha.org/news/headline/2024-08-06-analysis-medicare-advantage-prior-authorization-requests-increase-9-million-3-years

108 Lagasse, J. (2024, February 13). Class action lawsuit against UnitedHealth's AI claim denials advances. Healthcare Finance News.https://www.healthcarefinancenews.com/news/class-action-lawsuit-against-unitedhealths-ai-claim-denials-advances

109 HFS Research. (2024, December 9). UnitedHealthcare's AI use to deny claims is center of industrywide debate. https://www.hfsresearch.com/news/unitedhealthcares-ai-use-to-deny-claims-is-center-of-industrywide-debate/

110 Grand View Research. (2024, October). AI in revenue cycle management market size, share & trends analysis report by product, type, application, delivery mode, end use, and segment forecast, 2025–2030. https://www.grandviewresearch.com/industry-analysis/ai-revenue-cycle-management-market-report

111 DataM Intelligence. (2023, October). Revenue cycle management market size, share, industry, forecast and outlook (2024–2031).https://www.datamintelligence.com/research-report/revenue-cycle-management-market

112 HealthCare Dive. (2024, October 15). *'AI arms race' underway as payers, providers jockey for upper hand.* HealthCare Dive. https://www.healthcaredive.com/news/artificial-intelligence-claims-review-payers-providers/730872/

Chapter 24

113 Biro, J. M., Handley, J. L., McCurry, J. M., Visconti, A., Weinfeld, J., Trafton, J. G., Ratwani, R. M. (2025). Opportunities and risks of artificial intelligence in patient portal messaging in primary care. *npj Digital Medicine*, 8, 222. https://doi.org/10.1038/s41746-025-01027-7

Chapter 25

114 Frueh, S. (2025, October 12). Interview with Fei-Fei Li: "AI is a tool, and its values are human values." Issues in Science and Technology. https://issues.org/interview-godmother-ai-fei-fei-li/

115 Armitage, H. (2025, June 5). Clinicians can 'chat' with medical records through new AI software, ChatEHR. Stanford Medicine. https://med.stanford.edu/news/all-news/2025/06/ai-chatehr-medical-records.html

116 Ross, C., & Herman, B. (2023, November 14). UnitedHealth used a flawed algorithm to cut off Medicare Advantage patients' rehab care, lawsuit alleges. STAT. https://www.statnews.com/2023/11/14/unitedhealth-class-action-lawsuit-algorithm-medicare-advantage/

117 Grassley, C. (2024, July 17). Grassley pushes for answers on UnitedHealth Group's Medicare Advantage billing practices. U.S. Senate Committee on the Judiciary. https://www.judiciary.senate.gov/press/rep/releases/grassley-pushes-for-answers-on-unitedhealth-groups-medicare-advantage-billing-practices

118 Eckrote, M. J., Nielson, C. M., Lu, M., Alexander, T., Shah Gupta, R., Low, K. W., Zhang, Z., Eliazar, A., Klesh, R., Kress, A., Bryant, M., Asiimwe, A., Gatto, N. M., & Dreyer, N. A. (2024). Linking clinical trial participants to their U.S. real-world data through tokenization: A practical guide. *Contemporary Clinical Trials Communications*, 41, 101354. https://doi.org/10.1016/j.conctc.2024.101354

Conclusion

119 Schumpeter, J. A. (1942). Capitalism, socialism, and democracy. New York: Harper & Brothers.

Additional References

HCC Coding 101: Hierarchical Condition Category Coding, https://www.imohealth.com/resources/hcc-101-what-you-need-to-know-about-

Health Level 7 (HL7) Fast Healthcare Interoperability Resources, https://www.healthit.gov/topic/standards-technology/standards/fhir

FHIR® – Fast Healthcare Interoperability Resources, https://ecqi.healthit.gov/fhir